D1457514

Cambridge Studies in Historical Geography 5

EXPLORATIONS IN HISTORICAL GEOGRAPHY

Cambridge Studies in Historical Geography

Series editors:
ALAN R. H. BAKER   J. B. HARLEY   DAVID WARD

Cambridge Studies in Historical Geography encourages exploration of the philosophies, methodologies and techniques of historical geography and publishes the results of new research within all branches of the subject. It endeavours to secure the marriage of traditional scholarship with innovative approaches to problems and to sources, aiming in this way to provide a focus for the discipline and to contribute towards its development. The series is an international forum for publication in historical geography which also promotes contact with workers in cognate disciplines.

EXPLORATIONS IN HISTORICAL GEOGRAPHY

Interpretative essays

Edited by

ALAN R. H. BAKER

University Lecturer in Geography
and Senior Tutor of Emmanuel College, Cambridge

and

DEREK GREGORY

University Lecturer in Geography
and Fellow of Sidney Sussex College, Cambridge

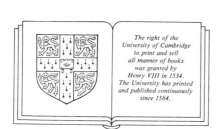

The right of the
University of Cambridge
to print and sell
all manner of books
was granted by
Henry VIII in 1534.
The University has printed
and published continuously
since 1584.

CAMBRIDGE UNIVERSITY PRESS

CAMBRIDGE
LONDON   NEW YORK   NEW ROCHELLE
MELBOURNE   SYDNEY

Published by the Press Syndicate of the University of Cambridge
The Pitt Building, Trumpington Street, Cambridge CB2 1RP
32 East 57th Street, New York, NY 10022, USA
296 Beaconsfield Parade, Middle Park, Melbourne 3206, Australia

© Cambridge University Press 1984

First published 1984

Printed in Great Britain by the University Press, Cambridge

Library of Congress catalogue card number: 83–19003

British Library Cataloguing in Publication Data

Baker, Alan R. H.
Explorations in historical geography. –
(Cambridge studies in historical geography; V.5)
1. Anthropo-geography – Great Britain
2. Great Britain – Historical geography
I. Title II. Gregory, Derek, *1951*–
304.2′0941   GF551

ISBN 0 521 24968 6

UP

Contents

Preface

The active debate in recent years about the purpose and practice of historical geography has focused upon the progress to be made in the discipline through an adaptation to new problems, new methodologies, new techniques and new sources. This volume of interpretative essays extends the debate still further by exploring in tentative and speculative fashion some basic methodological and substantive issues from essentially interdisciplinary standpoints. In any exploration, risks have to be accepted as an integral part of the enterprise. All of the contributors to this book take pleasure in one another's polemical company, principally at Occasional Discussions in Historical Geography in Cambridge, and each essay explores a wide field while being soundly based in personal research. Our hope is that some of our pleasure will be shared by those who critically read these essays.

We should like to take this opportunity to express our thanks to the contributors to this book, for their cooperation and patience. In addition, we are grateful to Arthur Shelley and Michael Young for drawing the maps and diagrams and to Felix Driver for compiling the index.

Cambridge   ALAN R. H. BAKER
Good Friday 1983   DEREK GREGORY

vii

1

Reflections on the relations of historical geography and the *Annales* school of history[1]

ALAN R. H. BAKER

Presentation of a paradox

The intellectual *frisson* experienced by those historians and geographers engaged in major philosophical and methodological debates during the 1920s and 1930s may be understood, even shared vicariously, by those who have witnessed, or better still participated in, critical discussions about the roles and relations of history and geography during the 1960s and 1970s.[2] The changing intellectual landscape of the inter-war years included some remarkable features: for example, the publication of Lucien Febvre's *La Terre et l'évolution humaine: introduction géographique à l'histoire* in 1922, of Carl Sauer's *The Morphology of Landscape* in 1925, of Marc Bloch's *Les Caractères originaux de l'histoire rurale française* in 1931 and of Clifford Darby's *An Historical Geography of England before A.D. 1800* in 1936.[3] Given that charisma and context may be the root explanation of any intellectual 'great leap forward',[4] then a primary role in the development of history and of historical geography may readily be attributed to Febvre and Bloch, to Sauer and Darby, each of whom has exerted enormous charismatic impact directly through his own writings and teachings and indirectly through the endeavours of his many pupils, but all of whom should be viewed contextually as intellectual innovators, intent on promoting a new kind of history in the case of Febvre and Bloch and new kinds of cultural and historical geography in the cases of Sauer and Darby.[5]

In 1930 there took place the First International Congress of Historical Geography: it was held in Brussels, its proceedings were in French, and most of its participants came, significantly, from France or Belgium. Among the participants was a Welshman, young Clifford Darby, keen as a pioneer to explore unknown archival avenues and uncharted methodological mains, eager as a missionary to lead the search for a new historical geography. Darby himself has recently reflected that with the general development of

academic geography in the English-speaking world in the 1920s and early
1930s came the particular rise of historical geography as a self-conscious
discipline.[6] Only a year before that meeting in Brussels, Febvre and Bloch in
Strasbourg had launched their revolutionary *Annales d'histoire économique et
sociale* and in doing so laid the foundations for a new kind of history, which
was intentionally opposed to the idolatry of facts and to the isolationism of
specialization, and in favour of a problem-focused history which would
explicitly employ theoretical concepts, imaginative interpretations and interdisciplinary approaches.[7] While English-speaking historical geographers have,
during the last fifty or so years, had many and fruitful contacts with English-
speaking historians, they have shown scant awareness of the work of the
Annales school of history.[8] In France itself, the birth and burgeoning of this
school has paradoxically been paralleled by the relative decline and decay
of the practice of historical geography in France.[9] It is somewhat absurd
that *Annalistes* seem to have both learned and practised Paul Vidal de la
Blache's principles of human geography more soundly and faithfully than
have many French geographers.

This paradox will be explored in this essay partly on the assumption that
historiographical understanding is an important and integral part of our
endeavour to study people and places in the past, and partly in the belief
that methodological consciousness should be allied with – and not put in
antithesis to – scholarly craftsmanship. Methodological debates may sometimes result in confusion but this is not to deny the intention behind them,
which is to improve the ways and means by which we can achieve our ends,
the researching and writing of better historical geography. This essay will
initially examine the nature of the interdependent but uneven development
of the *Annales* school of history and of historical geography in France. It will
then ponder whether it would be possible, equipped with this retrospective
historiographical survey, to begin prospectively the task of laying the foundations for the making of a new kind of historical geography. It will conclude
by looking briefly, as a case study, at rural France in the nineteenth century.

The *Annales* school of history

Creation of the 'Annales' school

People and events need to be assessed in their contexts. Febvre and Bloch
in 1929 founded a journal, the *Annales d'histoire économique et sociale*,
which has come to be seen as marking a significant turning-point in French
historiography. During that year Febvre celebrated his fifty-first birthday and
Bloch his forty-third: the barricades of traditional French historical scholarship were being assaulted not by young and headstrong revolutionaries but
by mature and experienced revisionists. The roots of the *Annales* can be

traced back at least into the last decade of the nineteenth century, for it was modelled to some extent upon three French journals founded then in reaction against the philosophical and methodological orthodoxies current within the humanities: the *Annales de géographie*, launched by Vidal de la Blache in 1891; the *Année sociologique*, by Emile Durkheim in 1896; and the *Revue de synthèse historique*, by Henri Berr in 1900. The ideas and writings of this triumvirate of intellectuals had a particularly formative influence upon both Febvre and Bloch, who encountered them initially as students in the early 1900s and subsequently as colleagues.[10] Febvre and Bloch were precocious participants in the broadly based reaction which spread in France during the early twentieth century against the positivist methods of historical scholarship. A desire to go beyond the documents and to conquer the distrust of historical generalization characterized Berr's *Revue de synthèse historique* and his *L'Evolution de l'humanité*, which was launched in 1913 as a synthetic history animated, as Keylor puts it, by 'a passion for recapturing the complexity of past epochs through the broad sweep of historical narrative'.[11] Bloch and Febvre were both early contributors to the *Revue* and to the *Evolution* series, addressing themes ignored by earlier generations of historians and offering interpretations based as much upon imagination and intuition as upon documentary evidence. Two particular works by Febvre should especially be viewed as foundation stones for the *Annales*: 1912 saw the publication of his thesis, *Philippe II et la Franche-Comté*, the novelty of which lay essentially in its interdisciplinary and problem-solving approach, its narrative style and its concern with a geographical region; and 1922 saw the publication of *La Terre et l'évolution humaine; introduction géographique à l'histoire*, an extended attack upon determinism and a forceful advocacy of possibilism, emphasizing the close links between history and geography.[12]

The founding of the *Annales* in 1929 needs, therefore, to be seen as a specific event which followed logically from a general process of intellectual revisionism[13] and of close cooperation between Febvre and Bloch, who first came together in the autumn of 1920 as newly appointed teachers and researchers in the exhilarating intellectual atmosphere of the University of Strasbourg in recently liberated Alsace. In 1933 Febvre left for Paris, to take up a post at the Collège de France; Bloch followed soon afterwards, in 1936, to an appointment at the Sorbonne. During the first ten years of the *Annales'* existence, Febvre and Bloch devoted their energies to ensuring the journal's success. Checked by the Second World War and especially by the death of Bloch, who was executed by the Gestapo in 1944, the *Annales* continued to be edited by Febvre until he died, in 1956, when Fernand Braudel took over until 1968. For almost forty years, therefore, the *Annales* had been directed by only three, like-minded, men. Furthermore, the spirit of the *Annales* was institutionalized in 1947 with the establishment under the direction of Febvre of the Sixième Section of the Ecole Pratique des Hautes Etudes, a focus for cooperation among social scientists with historians playing the leading roles. In one sense, the *Annales* were established in 1929 to fight the historical establishment; by 1947 the *Annalistes* had themselves become the new establishment.

It is, however, misleading to refer to the *Annales* paradigm, if that term is used in the Kuhnian sense to denote a generally accepted set of assumptions and procedures which serve to define both the subjects and the methods of inquiry.[14] The closer the inspection, the less apposite this concept appears in relation to the work of *Annalistes* precisely because it is too broad. The *Annales* school has never been monolithic and is unlikely to become so. Nonetheless, the existence of some widely held views about the purpose and practice of historical inquiry does make it appropriate to refer to the *Annales* school, to a broad community of historians, while recognizing that it was explicitly not the intention of its founders to erect barriers between well-defined academic territories. Bloch and Febvre, together with their associates and disciples, renewed historical research and writing; they provided the study of history in France with a new status and self-awareness: in occupying the middle ground between nomothetic and hermeneutic traditions of historical inquiry, the *Annalistes* combined imaginative sweeps with a close attention to detail.[15] The *Annales* school has not, however, been universally acclaimed. Before any appraisal of the school is attempted, its characteristics need to be brought more sharply into focus.

Characteristics of the 'Annales' school

In reacting against positivist history – which believed that the 'hard facts' of historical reality were contained within documents, that they were self-explanatory and so did not require the mediation of interpretative theories, and that the historian's role was to locate, accumulate, collate and authenticate documents so that history could be written 'as it really was' – Bloch and Febvre laboured consciously to promote the study of a total history, a synthesis based upon interdisciplinary analyses and upon the interpretation of historical patterns, processes and structures, both ideational and artefactual. In addition, the *Annales*' purpose was specifically to encourage debate among historians and between historians and other scholars, and to discourage the isolation of the specialist.[16] But viewing history as the science of man in society has enabled the *Annales* to exercise an intellectual hegemony over the other social sciences, because the synthesizing role of history endows it with a superiority over other, analytical, disciplines. Surprisingly, it has even done so over geography, despite its being history's epistemological twin.

The new history developed by Febvre and Bloch was closely related to the new geography envisaged by Vidal de la Blache. As Burke has pointed out, the traditionally close link between history and geography in French education helps to explain why Febvre and Bloch discovered the social sciences through geography.[17] As students at the Ecole Normale Supérieure in Paris before the First World War both Febvre and Bloch – but sequentially rather than simultaneously – graduated as *agrégés* in geography as well as in history and in so doing encountered, as teachers at the Sorbonne, Paul Vidal de la Blache and Lucien Gallois, one of Vidal de la Blache's first pupils, co-editor with him of the *Annales de géographie* from 1894 and author in 1908 of an influential book on natural regions and regional nomenclature.[18] The vigour of the new history being developed in the *Annales* was fortified in substantial measure by its digestion of some of the geographical concepts offered by Vidal de la Blache and his disciples: the notions of *milieu* and *mentalités*, of *sociétés, genres de vie, circulation* and *civilisation*, as well as of geographical distribution, diffusion, differentiation and *personnalité* pervade much of the work of the *Annales* school.[19] Both Febvre and Bloch were remarkably attentive to geographical thinking. For example, Febvre drew sustenance from it for his *La Terre et l'évolution humaine: introduction géographique à l'histoire*, which geographers saw as an affirmation of Vidal de la Blache's critique of environmental determinism and historians as a confirmation of the need to evaluate man's perception and use of his physical resources, to situate histories within their geographies; and Bloch's survey of the origins of French rural history drew considerable inspiration from geographical concerns with landscape and regional distinctiveness.[20] Later, Febvre was to make quite explicit his own recognition of the intellectual debt owed by history to geography: 'En fait, on pourrait dire que, dans une certaine mesure, c'est la géographie vidalienne qui a engendré l'histoire des *Annales* – l'histoire qui est la nôtre.'[21] In her extended assessment of French geography, Buttimer argued that Febvre made the Vidalian tradition accessible to historians, and Claval has suggested that Febvre should be seen both as one of the founders of the *Annales* school and as the theoretician *a posteriori* of the Vidalian conception of geography.[22]

For almost thirty years, while under the editorial control first of Febvre and Bloch together and then – after the death of Bloch – of Febvre alone, the *Annales* consistently contained reviews by geographers, reviews of works by geographers and notes on conferences and other geographical research activities. The pattern was established in the very first volume of the *Annales*, which included reviews by Albert Demangeon and Henri Baulig, reviews by Bloch and Febvre of recently published geographical monographs, and notes on the work of the International Geographical Union's Commission on Rural Settlement and on the International Geographical Congress which had been held in Cambridge in 1928. In reviewing Daniel Faucher's regional monograph on the middle Rhône Valley, Bloch took its author to task for his insistence that geographers should never forget that their proper concern was to write geography, not history. Bloch could see no value in such a distinction between two disciplines whose combined purpose was to construct a science of man in society.[23] Precisely the same view was to be expressed in the *Annales* almost twenty years later in Robert Mandrou's admonition of Etiene Juillard for recognizing the existence of a frontier between history and geography and of Clifford Darby for placing boundaries between different categories of historical geography.[24] Such separatist and divisive claims were contrary to the creed of the *Annales* school. Mandrou's conviction that social history and human geography are – or ought to be – inseparable reflected the approval which had been given earlier by Febvre to Roger Dion's inaugural exposition of historical geography as retrospective human geography.[25] For virtually three decades, from 1929 until 1957, on average between 5 and 7 per cent of the pages of each annual volume of the *Annales* were devoted to geographical reviews, notes and comments. From 1957, when Braudel assumed editorial control, the proportion rapidly and significantly declined to less than 1 per cent. Braudel's love–hate relationship with geography as practised in France was remarkably astute. His positive acceptance of the need to situate histories contextually within their geographies is evident both in his own writings (notably his panoramic reconstruction of the Mediterranean world during the sixteenth century) and in his supervisory insistence that one of his graduate pupils, Emmanuel Le Roy Ladurie, should view the peasantry of Languedoc in their distinctive geographical setting.[26] For Braudel, geography was much more than simply a stage, a physical environmental space, upon which historical dramas were enacted: his study of the Mediterranean put into practice the programme which Febvre had set forth for a continuous inter-weaving of geography and history, achieved through cognition of the changing ecological components of the physical environment, of the role of environmental perception and of natural resources (including time and space) as cultural appraisals, and of the constant interplay of human and non-human forces in the making and the changing of the distinctive Mediterranean milieu. This combined emphasis upon what Braudel termed *géohistoire* and upon the writing of regional historical syntheses has become a distinctive characteristic of the *Annales* school.[27] So much so, that the school has been accused of annexing geography.[28] Braudel's embrace of geography was certainly not warm enough to include the works of many geographers. He was critical of traditional regional monographs, on the grounds that they were too solid, too particularistic, too formal. He also decried the academic isolation of French regional geographers and their betrayal of Vidal de la Blache's principles. Surveying history and the social sciences, Braudel stressed the need to refer any social reality to the space, place or region in which it exists, to its geographical context. But, he regretted, 'geography unfortunately too often thinks of itself as an independent world. It needs someone like Vidal de la Blache, who, for this purpose, instead of the concepts of time and space, will use place and social reality.' Braudel also argued that spatial models ought to be more widely known and used by historians and social scientists:

I have often thought that one of the chief assets to France in the domain of the social sciences was the school of Vidal de la Blache and we shall never be able to make good our betrayal of its spirit and teachings. All the social sciences, for their part, will have to make room for an increasingly geographical conception of humanity; Vidal de la Blache was pleading for this as early as 1903.[29]

The inseparability of geography and history, their combination in the form of regional histories, is a fundamental tenet of the *Annales* school and directly reflects its search for synthesis, its trust in total history. Such an holistic conception of the study of history was inevitably associated with advocacy of an interdisciplinary approach which soon extended beyond collusion with geography to cooperation with the full spectrum of academic disciplines, all of which were considered as potential handmaidens to history.[30] The pages of the *Annales*, as well as other writings of *Annaliste* historians, are products of multiple cross-fertilizations of history with the environmental and social sciences and with the humanities, progenies of a view of a history which acknowledges the existence of no boundaries between itself and any other discipline. Explicit adoption of the comparative method by researchers of the *Annales* school broadened and deepened the problems, sources and techniques of historical inquiry.[31] The all-inclusive nature of total history quite simply meant that no problem, source or technique could legitimately be omitted from the ultimate synthesis: which is not, of course, to say that all problems, sources and techniques had to be admitted into each and every historical analysis. While the diversity of the *Annales* school cannot be denied, it is quite impossible to describe it at all accurately in a few sentences. Some idea of its richness may be obtained, by way of example, from the subjects of the ten special themes occurring in the *Annales* during 1969–74. They were as follows: biological and demographic history; history and urbanization; prosopography; history and structure; family and society; non-written (archaeological, symbolic, cinematic, oral) history; reinterpretations of the Ancien Régime and French Revolution; environmental history; sexuality; heresy; religious history. The range of concerns for historians of the *Annales* school is, theoretically, limitless. In practice, however, certain themes and approaches came to receive more emphasis than others and to be regarded as distinguishing characteristics of the school.[32] Such would be the case, for example, with the *Annalistes'* concern for the reconstruction of the *mentalités* (or collective consciousness) as well as of the material conditions of past societies; with their encompassing of all groups within society, rather than merely or even mainly of its elites; and with their endeavour to unravel layers of meaning, and hence of understanding, from both conscious and unconscious categories of evidence, employing interpretative theories from cognate disciplines in order to do so.

Additionally, the *Annales* acted as an open forum within which ideas could be readily exchanged and their value established. *Combats et débats* among historians and between historians and other scholars were actively promoted by Bloch and Febvre; so much so that a pleasure in polemics, a delight in debate – not for its own sake but as a means towards improved historical understanding – has become a characteristic of the *Annales* school.[33] An historian's business, by its nature, is always unfinished, so that his mind must ever be open to new questions and suggestions: history's existence as a scholarly discipline depends upon a consensus among historians, but progress in studying history requires a constant questioning of its conventional wisdoms. Such a perspective upon history, which may justifiably be seen as an important trait of the *Annales*, has contributed significantly to the school's vitality and to its reproduction. So, too, has its self-critical search for improved research methodologies and better literary styles, its quest for a solution to the problem of historical description.[34] Although Bloch and Febvre declared that their aims in founding the *Annales* were to be achieved by example and in practice rather than by methodological discussions and theoretical discourses, the many debates generated by them and their successors have, unsurprisingly, been related not only to particular but also to general historical problems.[35]

Critiques of the 'Annales' school

Assessments of the *Annales* school have been as varied as they could possibly be, ranging from warm acclaim to cold derision. More precisely, the responses of individuals to the school as a whole, or to some of its particular products and practitioners, have been a mixture of admiration and reservation. This is well illustrated in the ambivalence expressed by Richard Cobb, who considered that the *Annales* school had 'produced some of the best and some of the silliest historical writings', and by Olwen Hufton, whose admiration for the achievements of the school was tinged by an intensely felt irritation with its literary style and conceptual self-consciousness. Both Cobb and Hufton recognized the importance attached by the *Annales* school to exploration and experimentation: for Cobb the work of the school was so marked by an overriding search for novelty that its results were often vulgar and pretentious, whereas Hufton accepted that risk-taking was part of the *Annales* creed, which reflected 'a state of mind alert to any new question, any potentially unexplored technique which might throw further light on man and his environment'.[36] Whether one looks back at the *Annales* school over the last fifty years in anger or in admiration, or simply – and perhaps more honestly – with ambivalence, the fact remains that its significance extends beyond the restricted realm of French history both into cognate disciplines (especially as practised within France) and into the conduct of historical inquiry elsewhere in the world.[37] Its contribution has come to be widely acknowledged, its model widely adopted, although not universally acclaimed.

One serious charge sometimes levelled against the *Annales* is that its pluralistic, even imperialistic, approach is too wide-ranging to offer any clear or firm leadership, that the school is all periphery and no core, and that some of its principal products do not in practice serve as models of historical scholarship, capable of being emulated.[38] Braudel's study of the Mediterranean world in the sixteenth century exemplifies this, for it has come to be recognized as a classic, as an attempt at a total structural and ecological history which demonstrates a sustained concern for organization, methodology, and for presentation, rhetoric. The detailed critique of Braudel's work recently proffered by Kinser acknowledges *La Méditerranée* as a masterpiece but as one which has inspired rather than informed other historians, for the study 'is not in the narrow sense a paradigm or an exemplary work. Nor has it been literally imitated by anyone, because it offers an image of *Annaliste* history more than a method.'[39] What such *Annaliste* work does is to inspire attempts by others to construct new and compelling broad visions of the past; original and convincing regional historical syntheses such as Pierre Goubert's study of *Beauvais et le Beauvaisis de 1600 à 1730* and Le Roy Ladurie's study of *Les Paysans de Languedoc.*[40]

Although *Annalistes* are concerned with particular people, places and periods in the past, the writing of total history in practice involves a concern for the general as well as for the particular. The *Annales* emerged, as has been mentioned, in reaction against what came to be termed 'the sin of eventism', against a narrow event-dominated narrative (and essentially political) history. Nonetheless, *Annalistes* have striven to occupy the middle ground between historicist and structuralist approaches to history, between an exclusive emphasis upon the uniqueness of events and an insistence upon the universality of laws.[41] This has laid the *Annales* school open to the criticism that it has neither employed nor developed any coherent theory of history, of social and economic change.[42] Such a charge is misdirected, for it ignores the fact that *Annalistes* are, as Iggers has emphasized, fundamentally historicists whose purpose is to try to understand specific historical situations rather than to formulate general historical theories.[43] For the *Annalistes*, however, understanding of the past would be considerably enhanced by the identification and explication not merely of historical 'facts' and 'events' but also of the patterns which they form and of the processes – both determined and contingent, both intended and unintended – which underpin them. Although Febvre and Bloch had expressed some reticence about methodological discussions, the *Annales* became an international forum for interdisciplinary methodological debates and it was Braudel who presented the most explicit model of historical explanation with his tripartite division of temporal duration into short-term events (*événements*) and medium-term and long-term patterns and structures (*conjonctures et structures*).[44] This identification of processes operating on different time-scales is, of course, somewhat reminiscent of – and logically should be related to – the identification by geographers of processes operating on different spatial scales. Although not amounting to a theory of history and although not providing an indispensable model, Braudel's general ideas about time and space, period and place, have both imbued and improved much of the work of the *Annales* school.

The approach to history associated with the *Annales* is in many respects compatible with that adopted by Marxists.[45] Both schools, as Birnbaum has stressed, share the idea of an historical formation as a totality which is assumed to have several levels, not all of which are immediately available to analysis, and both reveal a deep-seated interest in the study of long-term historical development, even if *Annalistes* tend to emphasize continuities and structural evolution while Marxists tend to emphasize discontinuities and catastrophic changes.[46] In practice, the relations between *Annaliste* and Marxist historians have, as McLennan has argued, been mixed, often turbulent and sometimes confused. Given their mutual interest in, for example, the transition from feudalism to capitalism, it is remarkable that the dialogue between *Annalistes* and Marxists has not been more fruitful. McLennan considers that 'Braudel often does utilize conceptions consonant with a broadly Marxist perspective. And where his own distinctive formulations about capitalism are in evidence, Marxists can still learn from them. It is thus not absurd to posit an affinity between Braudel and historical materialism.'[47] The *Annales* school has not, it could be argued, been as open as it might have been to the ideas and writings of Marxist historians and theorists.[48] The relations between the *Annales* school and Marxist thought are being explored by Michel Foucault. Convinced that it is impossible at the present time to write history without using a whole range of concepts directly or indirectly linked to Marx's thought, Foucault is integrating and extending the ideas of *Annalistes* and Marxists about the character of historical transformations, building upon 'total history' what he terms a 'general history' in which the key notions required by historical research are no longer those of consciousness and continuity, nor those of sign and structure, but those of the event and the series viewed as being materially based, discontinuous and unpredictable.[49]

If *Annalistes* can, with some justification, be accused of not having taken seriously enough the work of Marxists, then other sets of scholars – British historians and French geographers – can rightly be charged with having neglected the work of the *Annales* school. Peter Burke has pointed out that it was a long time before the *Annales* school was noticed by British historians: the silence was broken by a largely negative response in the 1950s and by a more positive response in the middle or perhaps late 1960s, although even in the 1970s work by *Annalistes* did not receive by any means an undiluted welcome from British historians. Burke argues that English Marxist historians have been quicker to welcome the *Annales* approach than have most of their non-Marxist colleagues.[50] One ardent supporter of the approach was Gareth Stedman Jones, who claimed that the *Annales* school was 'perhaps the most successfully revolutionary group of modern historians'. Stedman Jones considered, however, that the new kind of history being conducted in France was being warped by the English historical climate, and argued that the influence of the *Annales* school had finally been transmitted to England in the form of a clumsy parody, through the medium of the Cambridge school of historical demography: 'what in France . . . now forms one cornerstone of an attempt at total historical interpretation, in England is quickly becoming yet another form of historical specialisation'. More surprising than the neglect of the *Annales* school by British historians, however, is the scant attention paid to it by French human geographers in general and historical geographers in particular.[51]

The French school of historical geography

Geography and the historians

For more than a century, the links between geography and history within the French educational system have been intimately close, with students graduating jointly in both subjects. Vidal de la Blache, founding father of the French school of geography, had graduated in history and geography at the Ecole Normale Supérieure in Paris in 1865.[52] To a substantial extent, as Burke has pointed out, Febvre's 'geographization' of history had been preceded by Vidal de la Blache's 'historization' of geography.[53] According to one of France's leading historical geographers today, the French school of geography – more than any other – has been imbued with history.[54] This makes it all the more remarkable that R. Harrison Church concluded from his mid-twentieth-century review of the French school of geography that surprisingly little had been achieved in the field of historical geography and that De Planhol declared despondently and regretfully that

French historical geography today [1972] seems to be in large measure a residual discipline. It has not established a set of principles. Its progress depends upon isolated individuals following their own initiatives. Historical geography [in France] has, it is true, produced some notable studies. It still produces them. But one would have expected more in view of the particularly propitious environment in which historical geography in France developed.[55]

It is undeniably the case, for example, that the fortunes of historical geography in France and England have been markedly different. Virtually half a century ago this was reflected in the contrast between Léon Mirot's *Manuel de géographie historique de la France* (1929) and Darby's *An Historical Geography of England before A.D. 1800* (1936).[56] With its distinctive emphasis upon France's changing political boundaries and administrative sub-divisions, Mirot's work remains today the only book-length treatment of the historical geography of France, whereas Darby's has been replaced by his own *A New Historical Geography of England* (1973), and extended both by R. Dodgshon and R. A. Butlin's *An Historical Geography of England and Wales* (1978) and by M. Dunford and D. Perrons' *The Arena of Capital* (1983), this last being a Marxist account of the historical geography of the development of capitalism in Britain.[57] In short, it can hardly be argued with justification – as Buttimer has tried to do – that 'the superb quality' of French social history and French historical geography provides ample evidence of the mutual benefits derived from a dialogue between historians and geographers, for the exchange of views has been too one-sided.[58] The reasons for this deserve appreciation: one is the extent to which geography was appropriated by historians.

Until the closing years of the nineteenth century, geography within French higher education was taught primarily by people who regarded themselves essentially as historians and who viewed geography as the physical stage upon which history was played. Between his arrival as a teacher at the Ecole Normale Supérieure in Paris in 1877 and his death in 1918, Vidal de la Blache strove to transform the status of geography and especially its relation to history. His inaugural lecture at the Sorbonne in 1898 emphasized, *inter alia*, his interest in man's role in actively modifying his physical environment through time, his view that understanding the geography of a place in the past can illumine our appreciation of it today, and put forward his suggestion that in certain circumstances research can be undertaken productively by working from the present day backward into the past. These historical themes were, of course, to be investigated in particular places, with *pays* and regions being seen by Vidal de la Blache as acquiring distinctive characteristics, products of man's interaction with his physical environment over centuries.[59] This idea was extensively employed in his own contribution to Lavisse's *Histoire de France* (1903), an essay on the 'geographical personality of France', a phrase apparently adapted from a reference by the historian Michelet to France as *une personne*.[60] The essentials of *la tradition vidalienne* are well known and need not be rehearsed here: all that is needed is to draw attention to its conception of geography as a social science and to its production of historically informed regional monographs. The first of these – Demangeon's *La Picardie* (1905) – came to be used as a 'model', for others subsequently emulated its focus upon themes of landscape change (such as clearing the wood and draining the marsh), its acceptance of the past as holding the key to the present, and its considerable and effective use of archival sources. It is worth citing Demangeon's conclusion about Picardy: 'There has been a transformation of the natural scene in which human effort has been the primary cause – it is from the combination of these two elements, by their relations and interactions, that the Plain of Picardy has obtained its geographical personality.'[61] Around 1900 few French historians were studying man's relationship with his physical environment or writing histories within regional (as opposed to national) contexts. Consequently, geographers, as André Meynier put it, became their own historians:[62] Demangeon, for example, devoted his secondary thesis to unpublished historical sources on the geography of France deposited in the National Archives.[63]

The nexus of concepts propounded by Vidal de la Blache was intended to be applied to particular places and studied in terms of historical evolution, the ultimate aim being a humanistic synthesis. Given the omnivorous character of the new history emerging in France during the early decades of the present century, it is hardly surprising that some – indeed many – of Vidal de la Blache's ideas were rapidly adopted by historians and effectively integrated into their own broad, and equally visionary, projects. The *Annales* school, as has been noted already, owed much to Vidal de la Blache, perhaps most obviously in its development of the field of ecological and environmental history, in its sensitivity to the significance of geographical distribution and diffusion, in its elaboration of the concept of *géohistoire*, and most especially in its embrace of the region as the appropriate context for historical inquiry. Historians of the *Annales* school drew inspiration and strength from acquaintance with the ideas of Vidal de la Blache: for example, the flourishing of regional history (or, at least, of regionally based history) in France may be traced directly to Febvre's study of Franche-Comté but indirectly to the regional concept within geography. By contrast, many geographers neglected the broad range of Vidal de la Blache's ideas, and after his death French geography entered into a period of stultifying intellectual isolation.[64] As French geography turned in upon itself, the regional monographs which it produced tended to become decreasingly interpretative and increasingly factual, with academic reputations being made by collecting more bricks rather than by building better bridges.[65] The geographer's equivalent of the historian's 'sin of eventism' was celebrated in fundamentally factual monographs recording the geography of a place 'as it really was'. It is an irony that the essence of Vidal de la Blache's conceptualization of geography was nurtured far more successfully by many historians than it was by some geographers. But the limited development of historical geography in France stems not only from the extent to which geography was annexed by historians[66] but also by the ways in which geographers responded – or failed to respond – to history.

History and the geographers

Two elements of the attitude of French geographers towards history merit attention: first, the pressing of history into the service of a geography focused upon the present rather than the past; and, secondly, the reluctance of geographers to engage in debate about the relations between history and geography. It is undeniably the case, as Claval has observed, that some of the most remarkable studies to have been produced by French geographers have been historical in approach.[67] From its beginnings, the aim of the regional monograph was to explain the present-day geography of a place by considering its historical development. History played the role of hand-maiden to a geography which distinguished itself from history by its explicit focus upon the present rather than the past. This perspective was even the one adopted by Dion who, more than anyone else, was responsible for giving historical geography in France a sense of identity, a degree of independence from both history and geography.[68] Nonetheless, when Dion inaugurated his Chair of Historical Geography at the Collège de France in December 1948 he lectured on *la géographie humaine rétrospective*, arguing that present-day cultural landscapes must be understood as reflecting their histories and that 'la géographie humaine de la France est nécessairement une géographie historique', a view echoed later by Darby in his famous claim that 'all geography is historical geography'.[69] Similarly, almost ten years later, Dion argued in a general essay that *la géographie historique* was in essence a retro-spective human geography and that it was geography rather than history because its concern was primarily to explain the present scene: 'Mais, et c'est en quoi la géographie historique ainsi est vraiment géographie, elle ne s'intéresse à l'activité des hommes d'autrefois que dans la mesure où les effets en sont sinon matériellement perceptibles dans la géographie humaine actuelle de notre pays, du moins indispensables à l'intelligence de celle-ci . . . son objet est d'expliquer les choses en retraçant leur genèse.'[70] These two methodological statements by Dion gave historical geography in France a logical but limited realm. They also tied historical geography closely to contemporary human geography, which placed it at a disadvantage when the latter (during the post-Second World War decades) turned towards planning and applied geography, towards *la géographie humaine prospective*. In prac-tice, even Dion escaped for increasingly long periods from the epistemological prison which he had himself constructed: his own research and teaching developed an unambiguous interest in geographical problems in the past for their own sake rather than for their illumination of the present.[71] Regrettably, Dion's expanding view of historical geography was not formally expounded in a way which would have enabled it to be more widely shared and to give direction to the subject. Within geography, Dion became more and more isolated, more and more regarded as an historian.[72]

The paucity of substantial studies concerned exclusively with the historical geography of France (or even of an area of France) is paralleled by the limited amount of methodological debate within French historical geography, the general acceptance of Dion's portrayal of the subject as restrospective human geography, and the relative absence of an explicitly reflexive critique. One can point only to a handful of essays that offer surveys of the progress being made within particular sectors of French historical geography.[73] There are similarly only a few assessments of the purpose and practice of historical geography in France to add to the two by Dion already signalled. Maximilien Sorre, briefly exploring the role of historical explanation in human geography, described and praised Braudel's manner of conceiving history as a succession of geographies, and he pleaded for 'a true collaboration for common profit' between history and geography while retaining 'clear awareness of the autonomy of each discipline'.[74] Juillard's observations on the relations between history and geography stemmed directly from his contacts with Darby at University College London during the 1950s, when the latter was systematizing some methodological approaches to historical geography.[75] Juillard broadcast to a French audience Darby's four-fold classification of historical geography (geography behind history, geographies of the past, changing geographies, and the past in the present): he usefully reviewed Darby's ideas, relating them in turn to work by French geographers, but offered little by way of their elaboration or extension. Likewise, De Planhol's assessment of historical geography in France was conducted within a similar methodological structure, even though it proved necessary to consider separately the specific contribution of Dion, which might in turn have suggested that Darby's was not an entirely suitable framework within which to evaluate French historical geography. It was perhaps inappropriate to consider Dion's work almost as an appendix to a critique of French historical geography while at the same time arguing that he was the only French geographer who had faithfully embraced historical geography and placed an historical perspective at the centre of all his work.[76] It is also, perhaps, symptomatic of the isolationism of French historical geography that De Planhol's critique showed no awareness of the partial but provocative survey of the field of historical geography undertaken by Higounet, a medieval historian.[77] That both De Planhol and the present author[78] might have been unduly pessimistic about the condition of French historical geography could be inferred from a reading of Mollat and Pinchemel's enthusiastic appraisal of encounters between geography and history in France; but such enthusiasm in part reflected their essay's status as an official report on French geography prepared for the 1972 International Geographical Congress in Montreal.[79] Nonetheless, there has perhaps begun at last that long-overdue reappraisal of French historical geography which is necessary to prevent it from becoming a residual discipline: for Boyer has recently examined its condition and diagnosed that it needs to be more directly related both to the practice and progress of historical geography in Britain and North America and to developments in contemporary human geography generally.[80] The last ten or so years have seen a growing self-consciousness and confidence among

French historical geographers, and Clout has recently stated that there is 'abundant evidence of the vitality of our French colleagues and the diversity and rigour of their approaches to understanding the evolution of the cultural landscape'.[81] Additionally – and perhaps in the long term of more fundamental importance than renewed gains on the empirical front – one can point to the opening up of a theoretical salient, a proposal for a 'critical paradigm' within human geography which requires not merely the employment of an historical perspective in human geography but the construction of 'a model of geo-historical reality'.[82] A long-awaited dialogue, has, it seems, begun. The strength of the *Annales* school, it will be recalled, lies fundamentally in its constant posing of questions, in its commitment to *combats et débats*, in its conduct of history as an inquiry and a search.

Search for a method

Pragmatic historical geography

Methodological questioning – a reflexive critique – has come to play a significant role within the practice of historical geography. While only a minority of historical geographers participates in methodological debate and a few openly confess their distaste for it, most acknowledge its function explicitly and all are unavoidably affected by it implicitly. The last twenty years have witnessed considerable interrogation of the methodology of historical geography:[83] numerous papers have been published on this issue since the scope of the discipline was defined two decades ago by Darby.[84] To some extent, the present strength of what Paul Claval has referred to as 'la puissante école de géographie historique britannique' rests on the sure foundation of methodological questioning in historical geography laid by Darby in a quartet of papers which collectively constituted a search for a method in historical geography.[85] Recently Darby has reflected that, beginning in the 1920s and 1930s, he promoted the rise of historical geography as a self-conscious discipline, aided by a small group who worked with the 'dogmatic fervour of new converts to a faith' but who were 'dissatisfied with professing the faith without attempting good works'.[86] Profession and practice, rhetoric and reality, were established as twin pillars of wisdom in historical geography and manifested in a novel account of the historical geography of England, intentionally organised as a series of cross-sectional reconstructions of the geography of England at selected periods in the past.[87] But the very act of editing this work brought home to Darby the limitations of this particular methodology and led him to search deliberately for others, for a new testament.

This exploration had two closely related concerns: first, the ways of *organizing* the results of research; and, secondly, the problems of *writing* historical geography. In an essay on the relations between geography and history, Darby evaluated the merits and limitations of the cross-sectional approach and set these alongside those of narrative accounts of changing geographies.[88] At the same time, delimiting the frontier between historical geography and geography was seen to be difficult, both because the geography of the present is but a thin layer that is continually becoming history and because the characteristics of different regions are the products not only of physical but of human factors in time.[89] Considerable emphasis was therefore placed on the elaboration of 'vertical themes' of landscape change (such as clearing the woodland, draining the marshland, reclaiming the heathland, the landscaping of gardens, and the growth of industries and towns), with man as the principal instrument of landscape change in historic times.[90] While Darby's purpose was to differentiate between geography and history, he fully recognized that 'these limits are not to be defined by nice methodological arguments or by jugglery with words and definitions. The limits are best set by the nature of a particular problem we are attempting to unravel or by the character of a particular landscape we are trying to describe.'[91] While a *general* methodology could be designed which successively interleaved 'horizontal' cross-sections with 'vertical' narratives, the choice of dates for *particular* cross-sections would have 'to be indicated by the march of the developing landscape, and by the nature of the available sources'.[92] The new testament on the historical geography of England was a compromise between the theoretically desirable and the pragmatically possible.[93]

Grappling with problems and sources led Darby to conclude that 'in the writing of historical geography there is no such thing as success, only degrees of unsuccess'.[94] Of strong literary bent, he portrayed a consistent interest in the technical aspects of writing and examined some of them in detail in his essay on the problem of geographical description. His concern there was to consider some possible solutions to Whittlesey's 'puzzle of writing incontestable geography that also incorporates the chains of event necessary to understand fully the geography of the present day'.[95] At least six possible kinds of solutions were identified by Darby – the method of sequent occupance, that of the introductory narrative, that of the parenthesis, that of the footnote, that of the retrospective cross-section, and that of the present tense – while at the same time he recognized that 'variants and combinations of these methods' provided 'challenges to literary skill and ingenuity'.[96] On a larger canvas and with a broader brush, Darby painted four methodological faces of historical geography: geographies of the past, changing landscapes, the past in the present, and geographical history.[97] Darby's search for a method in historical geography discovered a diversity of problems, of sources, of approaches and of techniques. His principal finding was an experimental and pragmatic scholarship. Its limitations were recognized by Darby himself: for example, he admitted that 'the implications of [Whittlesey's] question involve us at once in philosophical debate about the nature of geography as an academic discipline. I am not going to venture into these realms of higher thought. I should like to try to answer the question on a much more lowly level, by looking at what has been done in practice.'[98] Building upon this methodological component of the Darbian tradition, some historical geographers since the mid-1960s have extended the search beyond the realm of pragmatism and into that of philosophy.

Problematic historical geography

The orthodoxy of an historical geography grounded in source-based empiricism and methodological pragmatism has been increasingly questioned since the mid-1960s by those of its practitioners willing to interrogate it in the light of new developments within contemporary human geography and within social history and the social sciences in general.[99] Of course, the search for new sources and techniques with which to confront old problems has continued, but parallel with it has emerged a quest for a new problematic in historical geography. There has been a sustained debate about the roles within historical geography of explanation and understanding, of positivism and phenomenology, of materialism and idealism, which has led to the – possibly premature – suggestion that the foundations might be being laid for the making of a new historical geography.[100] This debate has been summarized elsewhere and there is no need to repeat it here. I want instead to focus upon those aspects of the debate which appear to be most significant, those which seem to demand a renewed emphasis upon man as an agent of landscape change, upon ideas as well as upon artefacts, upon attitudes as well as upon actions. Whether in the form of Collingwoodian idealism or of Marxian humanism, the search for a problematic in historical geography has focused attention upon people as much as upon period and place, upon the *social organization* of time and space rather than upon the *temporal and spatial organization* of society. While the idealist alternative to positivism initially acknowledges it unfortunately subsequently ignores the dual problem of reconstructing the actor's and of constructing the observer's view of the past. Individually, each of these two modes of inquiry would seem to be legitimate philosophically, but it might be more fruitful to marry them in a broader Marxian humanist approach, one which recognizes the reciprocal relations between human agency and social structure, providing what Gregory has called 'a genuine humanisation of the maps and models' of historical geographers.[101]

A few early reactions against the practice of geography merely as a positivist spatial science arrived like cuckoos heralding the arrival of a humanist spring in historical geography: Hepple argued that while historical geographers should endeavour to extend geographical models back into the past and build models of change over time, they should also develop what he termed the 'historical language band' of the epistemological spectrum; Harris argued that historical geography was more properly concerned with regional synthesis than spatial analysis and Clark warned that 'perhaps the most critical question for historical geographers today is the place of the regional study'.[102] Both Clark and Harris also emphasized historical geography as humanism, without providing the logically convincing critique needed to substantiate their case.[103] This has, however, been provided in a quintet of essays by Gregory. Rejecting the precepts both of positivism and of phenomenology led Gregory to explore the possible paths towards a structural historical geography and to suggest that 'a genuinely structural social science must be grounded in an explicit problematisation of discourse, one which refuses to take constructs and typifications of either past or present life-worlds for granted, but which relates them to social practices whose textures and rhythms reveal and reform their constitutive social structures'.[104] His argument led to the conclusion 'that there can be no general theory of structures; our discussions must be located in determinate situations . . . it therefore seems essential to abandon the search for some theory of spatial structure, and instead to consider whether there are any general spatial concepts which might help to identify a specific social structure, and which might reveal the transformations within it'.[105] This has led to the emphatic assertion that

spatial structures are implicated in social structures and each has to be theorised with the other. The result of this is a doubly human geography: human in the sense that it recognises that its concepts are specifically human constructions, rooted in social formations, and capable of – demanding of – continual examination and criticism; and human in the sense that it restores human beings to their own worlds and enables them to take part in the collective transformation of their own human geographies.[106]

Extending this argument, Gregory has suggested that the resurgence of a humanist tradition in geography has drawn its impetus from *la géographie humaine* of Vidal de la Blache and, by examining the connections between the two conceptions, he has demonstrated a common concern with the efficacy of human agency within an essential 'boundedness' of practical life; he has used a series of parallel developments within Marxian humanism to suggest that a scientific explication of the relations between agency and structure can be attained through the deployment of a concept of structuration, but this is seen in turn to require a concept of determination capable of incorporating 'economy' and 'culture' within a single system of concepts, which in Gregory's view presages a critical return to the traditional materialism of *la géographie humaine*.[107] These ideas have been explored further in an essay on action and structure in historical geography which defines the problem as a need to consider not only the intentions of historical actors but also the unintended consequences which follow from the fact that such actions take place within a structure. Gregory offers two solutions: the first, carrying strong echoes of the Darbian tradition, involves the renaissance of a concern with literary style, with the revival of narrative, in order to catch 'the sensuous swirl of contingency and determination'; the second, relying heavily on recent work in critical social science, employs a formal theory of structuration. Both the aesthetic form and the theoretical status of narratives in historical geography are in need of improvement.[108]

The specific implications of some of these general ideas have been pursued by Billinge. Revealing the philosophical naivety of those studies in historical geography situated in behaviouralism and idealism, he has argued that if as historical geographers we wish to study object assemblages, communities or social structures with partly observable, partly hidden and partly experiential attributes, then our frame of reference ought to be structuralist rather than phenomenological.[109] What this would mean in practice has been considered by him in an essay on the problems of reconstructing societies in the past. Billinge is critical of studies in urban historical geography which take as their central concern the identification of residence and similar spatial patterns as evidence of social (and by implication class) segregation, above all because they have 'elevated to the level of a problematic the *spatial expression* of class consciousness at the expense of the issues of *class formation* and *class consciousness* itself'. He argues that the critical need is to investigate 'the mechanisms of intentional social reproduction which underlie the more immediate patterns of perceivable spatial relations' and that we need to draw upon concepts from sociological analysis in order to do so effectively. In particular, he examines the concepts of class, community and institution in his search for a

cognitive lead towards the solution of the fundamental problem of how *individuals* in their contributions to the reproduction of specific institutions also change the nature of their (the institutions') personalities and in turn contribute to the reproduction of society more widely. In short, a vital link can be forged between the individual *client* (agency) and the social *context* (structure) in which his actions and transactions take place.

Thus social institutions in the past, whatever their overt purpose, provided, according to Billinge, a means of contact and entry into the organized system of power, whereby individuals can relate first to their own community, next to their own social class, and finally to society generally. While such individual and collective life-paths may find spatially patterned expression, they do not inevitably do so: there is need, therefore, for a more sensitive community-based approach.[110]

Both Gregory and Billinge have drawn explicitly and extensively upon critiques of social theory provided by Giddens.[111] Travelling by a rather different route, I seem myself to have arrived at almost the same destination. Stemming essentially from a developing awareness of new work within social history in general and within the *Annales* school of total history in particular, my own concern has been to extend the Darbian tradition of historical geography in a way which will allow it explicitly to embrace social as much as economic themes, attitudes as much as actions, ideas as much as artefacts, man as an agent of landscape change as much as landscapes transformed by man.[112] This leads, for example, to a recognition of the need to totalize historical geography so that it incorporates not only man's conflict with 'nature' (the making of cultural landscapes) but also man's personal struggle with 'conscience' and his social struggle with 'class'. It leads, inevitably, to the suggestion that no historical geography – and least of all any historical geography of France – should avoid being concerned with liberty, equality and fraternity and to the view that we must be concerned with individuals engaged in the collective transformation of their own human geographies in particular periods and places. The search for a problematic in historical geography has moved towards a Marxian humanism, based mainly on English and French writings on social theory which emphasize action and structure, individual and collective consciousness and control. For historical geography to make progress in this direction it needs to employ a formal theory of social analysis. Fully aware of the risk of being accused of carrying coals (from both theoretical and empirical seams) to Newcastle (or – in this context – Saint Etienne), I want in the remainder of this essay to draw upon some concepts from Sartre's existential Marxism, particularly for the light which they might throw upon some aspects of the historical geography of rural France in the nineteenth century, because it is this particular period and place that I am endeavouring to understand.

Towards a social historical geography

The duality of agency and structure is reflected in that between individuals and society. The fundamental character of the difference between these binary oppositions can only be partially resolved by regarding the problem as one of scale, with a consequent advocacy of the necessary linkage – on both temporal and spatial axes – of micro- and macro-scale studies. The problem of moving between agency and structure is not simply a question of scale to be resolved by moving between alternate short-term and long-term studies of social change or between local and regional (or even national and international) studies of social structure. While such alternation may contribute to a solution to this problem it does not itself constitute a complete answer. Such essentially temporal and spatial solutions, being partial, need reinforcement from the more explicit endeavours of social theory to provide a model of the links between action and structure, between individuals and society.

One such approach was elaborated by Sartre as the progressive–regressive method.[113] Forging links between Marxism and existentialism Sartre argued that history is composed of human actions and material things, subjects and objects. The human actions constitute projects which he described as follows: individuals are set in specific situations (objectivity), which they interpret in given ways and act within and upon (subjectivity), which in turn places them in new specific situations (objectivity). Individuals act by making 'projects': these consist of perceiving situations, choosing to interpret the resultant perceptions according to sets of values, and then acting out the choices to which they give rise; the project, as a mediation between two moments of objectivity, accounts for history. Sartre's progressive–regressive method involves going back and forth from the social totality to the individual and from the individual to society in search of the mediations that could account for 'present' circumstances: it begins with the social structure and traces its markings in the individual; it then returns to the individual and follows his impact upon the social structure. 'The movement of comprehension', Sartre insisted, 'is simultaneously progressive (towards the objective result) and regressive (I go back towards the original condition).' Sartre is seeking to connect the individual and society (or history), to elaborate the penetration of social forms in individual life and therefore the complete involvement of the individual in history. For Sartre, individuals perceive and act more significantly in groups than in isolation. Individuals are seen as socializing in order to overcome scarcity and preserve their own freedom rather than to appropriate a surplus and promote society as a whole. Individuals act collectively in order to make history: it thus becomes critically important to study the groups that emerge to mediate between the individual and society. The struggle against scarcity and between groups is seen, *par excellence*, in terms of class struggle, but conflicts between other groups also demand the attention of those whose concern is with total historical geography. The range of such groups is wide, but Sartre provides a general scheme which could usefully serve as a check-list for a truly social historical geography. He provides a typology of groups, organizations and institutions which ranges from the family to the State, from the personal and immediate to the impersonal and remote. The formation, function and reproduction – the beliefs and actions – of groups, organizations and institutions become the key concern of historical analysis because of their vital role in social change and social control, in the allocation of scarce resources (including time and space).[114]

Such *social processes* are so crucial to historical understanding that their study cannot usefully be restricted to – let alone be based upon – those which have a mappable *spatial structure*: to focus attention upon the latter carries with it the danger of overlooking groups whose social significance might have been considerable although not expressed in a spatially patterned way. Group formation and consciousness have a potential significance which is not conditional upon their having spatial expression. Consequently, the search for groups cannot both begin and end with the identification of their spatial patterning. That this makes the search more difficult but not less geographical will be accepted by those who practise historical geography as place synthesis rather than as spatial analysis. Within any specific period and place, therefore, an important task is to identify the relative roles of particular groups, organizations and institutions and the parts played by individuals within them.

The bonds fusing individuals into groups are potentially numerous, but relatively few have as yet received as much attention from historical geographers as they deserve. Individuals might form groups tied by any one or more of a number of bonds, such as: family; sex; occupation; class; creed; place of birth, of residence or of work; school; recreation. Networks of social relations based upon such bonds might be expected to extend across a spectrum of temporal and spatial scales. One method of approaching an historical geography of a particular period and place would therefore be to endeavour to reconstruct such networks, to search for an understanding of the beliefs and actions of social groups and to assess their roles in mediating between individuals and society. It will, perhaps, be helpful to illustrate very briefly some of these over-generalized ideas in relation to a particular place and period – rural France during the nineteenth century.

Fraternity in the French countryside during the nineteenth century

The transformation of rural France during the nineteenth century, embracing the disintegration of its social structures and the integration of its economic structures, constituted a sequence of changing *contexts* (or objectivities) for its peasant *agents* (or subjectivities). The nationalization – more specifically, the Parisianization – of France's regions and *pays* gave rise to a set of general processes, a totality, within which particular individuals acted in accordance with their perceptions of their specific situations. When examining particular periods and places, it becomes clear that the effectiveness of *general* processes was highly dependent upon the activities and attitudes of *particular* individuals. For example, the normally catalytic role of primary schooling in the transformation of rural societies varied in its impact within any specific commune with the charisma of particular teachers.[115] Similarly, the general industrialization of rural areas close to growing towns was most marked in those communes that came under the dynamic influence of especially enterprising and progressive individual developers.[116] Again, the politicization of the peasantry was a structural transformation in rural France during the nineteenth century, but the pace and direction of change in particular periods and places has been shown to have depended in considerable measure upon the rhetoric and energies of individual political agents.[117] Such examples illustrate the necessary concern with both context and charisma, with structure and action, with the social totality and with individuals. But it is also important to examine the groups which are established to mediate between these various poles. I want in particular to examine some groups whose bonds lay respectively in a *sense of class* and in a *sense of place*.

One of the basic structures underlying French rural history has been the conflict between individualism and collectivism. The nineteenth century has, in this respect, been referred to by Zeldin as a hiatus, a period in which collectivist traditions were suppressed while peasants struggled for individual ownership of land; the cult of individualism which triumphed with the French Revolution considerably damaged pre-existing concepts of collectivism.[118] Peasant farmers had long traditions of mutual assistance and in some regions even of organized cooperation in farming (as exemplified by the cheesemaking cooperatives of the Jura and the associations of *vignerons* of Touraine); but the concept of collectivism met considerable opposition during the nineteenth century in the alternative notion of individualism, enshrined in the recently formulated Civil Code which acted as a brake on the emergence of new forms of collective action, even when these were advocated as a means of preserving a class of individual owner-occupiers on their farms. Only very gradually did there emerge during the second half of the nineteenth century within rural France a range of agricultural *syndicats* in the form, for example, of livestock insurance societies, threshing syndicates, anti-Phylloxera syndicates and general purpose agricultural syndicates whose aim was to provide their members with supplies (especially of chemical fertilizers) of guaranteed quality and at reduced prices. Agricultural *syndicats* represent individual farmers socializing in order to overcome scarcity (to make the most effective use of limited resources) and in order to preserve their freedom (to ensure the survival of small, sometimes uneconomic, farms under pressure from competition from large and efficient farms not only elsewhere in France but also abroad, particularly in North America). The *syndicats*, groupings of peasants, mediated between the individual farmer and his social totality.

The function of these *syndicats* was by no means narrowly economic, for the lesson of solidarity was both taught by the State and preached by the Church in their struggle for the social control of the peasantry. High moral, social and political goals were to be achieved by economic means: the promotion of agricultural associations, cooperatives and syndicates represented materialism in the service of idealism. Few *syndicats*, it is usually argued, were organized by the peasants themselves: most were organized either by republican leaders of the political centre and left or by large landowners influenced by the paternalistic and corporatist ideas of Social Catholicism, and imbued with a right-wing desire to insulate the peasantry against the inroads of republican ideology. In studying these groups, therefore, two sets of individuals demand attention: first, those visionary teachers and preachers whose social links were with the urban world of politics as much as with the rural world of peasants; second, those enterprising and energizing local agents who acted to diffuse contagiously concepts of collective action which had been spread hierarchically.[119]

In general, the creation of *syndicats* served to heighten class consciousness within rural communities. In theory, many were founded on the concept of a single *classe paysanne*, quite distinct in its *mentalités* from the rest of French society. The activities of rural communities were to be regulated in order to ensure their own conservation.[120] In practice, most *syndicats* developed primarily economic functions and few included significant numbers of farm labourers within their membership, so that they served to harden class divisions within agrarian societies. The decline of traditional rural communities, with an internal social cohesion maintained by the existence of powerful external threats (for example, from the *seigneur*, the tax collector and the money-lender), was paralleled by the rise of a more explicit class struggle within the countryside.[121] The social totality of the rural community was clearly not fully comprehensive even at the beginning of the nineteenth century but it was much less so by the end of the century. Internal tensions within rural communities increased: 1848–51 saw the last major revolt of a poor peasantry protesting against the emergence of private, capitalist, agriculture, in defence of traditional, community, rights. From 1870 onwards agricultural strikes of a recognizably modern form by farm labourers contested the development of monopolistic capitalism and called for a more equitable distribution of the income from agriculture; from the 1920s some sections of the peasantry (some small owner-occupiers, some small tenant farmers) widened the social base of the protest movement and diversified it by engaging in direct action (demonstration, marches and occupations) in order to protect their interests.

To be comprehensive, a study of the geography of fraternity in the French countryside during the nineteenth century would need to extend beyond the agricultural *syndicats* to include both more traditional forms of sociability (such as religious festivals; markets and fairs; communal work in the fields, on the farms and in the villages; as well as the *cabarets* and the *veillées*) and other, more novel, categories of mutual aid and association (such as insurance societies; local corps of firemen; and musical, gymnastic, cycling and other recreational societies).[122] The growth of new forms of sociability may be seen as one of a range of responses and reactions to the processes which increasingly transformed – one could say, eroded – rural France during the second half of the nineteenth century. Disintegration of rural communities and intensification of the class struggle carried with it a significant change in the geography of social relations in the countryside. The *sense of community* in the early nineteenth century was bounded locally, and significant social relations were essentially of a neighbourhood or contagious kind and were immediately observable within the *pays*; with the development of a heightened *sense of class*, social relations became increasingly of a spatially remote or hierarchical and abstract kind. As social relations were increasingly forged among members of the *same class* but of a *different pays*, so an important transformation was to be expected in the *sense of place* as social links moved beyond the immediate locality and into the regional, the national and even the international arena. Any truly social historical geography of rural France in the nineteenth century must therefore embrace those groups that emerged to enable individuals to act collectively in their struggle against scarcity and against other groups; engagements in this class struggle were not confined to the immediate and personal locality of participating individuals. Groups such as syndicates, unions and political parties forged new sets of social relations which were not spatially contained within distinct *pays*. These groups were *agents* in the transformation of the social *structure* of rural France and played a significant role in the breakdown of the *pays*. They did so in conjunction with the nationally controlled endeavour to convert *le paysan* to *le Français* which has been closely identified with the spread of railways, schooling and military service.[123]

Some of these trends, identifiable within rural France, might be more readily recognized in those areas which underwent most industrialization and urbanization during the nineteenth century. Within such areas a new *sense of place* developed together with a new *sense of class*. They tended to be composed of people who were both geographically and occupationally mobile, people who could therefore be expected to be seeking – or at least willing to adopt – new geopieties and new social relations. Sewell has suggested that working-class consciousness emerged in France during the 1830s, a decade which saw both the identification of manual workers as *le peuple* (by casting them in the role of industrial serfs who should be emancipated from their exploitation by privileged proprietors) and the creation of new forms of fraternal association (free and voluntary societies based on the common will of the producers in the trade and on the idea of the collective ownership of the means of production).[124] Class consciousness emerged as an organized, unionized, force in industrial and urban France: strikes – a major weapon in the class struggle – came to be characteristic of certain *sectors* of the economy and of certain *regions* of the country.[125] Modern forms of *socialism* emerged in the industrial regions, for example, of northern France and in some Parisian suburbs, which were in marked contrast to the traditional forms of *sociability* identified in the Midi. The combination of new patterns of industrial activity and of an industrial work-force composed mainly of new migrants was fertile ground for the growth of regional working-class consciousness, as Lequin has demonstrated for the area in and around Lyons during the second half of the nineteenth century.[126] A new sense both of place and of class was cultivated by a variety of fraternal associations. In doing this, these groups were actively involved in the transformation of their own histories and geographies. The land of France during the nineteenth century was not as tranquil and empty as some historico-geographical accounts would lead us to believe.[127] It was 'full of sound and fury', it was full of people signifying something. All historical geography is, in essence, social historical geography.

Places in past periods were peopled. Their changing landscapes contained within them both social conflict and social cooperation among individuals and groups; and these relations should be seen as a vital part of the making of those landscapes. Reflecting upon the relations of history and geography fortunately serves the dual purpose of broadening the challenge confronting historical geography and of suggesting some ways in which that challenge might be met.

Acknowledgements

One version of this essay was read to a meeting of the Cambridge Occasional Discussants in Historical Geography held at the Swan Hotel in Southwold and another to the Franco-British Symposium on Historical Social Geography held in the Château de Morigny, near Paris. I am grateful to the participants at those meetings, as well as to Peter Burke, Anne Buttimer, Philippe Pinchemel and Hugh Prince for their comments.

University of Cambridge

2

Hegemony, class and power in late Georgian and early Victorian England: towards a cultural geography

MARK BILLINGE

The relationship of the bourgeoisie to the landowners . . . also poses problems. To what extent can the landowners (whose position rested on the success of capitalist agriculture conducted by their tenant farmers, but increasingly also on other forms of investment) be seen as a separate class, as opposed to a fraction of the bourgeoisie? How real was their apparent antagonism to the urban industrial bourgeoisie in the first half of the nineteenth century? The class determination of the landowner can perhaps be treated as an open question . . . what is important is to recognize their existence as a highly distinctive group, whose interests were strongly articulated and whose culture and values were in important respects different [from the bourgeoisie].

Robert Gray, *Bourgeois Hegemony in Victorian Britain*

Hegemony is then not only the articulate upper level of 'ideology', nor are its forms of control only those seen as 'manipulation' or 'indoctrination'. It is a whole body of practices and expectations over the whole of our living: our senses and assignments of energy, our shaping perceptions of ourselves and our world. It is a lived system of meanings and values – constitutive and constituting – which as they are experienced as practices appear as reciprocally confirming. It thus constitutes a sense of reality for most people in the society . . . It is, that is to say, in the strongest sense a 'culture', but a culture which has to be seen as the lived dominance and subordination of particular classes.

Raymond Williams, *Marxism and Literature*

This essay is not a complete argument, not even a complete exploration, still less an historiographic survey of the use of culture as a medium for historical divination. It is something of a companion to an earlier, essentially methodological, statement in another volume in this series, though it goes considerably beyond that necessarily sketchy outline in focusing not on the technical apparatus available for the recovery of social structures, but rather on the nature of social formation itself and the value of cultural theory in establishing a framework for its examination.[1] Two intersecting sets of ideas permeate the discussion: Giddens' theory of structuration and Gramsci's reworking of hegemony. Together they provide the materials for the restoration of 'culture' itself, though their treatment is scarcely equal. The former, with which geographers are now more familiar, is largely implicit in what follows, and since its broad arguments have been explored elsewhere[2] no detailed consideration will be given to it – though readers of Giddens will readily appreciate the extent of my debt to his clarification of the structure-agency problem. The latter – the production and reproduction of hegemony as social power – has become increasingly accessible in recent years, not least through the interpretative work of Robert Gray and Raymond Williams,[3] but it is more explicitly reviewed here with a view to rescuing 'culture' from its remote and at times purely superstructural role in historical explanation – that is to say its imputed value as a carrier of relatively formal social ideals or as a means of legitimating recurrent social practices. Nevertheless the thrust of this paper is primarily substantive, so that the most important sections are those in which the theoretical frame is set to work. Equally my exploration is one of period far more than of place: an attempt to prise the culture of an age away not from its general context, out of which it would be meaningless, but from the specifics of its location in metropolitan and provincial England. In order to achieve this, a quantity of theoretical equipment must be assembled. However, lest the direction of the general argument become in any way unclear, a brief statement of the path trodden in the exploration which follows may be usefully supplied here.

During the late eighteenth and early nineteenth centuries the hegemony of land was challenged by a vigorous and supremely successful force – that of capital. Throughout this period relations between the landed interest and the bourgeoisie were constantly renegotiated as the fortunes of the two 'classes' fluctuated in response both to the external vagaries of national economic performance and to the internal reorientations which the quickening pace of political development brought in train. Whether one subscribes to the view of E. P. Thompson (along with Gray and Poulantzas)[4] – that the landed interest constituted not a separate class but a fraction of capital during this period – or to the alternative view proffered by, amongst others, Weiner – that it was the rules and conventions of land that continued to supply the vademecum of middle-class social ambition and political aspiration[5] – depends in part upon theoretical sympathies (the conceptual room accorded to Marxist notions of *class* or Weberian formularies of *status*),[6] in part upon the explanatory power allowed to economy rather than culture in the definition of social delineations, and in part upon one's specific interpretation of certain key moments in the struggle between land and capital. Though on the whole there appears to be substantial agreement over the *outcome* of these social upheavals – that hegemony as well as overt political power (control of the

State instruments) passed from the landed aristocracy to the social amalgam generally styled the bourgeoisie – there is as yet no definitive view either of the mechanisms whereby this transference was achieved (aristocratic capitulation or bourgeois advance; social, political, cultural or economic force; *ad hoc* or institutional directives) or of its impact on the ideologies of the two groups subsequent to their hegemonic inversion. The argument pursued here suggests that the landed interest and the bourgeoisie remained throughout the eighteenth and nineteenth centuries separate social classes which (a considerable elision of economic interests notwithstanding) maintained different cultural traditions and ideological perspectives. The loss of political and hegemonic power did not, in other words, entirely subsume the landed interest within capital and its distinctiveness was maintained, albeit at considerable expense. Furthermore this essay suggests that the transference of power was itself achieved through cultural mechanisms as well as through economic ones. Though the economic decline of the landed interest opened up the possibility of bourgeois emancipation, the counter-hegemony of the middle class was essentially forged around cultural institutions and imposed through cultural media. Thus, like the political usurpation of the landed aristocracy at a higher level, the incorporation of the working class during the nineteenth century into what was in essence a bourgeois consciousness (together with the suppression of traditional patterns of social alignment associated with land, paternalism, a patrician society and the moral economy) was effectively a process of cultural restabilization. Indeed, by extension, the whole edifice of 'normal' social controls – the institutionalization of unequal relationships between groups – rests upon cultural values and their manipulation (conscious or otherwise) by dominant, hegemonic fractions. At the same time, it is important to establish two things: *first* that these developments do not amount to the working out of a consciously formulated plan: there is no suggestion here of the mechanical knowledgeability and rationality of procedure which considerably lessen the attractions of Foster's to some extent complementary analysis of bourgeois/working-class relations and their manipulation in the mid-nineteenth century. As we shall see, the crucial and wide-ranging power of culture as hegemony, uncoverable as it may be in retrospective analysis, is not tangibly present for its contemporaries to recognize, evaluate and direct – a feature which remains as analytically beguiling as it is practically essential. The power of culture as social norm is thus considerably strengthened by its essentially unconscious level of operation: a subjugating force which remains unrecognized and consequently unchallenged in its contemporary context. It follows then that the political and social development of the late eighteenth and early nineteenth centuries cannot be ascribed to entirely intentional actions by precociously knowledgeable agents. Hegemony is not mechanical, nor are its forms of extension primarily overt. *Secondly*, however, it is important to counter the monolithic tendencies of much class-development theory; both in terms of the division between social classes and of the internalized metamorphosis of group ideology. Indeed as we shall see, though the bourgeoisie emerged from its Victorian conflict with land the stronger and more viable force, it was not itself unchanged by that experience either in membership or in belief. Bourgeois consciousness by the mid-nineteenth century was not that of the late eighteenth: smoothed, diluted, reinterpreted, it was very different from the acute radicalism and extreme republicanism of its earlier manifestation. Equally, not all members of the bourgeoisie sought to inherit the political instruments for which the most advanced had fought. Thus the *grande bourgeoisie* (the older and wealthier commercial families of the early Industrial Revolution) found themselves increasingly drawn towards the values and prestige rewards of land[7] as increasing status brought more to conserve, and logically enough an increasing conservatism. Such families, once in the vanguard of the struggle for recognition and power, became in time (and again through cultural reorientation) more acceptable to the traditional landed interest, just as they themselves became less sympathetic towards the values of the bourgeoisie more generally. For the landed interest, successful negotiation with the acceptable face of commercialism, whilst it could not recapture the political initiative now well and truly lost to the middle class, could yet bolster that class's economic and cultural position and revive a flagging social confidence. If *mariage à la mode*, the conjunction of the landed and the loaded as it has been termed (normally a noble son to a dowry-laden daughter from the aspiring *nouveaux riches*), was founded upon economic necessity, it was not without ultimate advantage. For the bourgeoisie, too, class loyalty clearly came at a price and could be superseded as opportunity arose and definitions shifted, so that mutability was as much the keynote as ideological rigidity and abstract conviction. If hegemony shifted, then so did the ideology which its existence served to impose.

In short, then, this paper seeks to examine the important and hitherto much neglected class struggle waged between capital and land in the late eighteenth and early nineteenth centuries,[8] and in examining the course of that struggle it seeks to reinstate culture as an active channel of class formation, negotiation and exchange.

Hegemony, counter-hegemony and social power

Though originally confined to the relationship between dominant and client states in international politics, the theory of hegemony has been extended in Marxist analysis to embrace the connectivities between social groups and particularly the role of ideas in structuring and maintaining the inequalities between political elites and their subordinates.[9] Within this broad formulation hegemony is seen as socially collectivized rule and is normally seen as the object of a natural and active opposition launched by non-hegemonic groups seeking to break down the structure of dominance in order to establish alternative systems which may themselves in turn become hegemonic (though the ability of dominant classes to foresee and therefore to forestall such counter-interests is a measure of their own hegemonic strength). Hegemony is thus actively liberated in class struggle in that its location in most social organizations is seen as residing with the 'elite' (whether hereditary aristocracy or wealthy bourgeoisie), whilst 'alternative' or incipient hegemony is seen as existing ultimately within the working class.[10] This particular formulation has become something of a leitmotiv of nineteenth-century social history.

However, hegemony acquired a further and more significant refinement in the work of Gramsci, who drew the crucial and now widely recognized distinction between different, and not necessarily coincident, forms of social power: specifically between 'rule' (*dominio*) and 'hegemony' itself.[11] 'Rule', he suggested, is expressed directly in political forms and, in times of crisis – such as the eighteenth and nineteenth centuries in Britain frequently witnessed – in direct coercion. Such 'rule' is the constraining of subordinate groups in a visible, identifiable sense and is accordingly easy to recognize for what it is: the State machinery and its adjuncts; the apparatus of the dominant brought to bear on the lives and activities of the powerless majority in order to maintain the political status quo. In times of real social crisis 'rule' may be counter-productive in its very conspicuity (as an obvious grievance and a target for the attention of a focused opposition), and accordingly it may be neither the best nor the most commonly invoked form of social domination and constraint. Indeed, according to Gramsci, the more normal situation is regulation by a 'complex of deeply penetrative, interlocking controls'[12] which are hardly recognizable as constraints in the traditional sense but which are nonetheless active in the imposition of values designed to confirm the legitimacy of the dominant group. It is for the description of these interlocking controls and the mechanism of their liberation that the term 'hegemony' is reserved and so designated, it 'enjoys' a superficial resemblance to the concept of 'false' consciousness, familiar from the work of Foster,[13] though, as will become clear, a critical difference lies in the refusal of 'hegemony' to equate social belief with 'consciousness' alone.

This aspect of hegemony is important to us in two senses: in reaffirming the power asymmetries which exist in relations between social action and social structure (that is, the extent to which individuals and social groups retain the ability to shape their own accomplishments) and, secondly, in defining the relationship between hegemony and ideology in which the latter constitutes the system of values active in the projection of a particular class interest in attempts to define and maintain economic and hegemonic integrity. Ideology is normally seen[14] as a relatively formal and articulate system of meanings into which individuals are to varying degrees socialized and through which particular 'class outlooks' are maintained. Its systematic properties are frequently revealed through an analysis of what Williams terms 'typical, ideal or pervasive ideological traits':[15] a rather stark, structural account which, in emphasizing the coherence and shared rationality of this outlook, necessarily simplifies and generalizes the relatively mixed, uncertain and inarticulate consciousness of actual individuals. Clearly ideology has been a popular focus for social theorists precisely because its structured properties allow for its abstraction from specific contexts without fear of its fragmentation under the analytical microscope. It is possible, for example, to speak of bourgeois ideology in the nineteenth century (an amalgam let us say of political radicalism, nonconformism, utilitarianism, etc.) without asserting that every member of the bourgeoisie held such views in identical manner; and yet at the same time ideology is frequently invoked as the essential basis for directed social action by coherent social classes. A further advantage of this is that, once identified, 'ideology' can be reapplied as the governing principle of class action and association: that is, this sense of 'an ideology' is applied in abstract ways to the actual consciousness of both dominant and subordinate groups. Thus, in Marxist analysis, a dominant class is held to possess an ideology in relatively pure and simple forms, whilst a subordinate class either has nothing but this ideology (since the production of ideas is by definition confined to those who control the primary means of production)[16] or, in another and perhaps more persuasive version, has this ideology imposed upon its own very different 'natural' consciousness, which it must struggle to sustain or develop against the ideology of the ruling class.[17] Either way, both dominant and subordinate classes are said to show strong traces of an identifiable ideology (the essential qualities of which are equally traceable in individuals *per se*), so that its success and value in maintaining social configurations can be measured without direct recourse to contextual detail.

Analytically all this is very convenient though ultimately inadequate in its ability to respond with appropriate sensitivity to the wide range of (often ephemeral) channels and procedures through which information is conveyed, dominance asserted and subordination strengthened. The concept of 'hegemony', though in some ways close to these definitions of ideology, remains distinctive in a number of ways. In one sense it goes beyond ideology in incorporating and transforming its abstract ideals into *practice* (whilst simultaneously softening and legitimating its assertions through widespread dissemination and 'enforcement'); in another sense it transcends the formal consciousness which ideology implies. Thus, though hegemony by no means excludes the meanings, values and beliefs which ideology so conveniently summarizes, it chooses to involve them, together with the less formal, less reasoned and hence less abstractable elements of consciousness in a much more contextual analysis of social relations as they are lived and experienced in everyday life. Relations of dominance and subordination are seen accordingly:

in their forms as practical consciousness, as in effect a saturation of the whole process of living – not only of political and economic activity, but of the whole substance of lived identities and relationships to such a depth that the pressures and limits of what can ultimately be seen as specific economic, political and cultural systems seem to most of us the pressures and limits of simple experience and common sense.[18]

This expression of hegemony as a 'complete and lived culture' brings with it two immediate consequences which can be turned to advantage.[19] First, in seeing hegemonic control as culturally ingrained and to some extent commonly experienced, the whole question of class rule and of opposition to it is transformed, such that the normally invoked determinants of class formation – be they politics or economics – can be held insufficient to capture the rich subtlety of real social mediation. But, secondly, and equally importantly, it gives us an entirely new perspective from which to view the process of acculturation and the crucial importance of culture itself in shaping social ideals and social relations. Within much Marxist analysis culture and cultural activity have been seen as largely superstructural, in that they have been treated as reflections of a pre-formed economic and social structure:[20] that is to say, though the fundamental importance of cultural development has never been denied, its role has been circumscribed, being seen as descriptive and expressive of experience within a framework fashioned by other, more important, because more 'basic', political and economic forces. Within Gramsci's concept of hegemony these distinctions and functional inferiorities are suspended. Indeed culture is seen to be amongst the most basic of processes involved in the actual formation of relations between social classes, not least because in its everyday operation, it touches upon a much broader arena of experience than do the abstractions of social and economic theory. Thus cultural common denominators between social actors are just as fundamental in 'defining their interests as between themselves and as against other(s)'[21] as are half-formed and partially digested theories of political economy.

All told, the more sophisticated concept of hegemony which goes beyond ideology and class consciousness, renders more central and determining the cultural apparatus of social groups in their struggle for either domination or liberation and conveniently incorporates these values into its 'wholeness' of process. As Williams has it:

A lived hegemony is always a process. It is not, except analytically, a system or structure. It is a realized complex of experiences, relationships and activities, with specific and changing pressures and limits. In practice, that is, hegemony can never be singular. Its internal structures are highly complex as can readily be seen in concrete analysis. Moreover (and this is crucial, reminding us of the necessary thrust of the concept), it does not just passively exist as a form of dominance. It has continually to be renewed, recreated, defended and modified. It is also continually resisted, limited, altered, challenged by pressures not all its own. We have then to add to hegemony the concepts of counter-hegemony and alternative hegemony which are real and persistent elements of practice.[22]

For Gramsci, counter-hegemony was always located ultimately within the working class. In his view, society is thus characterized by an uneven though historically evolutionary struggle between two creative forces: an existing hegemony, which exerts powerfully repressive influences over the conduct of all subordinate groups, and 'working people', who, though themselves potentially hegemonic, have still to become a class, to develop counter-hegemony and eventually, through struggle and emancipation from the disruptive penetration of their 'natural' consciousness by alien values, to challenge the dominant groups.[23] Within Marxist thought generally that struggle is, of course, inevitably successful, so that 'natural' popular consciousness and 'legitimate' hegemony are held to be effectively synonymous, though how either is brought about remains something of an open question.

Investigations of hegemony in mid-nineteenth-century Britain (on both conceptually exploratory and substantively detailed levels) have generally supported Gramsci's abstract schematization, not least in terms of the location of hegemony and counter-hegemony and the specific constitution of those groups within the power bloc which can be said to design and build the functional architecture of dominance and subordination.[24] Thus in the mid-nineteenth century a relatively straightforward picture of the classic type is offered: a cohesive hegemonic alliance of the landed interest and the bourgeoisie (the position achieved after aristocratic 'capitulation' to middle-class pressures, the details of which will occupy us later) and, through exclusion, a counter-hegemony in active formation within the working class, which by this time had unquestionably attained the status of a fully articulate social class in its own right.[25] Straightforward as this might seem, the investigation of social relations at mid-century has not been without its conceptual difficulties, the solutions to which have in turn considerably advanced the practical application of Gramscian theory in more embryonic contexts. For our own purposes it is helpful to rehearse some of the more important strands of the argument before plunging into the murkier waters of the eighteenth century.

One crucial refinement to emerge from the intensive examination of mid-Victorian social formation has been Poulantzas' and Gray's distinction between the governing and hegemonic fractions of what is seen as a far from monolithic power bloc.[26] The power bloc – a collection of cooperative interest groups which together constitute all social power – is seen not as synonymous with the hegemonic group alone but more subtly as a shifting alliance between *politically* dominant, *culturally* dominant and *ideologically* dominant social sub-groups which may be drawn from different social classes. That is to say several 'niches' exist within the power bloc – one concerned with the direction of the State instruments (the government, judiciary, armed forces, etc.), one with the development of social 'policy' and one with the implementation of those policies through normal hegemonic channels. Though it is accepted that the sub-groups occupying these niches can, and indeed sometimes do, overlap and that at times they may even directly coincide,

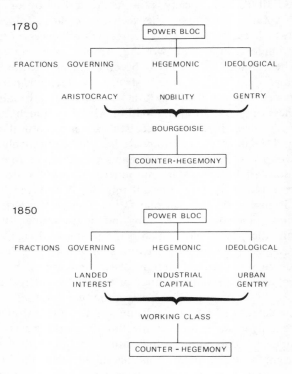

Figure 1

there is nevertheless the strongest suggestion that they need not necessarily do so, and that in the mid-nineteenth century they very significantly did not.[27]

The most appropriate schema for this period appears to be that put forward most recently by Gray, who suggests that the power bloc as a whole from the 1850s onwards consisted of both landed and bourgeois interests ('aristocracy' and middle class) in unexpected though highly structured alliance.[28] Gray further argues that the governing fraction of the bloc (those in established political office) was composed of the old landed interest together with the culturally assimilated and often directly related *grande bourgeoisie*, and certain elements drawn from the owners of commercial capital; the hegemonic fraction is seen as comprising the owners of industrial capital to an almost exclusive degree – it was their values that dominated social thinking and conventional socialization, and their agents who, through their provincial location, were responsible for the dissemination of hegemony to the subordinate working class. The social and political policies of the power bloc as a whole (the ideology of the dominant force) are seen as being the conscious creation of the 'intellectual' bourgeoisie (the 'urban gentry' drawn from several strata within the bourgeoisie), who, though not themselves directly involved in the central governmental process, were nonetheless instrumental in determining the future course of the power bloc's development. This division of 'responsibilities' into governing, hegemonic and ideology-creating fractions is summarized in Figure 1, though several features of it may require explanation. Thus, that groups ostensibly in government and theoretically in control of the entire State apparatus can in fact discharge their Parliamentary and civil duties without at any stage constituting the real locus of power (which is located as always in the hegemonic fraction whose puppet the governing fraction is), and without becoming the originators of social policy for the power bloc as a whole, might seem startling if not unnecessarily confusing and perverse. However, recognition of the validity both of these claims and of the distinctions which they imply takes us conceptually a major step forward in our attempt to understand the shifting nature of social power and social relations in this crucial phase of industrialization.

The same niches within the power bloc did of course exist in the late eighteenth century, though they were occupied by very different groups. Indeed the difference between the formations of the 1780s and those of the 1850s is both a mark of the real political emergence of the bourgeoisie and a measure of the explanatory task which confronts us. In the 1780s the power bloc consisted exclusively of the landed interest,[29] which constituted the State government and controlled State power both centrally and locally, either by direct presence or, more usually, through a series of quasi-medieval agencies, recruitment to which was carefully controlled and/or nepotic.[30] Like the power bloc of the 1850s it was not unitary but a marriage of convenience between social groups divided internally along specific though intermeshing political (Whig: Tory) and social (aristocracy: nobility: gentry: squirearchy) lines.[31] Responsibility too was divided between the various constituent fractions. Corporate ideology sprang generally from these groups in roughly equal measure, though it was specifically elaborated and reproduced in dominant form by the rural gentry. The aristocracy formed the larger part of the governing fraction (directly in the Lords, indirectly through the Commons and the Church), whilst the nobility constituted the hegemonic fraction.[32] Counter-hegemony (in formation though also increasingly in physical completeness) rested at this time not with the working class of Gramsci's universal formulation, but with the bourgeoisie fighting for recognition, identity and power.[33]

Precisely what this counter-hegemony of the bourgeoisie looked like in 1780 will occupy us shortly. Clearly though, it bears some resemblance to the hegemony to come of the 1850s – at least in terms of its ideological basis – in its powerful mixture of utilitarian value, rigid morality, political extremism and social and ecclesiastical radicalism. In 1780, this combination of values constituted a startling and ambitious manifesto; by 1850 it had become (with variations in the process) the orthodox code of everyday practice as well as the unexamined basis of ordinary social belief. The processes and events which we shall be observing in late Georgian and early Victorian England are all intimately bound up with this major transition: this passage from counter-hegemony to hegemony, this ousting of the landed power bloc. The parallel theme is of course that to which I have already alluded – the social legitimation of the *grande bourgeoisie* through cultural antagonism and reassimilation (about which more later) – though viewed from this perspective it is clear that (since it was the grande bourgeoisie who initially formulated the counter-hegemonic position) these themes are not 'parallel' at all but rather different aspects of precisely the same process: hegemonic exchange and transition. We need to know much more about the nature of these different classes and of the cultural agencies through which their struggle was directed, and it is to this that we must now turn.

Coningsby and Mr Gradgrind

The widely different character of landed and bourgeois society is a theme well articulated in late eighteenth- and early nineteenth-century fiction and comprehensively elaborated in Williams' rightly famous account, *The Country and the City*. The highly symbolic dichotomy lovingly elaborated by Mrs Gaskell (*North and South*) or Disraeli (*Sybil*), together with the earlier satires of a Peacock, a Surtees or a Trollope, gives clues to the contemporary awareness (amongst writers of very different social backgrounds and political persuasions) of shifting social tensions amongst the privileged classes of the nation, albeit tinged with essentially middle-class sentiment and the conventions of literary artifice. Now is not the time to assess the importance of such 'sources' for the illumination of social attitudes in the past, though one thing is clear: the character of a Coningsby or a Gradgrind (the one fighting for the restitution of a principled oligarchy and strongly disapproving of 'a crown robbed of its prerogative, a Church extended to a commission and an aristocracy that does not lead';[34] the other an arch-utilitarian whose faith lies exclusively in the ability of fact, rationality and a peculiarly rigid Benthamism to create a better society)[35] caricatures a widely established contemporary belief in the distinctive polarization of dominant types in the nation's higher echelons:[36] a point warmly supported by an older generation of historians – notably Bagehot[37] – and only recently suppressed by the theoretical rigidity of, amongst others, Thompson.[38] Thompson's commercialized aristocracy or Weiner's 'aristocratised bourgeoisie' notwithstanding, there is much to be gained from a recognition of this imperfectly negotiable division: a division recently redefined by Scott[39] and theoretically charted by Weber.[40] In literature these may indeed be caricatures, but, as Thompson admits of Gadgrind, 'it is of the best order of caricature which delineates the essential lines of truth'[41] and which, furthermore, penetrates deeper than mere outward appearance and convention, for contained within both Coningsby and Gradgrind are the expressions of inward mentality which had determined at least in part the success of middle-class incursions into what had been hitherto exclusively aristocratic domains. Whilst the aristocracy through Coningsby and his earlier manifestations found itself in a situation of defence – a situation justified only by appeal to tradition and an uneasy *status quo* and leading in turn to a marked inability to adapt to wider, uncontrollable social developments – the middle class through Gradgrind and his kind proved itself dynamic, enterprising (in all senses of the word) and above all remarkably open to change:

Mr Bounderby, the coarse and avaricious mill-owner of *Hard Times*, the type of the earlier industrial revolution, was now giving way to his more sophisticated cousin Mr Gradgrind. Gradgrind not only has power and wealth: he also has the theory to justify and perpetuate exploitation. The Victorian bourgeoisie had constructed from bits of Adam Smith and Riccardo, Bentham and Malthus a cast iron theoretical system which they were now securing with the authority of the State and the Law, and sanctifying with the blessing of religion.[42]

Not by coincidence alone were Gradgrind's own sons baptized as Adam Smith and Malthus Gradgrind. However, just as Coningsby and Gradgrind stand as symbols for the mid-nineteenth-century landed and bourgeois elements of the prevailing elite, so too are the terms 'landed' and 'bourgeois' merely a convenient, if inaccurate, shorthand for a whole series of political, ideological, economic, social and cultural orientations which, stated at their least subtle, appear in Figure 2.

Whatever doubts might persist about the nature of hegemony in the nineteenth century, there can be little dissent from the view that during the eighteenth century and for a considerable period before that the landed interest represented the patrician element in contemporary society.[43] Before the massive upheavals generally characterized as the Industrial Revolution, both rural and (to a lesser degree) urban spheres were either directly or indirectly ruled by the large estates and their agents. Parliament, the Church, the Press, education, the Civil Service, the armed forces laboured under aristocratic patronage, and the production of formal and informal ideas stemmed directly from the great houses, and were disseminated by a thousand and one hands through a thousand and one permanent and ephemeral channels. Though the nature of the aristocracy's role in a modernizing world was to change in time, the general image and life-style to which it adhered was slow to reflect those involutional reorientations in the wider economy, such that as the eighteenth century gave way to the nineteenth, the traditional interests and beliefs of this largely reactionary body (though significantly not their absolute fortunes) remained as distinctive as ever.

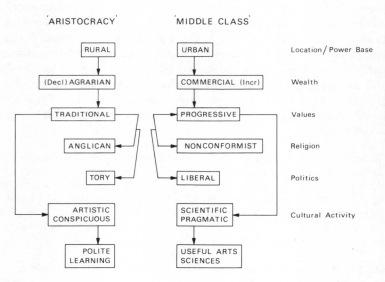

Figure 2

At least one part of this complex formulation is largely familiar. Society at Court, society in Bath and life on the great estates confirms a decidedly bucolic picture of the leisured life and the cultured manner.[44] To be sure, though riding to hounds, extravagant gambling soirées, galas, balls and the substantial expense of house renovation or collection building were more typical of the age of Charles Fox than of the age of Palmerston, conspicuous consumption in one form or another still accounted for a considerable proportion not only of estate expenditure, but also of the routine of daily activity with which it was closely associated. A society which raced its footmen as it raced its horses and protected its game as it did not protect its employees, gave symbolic expression to its cavalier attitude towards money in the regular loss and reacquisition of fortunes according to the laws of chance. The great libraries and galleries of aristocratic mansions continued to expand during the eighteenth century, and the latter in particular enjoyed a substantial fillip following the Classical Revival which accompanied the cultured Englishman's discovery of the ancient world, and the arrival in England of the Elgin Marbles – stolen from that most symbolic of cities by so symbolic a figure.[45] The nation and its aristocracy, in stark contrast to the harsher realities of eighteenth-century life, were only too happy to claim both continuity and solidarity with the traditions of government, empire, law and achievement established in the popular mind by classical allusion, and in the architecture of the Revival lay a symbolic stability much to be hoped for if unlikely to be realized in troubled times. If there was indeed to follow a 'Victorian Olympus' – when, for the first time since the Renaissance, the well-mannered man turned his earthly gaze towards the empyrean – then it was significantly still the traditional exponents of such cultural orientations – the aristocracy – who were to prefigure its arrival.

In short, throughout the eighteenth century it was the landed interest that found itself the rightful, willing and only weakly challenged protector of traditional cultural values: the *arbiter elegantiarum* of the English scene. When the aristocracy was not thus 'at play' it had, of course, an inherited role which, constitutionally at least, demanded its most serious attention. Before the Great Reform Act of 1832 (and for a considerable period thereafter) the aristocracy were the guardians of *political* power through the recognized channels of both Church and State. The ownership of land remained the key to national status, and through that status, allied to a carefully fashioned system of custom and law, the key to national political power. Whether directly through the House of Lords or indirectly through the purchase of boroughs, M.P.s and control of the Commons, the aristocracy continued to serve primarily themselves and, according to their own lights, the nation at large, as they continued to enact legislation and enforce a judicial system which principally strengthened their own economic and political position, furthered the interests of land more generally and only subsequently made possible the growth of industrialism.[46]

The alliance of wealth with essentially Tory politics and traditional values brought with it a strong political commitment (strategic if not necessarily theological) to the Church of England and to the prevailing latitudinarian orthodoxy.[47] For the largely chapel-going Nonconformist bourgeoisie, such a closing of the political circle represented almost insurmountable problems – not least those of political entry, where to the disqualifications of marginal status and 'landlessness' could be added the failure to observe acceptable religious practice. This close association of Church and State during the period of middle-class counter-hegemonic formation effectively removed one of the few potential 'courts of appeal' in a society now dominated by a unified and mutually reinforcing secular and religious authority. Thus, though the Church had arguably, at least in its institutional form, been little more than an adjunct of the State since Reformation times[48] (and by no means an uncorrupt or apolitical pillar of moral values set aside from the temporal affairs of State), throughout the eighteenth and early nineteenth centuries the strengthening bond of alliance, such that both Church and State espoused the values and supported the policies of the other, created a power relationship (moral as well as political) of a strongly repressive as well as a uniquely exclusive character. To the politically radical as well as to the spiritually nonconformist such a 'blockade' must have appeared unbreach-able. In constitutional terms, Parliament was committed until the 1820s to the preservation of the Church's monopoly through legislation which pre-vented non-Anglicans from entering into government and its adjuncts on any terms, suppressing at the same time the rights of Dissenters to attain public office, and strengthening in the process the ancient bond between land, Toryism, Anglicanism and privileged ideals.[49] Whatever debts the Church incurred in this manner were easily discharged through a loyalty in the country at large whereby a classic function of the local priest (in conjunction with or, given absence, in place of the local squire) was that of disseminating views by no means alien to the interests of the national power bloc.[50] Chadwick's argument that the nineteenth century saw a progressive watering down of such relationships and loyalties in the form of an active secularizing trend, though not completely without foundation, misses the essential point that such dissociations of the Church and politics came as a result of, not as a permit for, other, more subtle forms of Nonconformist middle-class pene-tration.[51] Equally, as the Evangelical and Oxford Movements attest, the desire to effect such a distancing, like the justification for its prosecution, came as much from forces within Anglicanism and Nonconformity as from a government hounded by public opinion to relinquish its open ecclesiastical control.[52]

Be that as it may, the progressive decline of the Church's political role during the nineteenth century did not lead to a parting of the ways for Anglicanism and Toryism as a main line of party advance. On the contrary, once the middle class, in temporary and fluctuating alliance with urban interests more generally, gained the political recognition it sought (see below), the creation of a Nonconformist Liberal bloc (as a fraction of the shifting national power bloc) crystallized Anglican and Tory interests, pushing them into still stronger defensive alliance both in Parliament and in the country. Such a 'package' remained the *sine qua non* of Tory politics throughout the century and in revitalized form became the basis of Disraeli's 'Young England' movement, of which Coningsby was the fictional embodiment. Though the actual membership of such a pact was subject to change, and was even occasionally split over major issues, the strength of the two institutions continued to be derived from their mutual and complementary interests. As Gray has written:

There were two main possibilities of mobilising political support during the period after 1850, corresponding roughly to 'urban' (Liberal) and 'rural' (Tory) political formations. But there was significant urban and even radical working class support for Toryism and Liberals often sought to weaken the land owners by claiming to represent the interests of famers and farm labourers thus splitting the rural bloc. The Whigs, as a party of big land owners in uneasy and shifting alliance with urban Liberalism, occupied a commanding but somewhat ambiguous political position. All parliamentary majorities had to be composed of some elements of both the 'urban' and 'rural' camps. Nevertheless, the difference between 'urban'/Liberal and 'rural'/Tory constituted the main line of political cleavage . . . until the changes of the 1880s and 90s once more threw party alignments into the melting pot.[53]

If the fortunes of the gentry (both political and financial)[54] were, in short, declining in the period of rapid industrial and social change, those of the bourgeoisie were correspondingly soaring. To begin with, commercial as well as industrial fortunes were increasing dramatically as the changes which began to relocate industry in more urban locations created spectacular fortunes for those individuals undertaking the problematical though lucrative transition from merchant to entrepreneur. Given the right circumstances such wealth could speak loudly for its owner, though not necessarily in the circles which ultimately counted. The amassing of personal fortunes was by no means entirely new in the late eighteenth century; nevertheless, the scale on which it occurred in the new provincial setting was startling indeed. In Manchester (not only the symbol of muscular industrial change but also arguably the most important commercial centre outside London in the early nineteenth century) the familiarity of the pattern of self-made fortunes is astonishing. If, for the working class, 'drink was the quickest way out of Manchester',[55] for the bourgeoisie fortune was the turnpike. Manufacturers, merchant-princes, bankers, professionals together created a cooperative climate in which the activities and households of the bourgeoisie flourished: Cottonopolis arose Venus-like from the Lancashire plain, and, as though to justify its Brobdingnagian transactions, a school of political economy bearing the city's name appeared. For contemporaries, no less than for subsequent commentators, the 'workshop of the world' was born. Indicative of the opportunities which such transformation brought is the way in which Nathan Meyer Rothschild journeyed to Manchester in the 1790s and there enjoyed the first successes upon which the English house of Rothschild was built. Equally typical, though perhaps less well known, is the example of self-made wealth provided by Samuel Reeves Brooke, a man who began life as the son of a modest manufacturer and ended it by leaving a personal fortune of over two and a half million pounds.[56] Other such examples could be adduced with ease[57] – so too with the myriad problems which the new urban bourgeoisie faced in their attempts to expand from their local power-base, and to transform their new-found wealth into social prowess and political muscle. Such problems and the stratagems adopted for their solution are more properly the subject of a later section of this paper, but it is worth noting at this stage that the opportunities extended to the bourgeoisie for advancement in any other than commercial arenas were strictly limited by both written and unwritten rules: by social convention (the product of landed hegemony) as much as by disabling legislation purposively granted by Parliament to its paymasters. Victories on any other front were, for the bourgeoisie, as hard-won as they were rare. In this way, the social and cultural isolation evident in the 'frontier' towns of the provinces was mirrored nationally in a political impotence consequent upon pre-Reform election arrangements (many towns had no M.P. before 1832 and no locally elected assembly until the Municipal Corporations Act of 1835) and in the tendency of the bourgeoisie to adopt Dissenting and often, amongst its articulate elite, Unitarian and Quaker religious affiliations. Clearly commercial wealth, utilitarian and Dissenting persuasions, together with a commonly emphasized humble origin and self-made status, were unlikely to receive the approbation of the more culturally central elements of the aristocratic/Tory/Anglican alliance; and even if the bourgeoisie as a whole was not entirely defined along the lines of a Bounderby or a Gradgrind, sufficient elements of those inflated characters persisted to render the commercial counter-hegemony in formation the most versatile yet the most isolated social group in the national hierarchy. Barred from traditional social circles by birth and belief, opposed by the working class as the architects of class oppression and exploitation (a view by no means discouraged by politicians and ideologies of the landed interest), they found themselves in a by no means comfortable half-way house – a problem which demanded immediate and radical resolution.

It is hardly surprising, therefore, that when political power did accrue to the *nouveaux riches*, fractions of it used such strength to begin the struggle to redress the imbalance and to dismantle where possible the continuing privileges which the landed/Anglican interest enjoyed at the expense of the majority of English society. The repeal of the Test Acts, the Corn Laws and the Navigation Acts, like the retaliatory factory legislation introduced by rural interests in the 1840s and 1850s are but the best-known examples of the constant, though now internalized (i.e. within the new power bloc), Tory/gentry, Liberal/bourgeois conflict which, within the governing fraction at least, deepened as mid-century was approached.[58]

The contrasts between these two identifiable patrician groups in late Georgian and early Victorian England having been drawn out, it is important to recognize those converse trends that were beginning to bring the interests of the two closer together. These were many and varied, though not the least was a common preoccupation with the problem of working-class control:

a subject of increasing concern given the working class's 'coming to itself' in these Promethean times.[59] The piecemeal response of the legislature to such threats bears considerable witness to the seriousness with which civil unrest was regarded as well as to the inexperience of those attempting its containment. The aristocracy for its part was less happy to leave the solution of such problems in the hands of either the traditional and cumbersome agencies (notably the militia) or the new bourgeoisie, once the protest movements of the nineteenth century began to spread from the towns into the countryside and out of industry into the heart of agricultural production. Certainly such developments landed the problems of the English proletariat as firmly on the marbled doorsteps of the great country house as on the stone steps of the Georgian urban mansion.[60] Increasing aristocratic indebtedness, together with an expanding (and partially enforced) aristocratic interest in commercial ventures (see below), was furthermore creating considerable common 'economic' ground between the traditional and new elites. Such commercial entanglements were to do much to undermine the prized economic independence of the nobility as a whole. For a generation of the new wealth, the shortfall in aristocratic capital brought about by the precocious development of some estates was to open the floodgates and allow them their much-sought-after point of entrée into prohibited circles, provided the necessary ideological transformations were satisfactorily accomplished during the passage from urban to rural environs. This process is dealt with in some detail below, but the general mixing of groups (which some see as the subordination of the landed interest within capital) was as complex as it was critical.[61] That it avoided the open class conflict which some contemporary commentators thought both imminent and inevitable is self-evident; that it markedly transformed the fortunes of the working class as well as the membership of the two participant elites has remained largely unrecognized. Critical, as always in these developments, were the specific mechanisms employed:

Given this or that, all might have happened in a different way. But in fact it did not. After the French Revolution evangelism blurred some of the differences between the Establishment and Nonconformity . . . Some of the manufacturers took their places on the Bench. Coal and canals brought the two together, as did commissions in the Volunteers, common services against Luddism, common resentment against the Old Corruption. Hence all happened as it did. Given the most perfect model of relations to the means of production ('basis') no one in 1760 or 1790 could have been certain as to how the cultural and institutional formations would in fact take place.[62]

It is precisely those cultural and institutional formations (for long neglected in historical analysis) that are the concern of the remainder of this paper; for, however aligned Establishment and Nonconformity were to become in the nineteenth century (a development easily overexaggerated), in the latter half of the eighteenth century it was within the cultural sphere that these characteristic ideologies were to find their strongest and most symbolic expression: as Wesley was to learn too painfully, latitudinarianism like its supporters left little room for radical commitment.[63] The fight of the Methodists within Anglicanism evokes much wider parallels. Here, in representative culture, was both the affirmation of social belief in proselytizing form and, simultaneously, the means through which distinctive concerns could be voiced and social niches created and occupied. Furthermore it was through cultural exploration and association in the first instance that the initial and most significant intergroup contacts were tentatively established. Examination of these and other issues requires a change of scale.

Manchester, science and bourgeois culture

The cultural disposition of the landed interest has been outlined already: essentially literate and artistic (as well as sporting), aristocratic patronage confined itself to the polite, the decorous and the amusing; though (as with most forms of investment) book-collecting and portraiture, as well as racing and estate expenditure, could be turned to profit should circumstances demand. Certainly sales of assets by aristocrats fallen upon hard times in the nineteenth century often realized sufficient capital to rescue family reputations,[64] though the *objets d'art* in question can hardly have been purchased with that eventually in mind. Interestingly enough, the buyers of such treasures after about 1820 were invariably members of the culturally assimilated *grande bourgeoisie* anxious to establish a family collection (and by implication a household longevity) in the shortest possible time. Any short cut which thus presented itself was seized with characteristic vigour.[65] Be that as it may, on the whole the boundaries of aristocratic involvement in cultural affairs were well defined, traditionally established and chiefly evident in literature, painting and music.[66]

The cultural concerns of the bourgeoisie up until the 1820s have generally been viewed as weakly developed, unenthusiastically pursued and merely pragmatic in intention. More recent work has done much to modify this superficial and grudging assessment. Equally, those accounts which have elaborated a view of bourgeois culture as, in all its essentials, directly imitative of aristocratic values have increasingly found their currency confined to a period earlier in the eighteenth century (when landed hegemony naturally encouraged such conformity with its own ideals) and before the bourgeoisie can be thought to have developed counter-hegemonic ideals in any serious sense. (Later, in the mid-nineteenth century, this imitation was again to become important for specific sections of the *grande bourgeoisie*, though, as we know already, its manifestation in these circumstances was part of a conscious acculturation designed to increase that fraction's acceptability within the governing fraction of the power bloc, not a casual and unintentioned conformity to the demands of hegemony itself.) For much of the late eighteenth and early nineteenth centuries, bourgeois culture, far from being imitative, was deliberately antagonistic, and its central pillar was *science* or, more accurately, *natural philosophy*.[67] Manchester has generally been considered not only typical of the provincial city in this regard, but also in every respect the spearhead and capital of bourgeois culture as it was to find scientific and Nonconformist expression. As no less a commentator than Benjamin Disraeli was to note, conscious no doubt of the full weight of the Classical Revival: 'What Art was to the ancient world, Science is to the modern . . . Rightly understood, Manchester is as great a human exploit as Athens.'[68]

The extent of Mancunian involvement in the scientific movement of the period has been exhaustively documented; indeed hardly a 'scientist' who lived there *bona fide*, self-styled or *poseur* has escaped the attention of rapacious historians and historians of science alike.[69] Rarely has the cultural significance of Mancunian science been realized. Some measure of the city's total rejection of traditional, primary, aristocratic culture, together with its complete acceptance and championship of the 'new science of the rational age' is given in Love's description of 1839 (other sources, though more fragmentary, can add considerably to this partial account),[70] which notes that, although the city (by now second only to London and growing twice as fast) could boast only two theatres and no purely literary or artistic societies, it managed to support ten major scientific societies amongst its cultural institutions and a plethora of smaller clubs equally dedicated to the furtherance of scientific knowledge.[71] The ten major societies were carefully arranged in a fairly formal hierarchy such that each was governed by the institution next highest in order and in such a manner that almost every section of the community could find an institution appropriate to its social and intellectual status. Significantly, however, there were more institutions aimed at attracting the patronage of the wealthy bourgeoisie than of any other section of this diverse community.

The task which confronts us is not to establish the validity of the assertion that Manchester was the central focus of both bourgeois aspiration and the scientific enterprise – for this much is indisputable – but rather to understand the rationale whereby radical politics, commercial wealth and Nonconformist affiliation aligned themselves with the scientific enterprise, and to delineate the processes which allowed this cultural assumption to be used in the continuing struggle for the attainment of counter-hegemonic status: for national recognition and for a political platform from which to voice the claims of wealthy urban interest.

Superficially such a connection is not hard to find or explain, but in this apparent ease of explanation lies an obvious, though hazardous, trap. Thus,

due emphasis having been given to the bourgeoisie's characteristic pragmatism, rationality and utilitarian concern, it is not perhaps unreasonable to
see in its scientific interests a direct and quantifiable link between theoretical
science, its application to technological improvement and an increased wealth
for its patrons through invention and innovation. Indeed, a whole school of
economic historians has continued, for many years, to emphasize a purely
mechanistic connection between the activities of 'scientists' (amateur and
professional) and the profit of technologists and entrepreneurs.[72] Such a view
does of course, at the very least, diminish the science movement – which
consisted of the establishment in almost every provincial town, regardless of
size or character, of a scientific academy of some description – to the role of
a narrowly constituted economic foundation of little or no wider cultural
importance. In other words, for the sake of a neat if simplistic explanation
which answers only to limited concerns, the proponents of such a causal
chain have sacrificed much of the contemporarily recognized complexity of
the movement and consequently relegated an important *social* institution to
a position of fringe interest, of direct concern only in so far as it produced
'useful' and ultimately profitable science.[73] This 'theory', generally associated
with the school established by A. E. Musson and Eric Robinson, fails to
answer to a variety of general and specific concerns.

Scientific patronage by the bourgeoisie was not associated with a simple
profit–return strategy, nor was it entirely disinterested or philanthropic. The
Musson and Robinson line, stemming as it does from a long historiographic
tradition in the writing of, amongst others, Ashton, Mathias, Schofield and
Bernal, has painstakingly documented known cases of scientific/technological
interaction both within and without scientific institutions.[74] It has been elegantly and consistently criticized by a number of authors in an equally long-
standing tradition, though there is scarcely space here to do justice to its
multiple twists.[75] Most recently Rupert Hall[76] has succinctly refuted the
claims of the 'applied' science proponents in an important review paper,
the conclusion of which is as emphatic as the argument which precedes it
is detailed:

The opportunity for engineers to [create new technology] . . . could not be postponed.
Hence they turned to calculation and experiment to discover what could be done,
drawing in a minor way on the ideas of the physical sciences, but employing also
their own experience and technical intuition of what constituted sound design. But
the point is that it was engineers and inventors who experienced the opportunity,
and who created the new design methods to exploit it. They did not find these
methods ready made to their hand in science. And it was they who chose, according
to their necessities, fragments of scientific theorization to fit into their new ideas of
engineering design – it was not the force of scientific truth which compelled them
to do this, but the desire to derive quickly a sound and economic answer to a design
problem. The history of the industrial revolution in Britain shows amply how

ready the technical innovators were to work out new ideas empirically when, as was so often the case, science had little guidance to offer.[77]

Equally Sir Eric Ashby:

There were a few 'cultivators of science' as they were called, engaged in research, but their work was not regarded as having much bearing on education, and still less on technology.[78]

Such conclusions do not of course disprove the existence of links between science and technology, either directly in the application of scientific theorems to practical problems, or indirectly through an increasingly secular and science-based curriculum in child and adult education which arguably rendered artisans more knowledgeable and more able to perceive potential improvements in the technology with which their daily activity surrounded them. However, such possibilities notwithstanding, increasing doubt has been cast on any interpretation which seeks to see scientific activity *only* as technical in purpose, and it seems likely that further research will continue to diminish the status of such an approach. Even when we turn to examine in some detail those institutions designed to promote scientific discovery (potentially of course the 'laboratories' of the Musson equation), the evidence available suggests that the conclusions of Usher, Ashby and Hall are more likely to be upheld than challenged.[79] Work on the most prestigious of Georgian institutions – the Manchester Literary and Philosophical Society – by the present author and others confirms that explanations of considerably greater subtlety than those so far advanced for the establishment and success of the Society will have to be sought.[80] Not least, such an alternative scheme will have to account for the curious structure of the institution: its poor record in terms of technological fecundity, its promotional anomalies, whereby the prestige of office and the benefits which tenure of such positions afforded did not necessarily accrue to those of the highest scientific achievement, nor yet those famed for technological ability, and its lineage, derived as it was from three singularly virile progenitors: a Dissenting academy, a Unitarian chapel and a prestigious infirmary. As Robert Kargon comments in a study which generally supports the view that Manchester science was significant (though not necessarily in this early period):

When, therefore, the vigorous British Association for the Advancement of Science met in Manchester in 1842, it exposed a dichotomy in the Manchester community. Institutional honours and control were held for the most part by men who had long been prominent locally . . . but who were far from the frontiers of their disciplines. When major scientists from Britain and abroad came to the city, they came to listen to new (and as yet not institutionally honoured) . . . voices.[81]

In short, rise to pre-eminence in such a major institution as the Literary and Philosophical Society seems to have borne little relation to the normally accepted process of scientific recognition (through publication, discovery and peer-group electives), being much more akin to those curious promotional mechanisms adopted in the social clubs and exclusive societies of the robust eighteenth century more generally. To what then did the leading lights of Mancunian society owe their position? It is a question of fundamental import to our broader cultural theme, and one which can be answered only with reference to a more detailed examination of the origins, growth, status-claims and objectives of the Literary and Philosophical Society, though in this sense it is merely a particular example of a generic type – a microcosm of the wider social picture.

Science, the Manchester Literary and Philosophical Society and elite formation

The Literary and Philosophical Society was founded in 1781 and inaugurated in rooms adjacent to the Cross Street Unitarian Chapel,[82] with genteel as well as scientific pretensions. Its membership, limited at first to fifty and then expanded as suitable candidates for election appeared, comprised in the main the acknowledged (though as yet unhonoured and untitled) elite of the town. Indeed throughout its history the Manchester Literary and Philosophical Society appears to have played Parthenon to the city's Acropolis. Francis Nicholson, an early, reluctant and by no means adequate historian of the Society, preserved from the original members' list (subsequently destroyed by bombing during the Second World War) the names of the founding fathers – some twenty-four in all.[83] On the whole it is the extra-societal connections of this early group that are most remarkable. It included the Reverend Thomas Barnes (1747–1810), minister of the Cross Street Unitarian Chapel and local notable; George Bell, M.D. (1755–1810), honorary physician to the Manchester Infirmary; Thomas Henry (1734–1815), apothecary to the Infirmary; Peter Mainwaring, M.D. (1696?–1785), honorary physician to the Infirmary and first President of the Society; James Massey (1713–96) first president of the Infirmary and one of the early presidents of the Society: Thomas Percival, M.D., F.R.S. (1740–1804), alumnus of the prestigious Dissenting academy at Warrington, friend and pupil of Priestley, honorary physician to the Infirmary and *vis motrix* of the Society, as well as a supremely successful local practitioner; and Charles White (1728–1813), honorary surgeon to the Infirmary and one of four Fellows of the Royal Society amongst the original members.[84] It was, to say the least, an exclusive and an impressive membership drawn from specific quarters of the city's social world; and if the manufacturer/entrepreneurial elements of the elite were initially missing from the rolls (later as their own status improved they would take their rightful place in the hallowed Pantheon, though their absence from the list of founders is significant in the light of claims for the Society's technical impulse), then the professional element of the local bourgeoisie more than compensated for their under-representation. Particularly striking, especially from fuller analysis, is the Unitarian (Cross Street Chapel) and medical (Manchester Infirmary) connection, and this relationship is worth pursuing a little further.

The building of the Manchester Infirmary in 1752 was part of a clinical movement which saw the establishment of similar institutions in Birmingham (1765) and Leeds (1768).[85] Positions in the new hospitals seem to have been widely coveted; especially those of honorary physician, surgeon and apothecary, since according to Brockbank tenure of these posts conferred a social standing within the community at large as well as securing financial gain and academic prestige within the medical profession more particularly.[86] It was, not surprisingly, to such positions that many of those individuals later familiar to us through their Literary and Philosophical Society connection aspired upon their arrival in Manchester from the 1750s onwards, and their eventual success in this regard clearly granted them a *savoir vivre* otherwise unavailable in so unfamiliar and uncompromising a provincial environment.[87] By 1825 the Infirmary could claim over 2,000 patients – more than the largest London hospitals – and the continuing prestige of office within it, as well as the status claims, personal ambitions and public interest which surrounded it, can be gauged from the election campaigns fought whenever posts fell vacant. In 1835, the successful candidate for a post as physician found it necessary to spend £690 on canvassing and transporting the 870 participant electors.[88] Such hospitals thus offered a successful member not only a badge of rank of considerable local currency, but also an early forum for like-minded discussion, where problems of marginality, undervaluation and social isolation could be sympathetically discussed and evaluated. The centrality of the Infirmary in effecting such transactions was only subsequently usurped by the Literary and Philosophical Society itself – a broader-based and more liberal institution with a less parochial appeal. The transfer of loyalties from one institution to the other was an unruffled and entirely logical procedure, so that it is hardly surprising to find a high degree of interplay between the members of both institutions in the early days. Indeed, in addition to the founding members named above, of the fifty-two serving officers of the Infirmary from foundation to 1830, thirty-six found their way into the ranks of the bigger institution. An analysis of those holding important office in the Literary and Philosophical Society merely confirms the enormous support granted by the local medical fraternity.[89]

Total domination of the infant Society by medical men was only prevented by the presence of an initially small though rapidly growing group drawn from the congregation of the Cross Street Unitarian Chapel. Though some medical men were members of this exclusive assembly as well, it was in particular non-medical trustees of the Chapel, together with a long succession of serving ministers, who occupied the remaining places of importance in the Literary and Philosophical Society – a society which, as Kargon and others have noted, was almost entirely 'a creature of its officers'.[90]

The Cross Street Chapel, though a somewhat older foundation, was, like the Infirmary, a highly exclusive establishment in its own right. Described as the national cathedral of Unitarianism (itself a highly exclusive religion attracting the wealthiest dissenters and, according to Priestley 'a feather bed to catch the falling Christian'), the Chapel attracted under its ample panoply the leading Dissenters of the city who, if financial success is anything to go by, had good cause to meet in praise of the ever-bountiful Deity. Just how much of their collective wealth was devoted to the furtherance of the Unitarian ministry is unknown, but during the latter part of the eighteenth century at least the Chapel never wanted for funds or trustees, while the surviving portraits of its ministers (there were always two at any one time) suggest that the services of God and an empty belly rarely if ever went hand in hand. Undoubtedly it was the focus of 'aristocratic dissent' in the city, the cause of many a business partnership, and as tightly knit a social entity as the Literary and Philosophical Society, in the fortunes of which the collective Unitarian congregation took a great and at times unnatural interest for so avowedly 'spiritual' a body.[91]

The Reverend Ralph Harrison, minister of the Chapel from 1771 to 1810 and loyal Literary and Philosophical Society alumnus, summed up the theological position of the Unitarians on matters scientific, when he suggested that 'The Deity has rendered knowledge of natural philosophy a source of pure, exquisite and lasting pleasure'; but there is every reason to suppose that the interest of his congregation as well as his own in the affairs of the Literary and Philosophical Society had as much to do with things temporal – their marginal status and total exclusion from all other forms of social and political activism, for example – as with things spiritual and with duty done for the life hereafter.[92]

Laying aside the putative role of Quakers and Unitarians in business enterprise – a theme more than adequately surveyed by Raistrick and Holt amongst others[93] – it seems clear that the involvement of Dissenters in scientific societies was a cultural response to a social predicament. Certainly if the Unitarians had shunned the potential hospitality of the scientific community, which through the accumulated prestige of its members was coming to dominate local proto-politics as well as local society, then it is difficult to suggest what other form of social outlet might have been available to them. The ensuing loyalty both to science in general and to the Society in particular seems therefore to have been the result not so much of chance or choice as of opportunism and necessity. For the Literary and Philosophical Society such a state of affairs had undoubted advantages: not least for its finances and stability. The strength of the Unitarian clique, like that of the medical fraternity, is everywhere apparent in the transactions of the Society –

though at first not in sheer numerical terms, but rather in terms of decision-making office. Thus, though only four of the twenty-four founding fathers professed the faith, they were amongst the Society's prime activists, the three most notable being Thomas Percival, Thomas Henry (a convert from Anglicanism) and Thomas Barnes, a minister. In time every serving minister of the Chapel (from 1781 to 1851) – seven in all including William Gaskell, husband of authoress Elizabeth Gaskell – would join the Literary and Philosophical Society with a single exception: John Hugh Worthington, who had a suspiciously brief stay at the Chapel – a mere two years.[94] Anglican representation in the Society was, on the other hand, usually small and markedly ephemeral.

It seems then that, in Manchester at least, membership of and success in its most important bourgeois institution had as much to do with social background, ideological orientation, religious affiliation, cultural value and conspicuous wealth as with scientific expertise or technological interest. To be sure, most of the members either attended the scientific discussions or dabbled in science in a minor, dilettante fashion, and though others were more active than this (being early devotees of a precocious type), by far the majority of elected members adopted a passive role, publishing little, discovering little and in many cases probably understanding even less. Crises of attendance, though significantly not of membership, were not unknown, and for many membership alone was the prize offered by subscription. This picture, furthermore, does not appear to be untypical. A number of similar studies in other provincial settings are beginning to suggest the general applicability of the syndrome, though much still needs to be done in the light of the multiplicity of institutions both large and small.[95]

For medical men the pursuit of science as a rational cultural activity is easily explained – as an activity which furthered their social ambitions and at the same time kept them closely in touch with scientific developments closely related to their own interests. To an essentially pragmatic generation such a justification for suspiciously pleasurable activity was welcome enough, and, to put a familiar aphorism into an unfamiliar context, had science not existed someone would have had to invent it. But why, generalizing to the nation as a whole, should science capture this central primacy in bourgeois consciousness? Clues are provided certainly by the interest of the Unitarians in particular and of Nonconformity in general, but the full answer lies somewhat deeper and specifically in the ideological appeal of science to a group in every way starkly contrasted to the culture, values and life-style of the landed interest. There is, in other words, a strong element of cultural opposition, of antagonism, of proselytism, in this bourgeois stance – an attempt to found and develop a rival and radically different culture which, like the aristocracy's own, would symbolize, mirror, announce and legitimize the social and political beliefs of its adherents. In this respect the seeds of the remarkable success enjoyed by the rival culture (which with the bourgeois hegemony of the mid-nineteenth century would capture an absolute primacy in popular thought) lay in the image of the scientific community and the broad social background of the bourgeoisie (for whom science was one of the few value-transcendent pursuits open to talent) and in the republican image of science itself as an ideologically revolutionary activity conducted within a merito-cratically structured institutional framework.

Ideology and the creation of counter-hegemony

This latter idea – that of the image of science as revolutionary – requires elaboration. Since natural philosophy and the sciences more generally did not (except in a few exceptional circumstances) fall into that category of activities directly patronized and thus indirectly moderated by the landed interest, it remained in the eighteenth century one of the few respectable pursuits open to 'outsiders'.[96] Unlike the restrictive, quasi-feudal professions which required connection and favour in at least equal proportion, contributions to what Brougham was later to christen 'The March of Mind' could, it was believed, be made by anyone, whatever his status in society. A covert hostility towards the ancient professions (as well as a suspicion of 'professionalism' generally) occasionally surfaced more explicitly in the organs of popular science which began to appear from the mid-eighteenth century onwards, and for precisely this reason,[97] whilst the unremarkable origins of many of the more eminent contemporary 'scientists' (often as fictitious as they were romanticized) became emphasized in favourable contrast to the elitist tendencies and aristocratic wardenship of all other forms of professional and culture activity. The received wisdom of these Georgian precursors of the full-blooded Victorian melodrama filtered through the ranks of the middle class as a modern catechism: time and again the names of the blessed rang through the class-room and the drawing-room, taking their place alongside those of the official saints of a former, more theological age – Herschel, Priestley, Black, Dalton, Davy, Faraday and Watt. These were the men who forged the trail, who succeeded in transcending the common code of social stasis in an age otherwise dominated by hierarchy and a strictly limited sense of social mobility. In this, their very success contributed profoundly to the emergence of a widely shared image of the scientific community every bit as important as the image of science itself. Meritocratic, anti-authoritarian and committed to a rationally unfolding progress (daily reconfirmed in the discovery of scientific order in natural chaos), the communion of science turned its back on an increasingly outmoded theologism and embraced instead a radical modernity which amounted in many minds (particularly the Liberal and Nonconformist) to a tacit critique of the broader oligarchic State. In this way the parallels which could be drawn between the acknowledged procedures and axioms of the scientific community as a social system and the vision of a changed and rationally designed society contributed profoundly to both the level of patronage which science received and the role of natural philosophy as an engine of modernity. Thus, the wide appeal of science as culture amongst progressively-minded elements of the bourgeoisie had less to do with a strictly utilitarian belief in its usefulness than with a firm belief in its ability to point forward to an alternative and (in their own terms) more justifiable, hegemony.

Yet even this formulation, which takes more account of science's clientele than of its content, is too simple; for the message and the spirit of science went still further, and its symbolism was, critically, more protean. The Newtonian model of science as it was received in the salons was a subtle creature capable of answering soothingly to the two most basic middle-class concerns outlined earlier: that is, the desire for social recognition commensurate with its new-found wealth; and the fear of working-class insurrection in the rapidly expanding and horrendously unpredictable provincial towns. In the case of the former it was to become both a lever and a justification for social upheaval; in the latter it became a powerful instrument of social control. Thus, a great attraction of the Newtonian model was its flexibility: it could rationalize as well as justify the inevitability of evolutionary progress (and thereby provide the first legitimate basis for attacking the old, almost divine view of society favoured by landed establishment interests); but it could also, by reinterpretation, justify the promulgation to lowlier elements of the value of a much-needed *status quo*. After all, in such a 'gospel' did not every cog have its place in the delicate, easily fractured mechanism? Was not the system dependent upon the controlled cooperation of all the parts? Could it not be jeopardized by the malfunction of just one part, no matter how small, with disastrous consequences to the whole system? Equally did not the earth travel around the sun in constant obligation, being forever *destined* so to do? Or in a more immediate analogy, what of the power of steam? Confined by the system it retains the potential to move mountains; released from its confinement it dissipates and is mere vapour. As with steam, so with people. This, and much more the voice of the *un*enlightened bourgeoisie to their working-class employees. As a rhetoric for dissemination through Mechanics' Institutes (themselves designed to appeal only to those vocal, intelligent and potentially dangerous elements of the working class; and organizations significantly granted greatest financial support by the bourgeoisie during periods of acute social tension),[98] the Newtonian epistles preached stability, containment and (allied to a strictly curtailed version of self-help) improvement within safe social limits.[99]

At the very least, the worker could be turned away from 'the tavern, the gambling table and the brothel', but, more than that, he would be given the kind of edifying instruction which would 'have the pleasing effect of removing prejudice, of softening the asperity of party feeling, and of fixing the public attention upon an object with regard to which violent differences of opinion can hardly be expected to arise'.[100] Furthermore (and this was certainly crucial), all such cosmetic social surgery could take place 'without any ill-consequence to his superiors'.[101] Thus, scientific and technical education for adults in Mechanics' Institutes – like the education of children in the Lancaster and Bell schools (named appropriately enough 'factory schools', not only because of their regimented teaching methods but equally because of their avowed aim to prepare the 'little pitchers'[102] for later work in the factories) – was designed to make them good citizens and to teach them the nature and

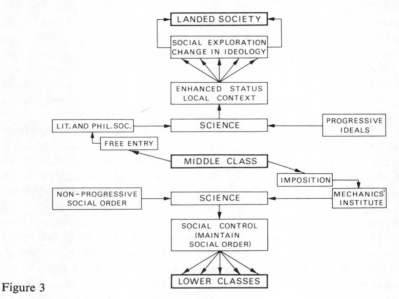

Figure 3

extent of their duties – a remarkably different interpretation from that which the bourgeoisie put upon their own use of science. As Joseph Priestley, chastened no doubt by his experience of aristocratic opposition to his radical programme, put it: 'the English hierarchy – if there be anything unsound in its constitution – has . . . reason to tremble even at an air-pump or an electrical machine'.[103] This dual function of scientific knowledge and its special place in bourgeois conceptions of change and control is imperfectly expressed in Figure 3.

Modes of re-acculturation: the renegotiation of aristocratic and bourgeois values

Given the great schism evident between the rural and urban patrician classes in the late eighteenth century – a schism based, as we have seen, upon both natural tensions and deliberate bourgeois opposition in cultural, economic and increasingly political terms – the scene might well have been set for a continued and deepening class struggle. In the event, however, the weakening financial position of the aristocracy (see below), together with the desire amongst some protagonist elements of the *grande bourgeoisie* to transcend their own cultural values, prevented such developments through a process of generationally patterned social legitimation which, through the granting of social 'visas' created a 'new' or 'bourgeois' aristocracy later to be fully absorbed within the landed interest. For science in Britain this was to have important repercussions. Only with the removal of the *grande bourgeoisie* from office in the great hierarchy of scientific establishments was science itself left free to develop as a specialized academic profession (a process evident in the rest of Europe a century or so earlier), concomitantly losing its position of cultural fundamentality in the country at large along with its responsibility towards the reinforcement of middle-class social attitudes. Amongst the remaining 'amateur' middle-class patrons, only the Field Naturalist and Statistical Societies survived as evidence both of their former involvement and of their continuing fears over working-class social unrest.[104]

More immediately important from our point of view is the exact character of the means employed to facilitate the creation and supervening incorporation of the 'bourgeois aristocracy'. The first of these has already been considered, since the creation was explicitly the product and rationale of scientific institutions which, in first delimiting an elite and then granting preferential status to its members (through the tenure of office), regulated the complex weaning operation which prepared high-ranking members for duty in the wider social life of the city. The second process – that of legitimation and absorption – was less easily, and certainly less mechanically, achieved. It involved not only consolidation of local social status through politics (significantly after the Municipal Corporations Act it was those institutionally honoured by scientific academies who quickly colonized the newly created posts in local government),[105] but also exploration of wider national interest groups and opportunities; suitable changes in political persuasion, religious belief and cultural value; and finally transformation (after pupation) into a social 'butterfly' able to find acceptance within landed elite circles and quite unrecognizable as the dowdy caterpillar of earlier times. Typically such a metamorphosis took two or three generations to achieve, with periods of apparent stasis; rarely if ever did one man complete the cycle in a lifetime.[106]

Such a view, for which a great deal of evidence survives,[107] receives strong if unexpected support from a keen observer of contemporary opinion, Sir Robert Peel, who, in a moment of rare candour, made the now legendary remark that 'It takes two generations to make a gentleman.'[108] Clearly Peel was speaking from recent family experience: his grandfather, a staunch

Liberal Nonconformist and an early member of the Manchester Literary and Philosophical Society, would surely have had interesting views to exchange with his knighted, Tory, Anglican grandson. Viewing precisely the same formulation from the landed point of view and with the benefit of hindsight, F. M. L. Thompson seems equally persuaded:

By no means all successful business men sought to set themselves up as landed gentlemen, but that a good many of the most able and forceful could do so was a source of great strength to the landed interest. Money placed in land could not of course always purchase automatic and instantaneous acceptance. Established county society often scorned newcomers as vulgar aspirants, and it might take two generations for humble origins to be forgiven, in the course of which it might become congenial or polite to sever connection with the business on which the family fortune was founded.[109]

It was precisely this aristocratic resistance that the acculturation process was designed to circumvent. Certainly amongst the membership of the Manchester Literary and Philosophical Society (by now a larger institution numerically, though still dominated by a few large intermarrying families) such a generational patterning (with final success achieved by the third generation) recurs with uncanny regularity. Limitations of space allow only one example, though the same basic story could be repeated for a number of cases with only minor variation.

The fortunes of the Greg family were first established in the 1780s when Samuel Greg became a modest fustian manufacturer on the site of the now famous Quarry Bank Mill at Styal, just outside the growing town of Manchester. He was a strong Unitarian, Cross Street Chapel member and trustee, and, by 1790, an established member of the infant Literary and Philosophical Society, having secured sufficient influence and favour to secure introduction and election. His Cross Street connections, not least through the minister Thomas Barnes, were not without value in this regard. Although he did not at first make an enormous impact at the Society's weekly meetings and did not publish a single scientific paper within or without the Society's eclectic *Memoirs* (such was his keen technical expertise), he did become a well established and respected citizen, in part through the Society's implicit sponsorship. Like many of his contemporaries, he sent two sons to the 'scientific' University of Edinburgh where (protected from the dilettante evils of an unreformed Oxbridge) they met a number of like-minded sons of the bourgeoisie in a city which spiritually and culturally had much in common with the radical intellectual climate of Manchester. Each of the Greg sons on his return to the parental home met and married into the family of another Unitarian, Literary and Philosophical Society member: Robert Hyde Greg to a daughter of Robert Philips (a happy amalgamation for two textile manufacturer fathers), and William Rathbone Greg to Lucy Henry, daughter of William Henry, Infirmary physician and one of the most wealthy and respected members of the community. Each son entered the family business (though their participation was considerably more ephemeral, and their positions more honorary than their father's) and was at length proposed and elected to the Literary and Philosophical Society, in the social rounds of which they were already typically enmeshed. Unusually, Robert seems to have been a man of considerable scientific stature with a keen interest in matters geological and horticultural. The bulk of his published papers lies in these fields, and evidence of his already widening attentions is provided by his active membership of the Geological Society of London (a subject and a society which exercised a distinctive fascination in the Victorian period and which afforded Robert a convenient excuse for frequent trips to the otherwise alien capital) and by his purchase of a large estate in Herefordshire on which he could practise, no doubt, his horticultural technique. Despite these less parochial connections, he retained many of his Mancunian allegiances (not least to the Geological Society there), and with profit, for in 1839 the now somewhat equivocally radical Robert was elected M.P. for the city, a position which, together with the scientific status he had acquired in Manchester and Edinburgh, made him a natural choice as founder-benefactor of a number of scientific institutions.

His brother – William Rathbone Greg – seems to have had no less illustrious a career, and no less active a life. He was first secretary and then President of the Manchester Statistical Society – an organization originally much involved in reformist endeavour and philanthropic works – and he also participated in the early activities of the British Association for the Advancement of Science, though he was by no means one of those 'new voices' which the major scientists of Britain and abroad came to hear in 1842. Nonetheless, the B.A.A.S. accorded William important connections outside the immediate social circles of his own town, so that, like his brother, he soon gathered ample pretexts for trips to London – a city in which he eventually settled as Comptroller of Her Majesty's Stationery Office during the early years of Victoria's reign. His connections with Manchester, its science and its society were henceforth obscure and at best passive.

Scientific interest and Literary and Philosophical Society membership did just survive into the third Greg generation, though not strongly, in the person of Robert Philips Greg, eldest son of Robert Hyde. Like his father he was educated first by a private tutor then at Edinburgh (though his own sons entered Oxbridge) and he joined the Geological Society of London. He was a founder member of the London Mineralogical Society and its treasurer for a number of years, but on reaching middle age he put such mundane associations aside and retired elegantly to the Herefordshire estate where his new-found interest in the Arts made him a more welcome and (business being more distant in his case) acceptable member of the local nobility than his father had been, despite his own pretensions to greatness. The remainder of

Robert Philips Greg's life was that of the squire with all the political and social values that such station demanded. The Gregs' connection with business, with Manchester, with Unitarianism and with science had ended. In this respect the Gregs are untypical of the genre. The Heywoods, a prosperous banking family active in the early scientific community, are yet more spectacular: through similar, though more skilfully timed, change and an early perception of the value of the public school system, they managed to become not only landed Tory M.P.s but even, by the third generation, peers of the realm.[110]

Though such a generational schema well illustrates the process of cultural coalescence, it does not of course furnish us with an understanding of the means of its accomplishment. Even accepting as convenient E. P. Thompson's theory, which attributes to the French Revolution as much as anything the realization of a need for stable, cooperative elite rule in the face of awesome proletarian struggle, we still require a precise explanation of why a hitherto powerful and unremitting aristocracy embraced the *grande bourgeoisie* rather than leaving it as a much-needed buffer and scapegoat between itself and the gathering working class. Equally, we need to know how and why hegemony passed from land to the owners of capital more generally. Certainly the threat of rural insurrection was an important stimulus to change, as was a growing crisis amongst the ranks of the Establishment, but in seeking such a directly capitulative mechanism, it would be folly to ignore the purposive dynamism and ingenuity of the *grande bourgeoisie* itself.

Capitulation and mechanism for advance

By far the most important determinant of the pace, both of hegemonic transfer and of *grande bourgeois* absorption, was growing aristocratic debt. However deep the crisis of the aristocracy appeared in the sixteenth and seventeenth centuries[111] there is reason to believe that it was in the eighteenth and early nineteenth centuries that the aristocracy, feeling the impact of industrialism on the national space-economy, faced their most severe financial threats. Certainly steps were taken to avoid financial embarrassment and the social estrangement this implied: extravagant expenditure was reduced to some extent,[112] and the major estates and their agents investigated the possibilities of exploiting mineral resources as a financial palliative,[113] though this itself (given the necessary levels of investment) could temporarily exacerbate whatever monetary crises existed. In this respect Lord Dudley and the Marquis of Bute were merely well-known exemplars of a common development.[114] On the whole, however, much estate expenditure (like investment in urban building) remained 'lumpy', so that the level of capital requirement, together with the extent of aristocratic indebtedness, remained high, and at times exceptionally so. For the aristocracy these unhappy facts of life had serious implications; for some of the less well connected fractions of the landed interest they might spell disaster. At the very least, the dependence of the landed interest generally upon outside sources of credit increased, and with significant results. The view of David Spring[115] that such escalating trends were reversed – that a reformed aristocracy appeared which ceased its extravagant expenditure and entered into a new age of careful frugality – does not seem to be borne out either by evidence of continuing sales of assets in the form of both land and collections (arguably a last resort) or by evidence of continued expenditure on the improvement, expansion and restoration of either urban or rural estates.[116] Typical of the latter is the Third Marquis of Bute (described as the greatest private patron in the history of British architecture),[117] who between 1868 and 1900 built or renovated no fewer than sixty buildings. Though many were financed from the profits of his Glamorgan coal estates, he was at times forced into massive debts, most notably during the rebuilding of Mount Stuart House, his ancestral home, which, having been partially destroyed by fire in 1877, was entirely reconstructed at a cost of over £900,000.[118]

On the whole there seems little doubt that recent scholarship has supported the view of aristocratic indebtedness first put forward by F. M. L. Thompson over twenty years ago:[119] that, although some encumbrances were reduced, many were not, and that those expenses which had been burdensome in the eighteenth century were (with rising interest rates and the movement of the economy against agriculture) by the middle of the nineteenth century as crippling as they were unavoidable. Running an estate, providing dowries, settlements and jointures was a costly business, the more so during the economic and social upheavals of the Industrial Revolution. The result for the aristocracy as a whole was a severe and deepening crisis; and whatever the specific causes of that crisis (and there were many) the outcome was, from our own point of view, catalytic.

The aristocratic life-style, together with the political power, social leverage and hegemonic status of land as a whole, relied for its support on the economic integrity of rural society. Increasing debt threatened both integrity and independence. At first loss of social and political power could be avoided by internalizing the circuit of credit and debit, but as whole sections of the gentry fell upon harder times such a capacity was severely reduced; and, with dramatic consequences, the call went out to the new owners of capital – the bourgeoisie. It was then, and only then, that the first significant cracks began to appear in the protective walls erected around the stately homes of England as tentative deals were struck, bargains agreed, concessions secured and relationships established. Strong enough to deny the overtures of the new commercialism the first time, such enfeebled defences could not hold out against a second, more calculated and more inevitable assault. The bourgeoisie, undoubtedly the most astute, ambitious and potent social force, now began to exploit that fundamental weakness and the opportunities it created, their wits sharpened by more than five decades of aristocratic denial. Bourgeois hegemony was by now at hand. If by the mid-1830s some members of the bourgeoisie were to be seen aping their betters in matters social and cultural (leaving behind, as we have seen, their rival cultural edifice) then it was because in matters economic they had already gained control of that much-vaunted engine of progress, the Industrial Revolution, and reaped the benefit of the power which it bestowed. For an increasingly uncertain country elite, on the other hand, debt and dependence meant capitulation on the social front to the *grande bourgeoisie* and wider political collapse in the face of bourgeois hegemony more generally. By admitting the *grande bourgeoisie* into their circle the aristocracy had bought economic and social survival; the *grande bourgeoisie* themselves had bought social recognition, but by throwing in their lot with the old hegemony had relinquished claim to the power now passing to the new one. For the remainder of the bourgeoisie – those factions identified by Gray as the industrial capitalists and urban gentry – the century was to witness the establishment of their own ideological perspectives in popular consciousness: a consciousness increasingly 'imposed' on the natural consciousness of the old and new landed elements of the governing fraction as much as on that of the subordinate working class.

For the bourgeoisie generally, then, the absolute guarantor of their success had been that which the aristocracy had initially most despised – their commercial wealth. The strength of their strategy, however, had lain in their ability to create to their own design a series of rival cultural institutions of sufficient complementarity in the wider sphere to bind together their own diverse interests and at the same time oppose the equally symbolic culture of the landed hegemony. For the *grande bourgeoisie* in particular, the extent and flexibility of their capital reserves had further allowed them to divert their investments at a later stage into areas more likely to advance their cause amongst the aristocracy itself. Typical of the way in which such a changing use of capital was effected was the construction and then, when appropriate, engineered decay of a rival education system – an important component in the schema designed to advance the acceptance prospects of the sons of the captains of industry.

Even by the mid-eighteenth century, the English education system was still essentially unmodernized, with theology the 'queen of the sciences' and preparation for the life of a gentleman the prime objective of an unchanging curriculum. Private tuition, sometimes private school, university and the grand tour constituted the processing machine through which the aristocracy fitted their offspring for wider service. Since curricular activities were largely effete and on the whole impractical (Dancing, French, Latin, Theology, Cosmography, Mathematics and Fencing),[120] the institutions responsible for their design were clearly unsuitable for the children of the late eighteenth-century bourgeoisie, whose anxious parents demanded a more practical education. Many institutions – most notably the universities – were forbidden territory for another and more obvious reason: their insistence upon allegiance to the Anglican Church in the form of an oath sworn either on matriculation (in the case of Oxford) or on graduation (in the case of Cambridge). In either case the Nonconformists experienced acute disabilities, and not by coincidence alone was the High Anglican revival of the 1830s centred upon and named after the University town of Oxford.

Pride as well as pragmatism demanded that the bourgeoisie themselves rectify such debilitating imbalance, and their first and logical response was to construct a viable, ideologically conditioned alternative which, however different in purpose, nonetheless retained some semblance of the institutional structure which had made the aristocratic system so resilient over the years. Thus each new institution had its aristocratic model – the private tutor, the dissenting academy, eventually the University College of London and even a European grand tour (which far from being a frivolous diversion was, initially at least, a deadly serious educative tour of the radical European universities).[121] It was a well established routine by the 1790s, and the sons of many of the most eminent manufacturers engaged in such well-conducted arrangements – Matthew Boulton Junior and James Watt Junior amongst them.[122] The Dissenting academies (of which one of the most notable was Warrington, joint progenitor of the Manchester Literary and Philosophical Society) were particularly important in so far as they combined the best possible practical scientific education (as would befit the potential man of commerce) with a strictly Nonconformist theological upbringing designed particularly for those 'desirous of entering the clergy'. In their almost equal combination of the sacred and the secular they were directly comparable with the stricter Anglican foundations, and the subject of continuing debate and speculation amongst educational theorists of the day: not least in the Literary and Scientific Societies. In Manchester the Literary and Philosophical Society devoted a considerable proportion of the contents of its first volume of *Memoirs* to plans for liberal education in the city. Teaching in the better academies was often in the hands of extraordinarily capable men, and the best could boast tutors of national as well as local importance. Warrington, for example, was the employer for a while of Joseph Priestley and Thomas Barnes; Manchester engaged the services of the young John Dalton. And yet, the system was not to survive the eighteenth century in anything but remnant form, for as the bourgeois sponsors of the system became increasingly beguiled by the possibility of landed acceptance after the turn of the century, and as their ambitions for their sons transcended those of technical accomplishment, so the strict utility and Nonconformity of the academies prompted reappraisal and withdrawal, and, important as these academies were for a generation, they disappeared with a speed as astonishing as it was unseemly.[123]

As an instrument in the broader scheme of bourgeois re-acculturation, the next stage of the educational transition capitalized on the achievement of the first, as middle-class families began to absorb additional aristocratic traits into their tutorial design. A by no means uncommon contemporaneous step was to send a particularly favoured son to public school where he might make advantageous social contacts with the sons of his superiors.[124] Robert Philips Greg's two sons, prior to their 'finishing' at Oxford and Cambridge, followed this precise route – one going to Harrow, the other preferring Eton. Such aspirations had in fact become evident at an earlier stage amongst advanced elements of the *grande bourgeoisie*: James Watt quickly perceived the advantages which an educational polish might bring to his son. The young James evidently displayed a lack of gentility and a poor public manner as a youth, so that, long before he reached the dangerous stage of adolescence, his father was to be found making preparations for his refinement. As he wrote to a potential schoolmaster:

Having a son at Winson Green School whom I want to remove to some other school where his learning and manners may be more particularly attended to than they can in so numerous a school, my friend Doctor Witherington has done me the favour to mention you as a person to whose care I may safely trust his education . . . I want him to be further instructed in Writing, Arithmetic, and Latin, and to be radically taught Euclid's Geometry, with such of the dependent Sciences as his time allows of . . . But what I most desire is that a strict attention be paid to his manners and his morals . . . When you do me the pleasure to answer this letter [I] shall be obliged to you to lett [*sic*] me know if you have any persons who teach French and dancing to your Scholars.[125]

Watt, as we have seen, undertook the grand tour, where doubtless his reformed manners were of invaluable service to him – not, however, in the way his father had envisaged. His facility with the French language was crucial in helping him to forge those contacts with the active revolutionaries that were to lead him not only to found the Constitutional Society in Manchester (his other affiliation outside the Literary and Philosophical Society) but also to develop politically as one of the strongest Jacobin sympathizers in the country. In some respects, however, James Watt Junior was precocious and untypical. If the normal impact of public school education was to soften the radicalism of middle-class sons, it was also more usually the third generation which enjoyed its hitherto forbidden fruits. Thus, as the second generation embraced the established values of the aristocracy, they demanded in turn a smoother passage for their offspring, and the contumelious image as well as the social profile of the public schools was set for the rest of the nineteenth century and beyond.

Another significant and increasingly prominent method of announcing ideological 'reformation' came in the form of the *grande bourgeoisie*'s embracement of the Art Movement;[126] since, as we have seen, art and the patronage of the arts was the hallmark of aristocratic high culture, it was predictable that, as the bourgeoisie desired to signpost their cultural renaissance, they should turn their attentions in this direction. A number of channels lay open to them, each with its own social pay-offs. To begin with there was the commissioning of family portraits; useful not only in its mimicking role, but also through judicious use of the retrospective, of immense value in establishing a fake family lineage on permanent public display along a staircase or in a hall. The photograph-album could never have served this purpose so well. A further benefit secured through involvement in the arts was the intimacy and acquaintance of the artistic community – and not a few bourgeois–aristocrat introductions were effected through mutual friends from such a community, who, given their broad social contacts, were the most useful of intermediaries.[127] A second and equally common arts programme concerned the appearance of the bourgeoisie at the so-called 'unpopular' concert. Concerts in the early nineteenth century were divisible into two types: the *popular* (consisting either of 'famous names' or light programmes, they were popular in appeal across a broad spectrum of social groups and consequently shunned by the aristocracy, being of little social 'value') and the *unpopular* (less proletarian, often deadly dull, avoided by the 'pleasure-seekers' and consequently a huge hit amongst the socially conscious whose interest in the performance was at best tangential anyway). The result of such a division was that attendance at either could be accurately predicted, and, by careful selection, the bourgeoisie were able to mix casually amongst the higher notables on neutral territory. Lack of musical knowledge (unlike lack of sporting 'form') was hardly a disadvantage since everyone was aware that the value of the concert lay in something other than the music itself.[128] The introduction of the reserved seat set the final seal upon the success of such a social forum, for this not only avoided the unseemly rush to sit next to the highest titled, but actually guaranteed in advance that one's partner for the evening (or perhaps one's daughter's) was a carefully chosen individual whose seat number had been discretely disclosed by the booking agency.

The dramatic increase in the number of unpopular concerts dates precisely from the period in which the aristocracy was opening up to such advances and the bourgeoisie was realizing its utility in issuing social credentials.[129]

In art patronage across a wide front, then, the bourgeoisie and the aristocracy found their first common currency. Those families intimately involved in the legitimation process became great collectors in their own right as they sought to authenticate their newly created 'ancestral' homes. Thus the Classical Revival received considerable support from an unexpected direction: those elements of the *grande bourgeoisie* who, feelings softened by the prospect of acceptance, now wished to proclaim a new 'Golden Age' as well.[130] It is perhaps fitting that these recent converts from proto-Benthamism still favoured in their artistic leanings the simplicity and relative functionalism of Classical Revivalist art and architecture, rather than the idiom of the Gothic Revival advocated a little later by, amongst others, Pugin and Morris,[131] and put to such startling use in the railway architecture of the Victorian age.[132] There was of course considerable ideological substance behind the appeal of the Gothic movement, but despite vigorous championship in certain bourgeois circles, it seldom attracted the patronage of the *grande bourgeoisie*. An interesting exception occurs inevitably in the ever perverse Mancunian community. Forever swimming against the tide, the city demolished a perfectly adequate classically proportioned town hall in order to construct one of the largest and finest examples of Gothic Revival architecture in Great Britain.[133]

Even so, it is significant that Manchester (still the symbol of radical dissent amongst those not ascended to the gentry and consequently avoided by the more socially ambitious amongst the middle class) was itself drawn into the cultural storms now brewing in the country as a whole. This was neatly underlined in 1823, by the foundation of the Royal Manchester Institution under the auspices of several Literary and Philosophical Society members. (Royal patronage was itself significant, as was the King's foundation gift – a copy of the Elgin Marbles.) The Royal Manchester Institution, later to become the city's municipal art gallery, was an intermediate and derivative cultural form, being a species of local quasi-scientific academy which yet emphasized the appreciation of artistic values and assembled a not inconsiderable collection of artworks. Such a softening towards the arts in general was further emphasized in a series of gallery concerts, a music festival and a regular subscription series which was to lead, albeit indirectly, to the foundation of a professional orchestra under the direction of Charles Hallé, a gifted pioneer who had recently arrived in the city. The Hallé Orchestra, as it was to become, was one of the first such permanent bodies in the country – a typically bold, though untypically charming, step for so austere a city.[134] Clearly the message was beginning to permeate unashamedly, as Sir Benjamin Heywood was only too aware: 'Literature and the arts tend, even perhaps more than the sciences themselves, to diffuse through the discordant elements of society a pervading emotion of friendly spirit and mutual satisfaction.'[135] His family was not but a few years short of its baronetcy.

Summation

Such dramatic cultural changes, such an abandonment of the severe and radical strictures of the first generation of Mancunian social architects associated with both the construction of the Literary and Philosophical Society, and that dogma which had denounced as unwarrantably fanciful and degenerate all non-pragmatic, non-scientific activity, emphasizes how complete, and in the event how painless, the absorption of the *grande bourgeoisie* had been. As a consequence, the aristocratic life-style had been preserved, if not its hegemony. If the *grande bourgeoisie* had lost the ideological distinctiveness of their own remarkable cultural construction (and willingly lost it at that) then they had gained wider access to the nation's political process in exchange. The aristocracy meanwhile had compromised both their independence and their 'principles' and bought in return only a little time and breathing space. Equally importantly, the bourgeoisie more generally had achieved the crucial position of hegemonic control within the newly defined power bloc. This was arguably the most important coalition in the history of English class antagonism and one which, upon its resolution, created a powerful, unified patrician class free to fight the social and economic demands of the labouring classes and the *petite bourgeoisie* both within and without Parliament. It deserves and demands closer attention.

Though necessarily brief, partial and sketchy, an analysis such as the foregoing illustrates the importance of an approach to past class relations which emphasizes not only economic determination, but also ideological persuasion and cultural cohesion in the development of social formation. It equally demonstrates the need to pass beyond the merely superficial in seeking satisfactory solutions to conventionally formulated problems. Much work still needs to be done – not least in terms of the operation of specific institutions (of all types and sizes); the locus of social mixing (for example, the important role of the county and spa towns in providing a captive and sympathetic aristocratic audience on neutral ground);[136] the other forms of cultural expression; and the orientations of shifting hegemonic blocs.

The nature of the source materials – scattered and piecemeal, disordered and frequently destroyed – is not likely to render such work popular amongst traditional historical geographers, for whom the concept of culture has, as yet, no specific place or meaning. Even so, such practical and conceptual difficulties cannot for long justify the total neglect of an important explanatory theme in the history of society.

University of Cambridge

3

Contours of crisis? Sketches for a geography of class struggle in the early Industrial Revolution in England

DEREK GREGORY

John Barton was not far wrong in his idea that the Messrs Carson would not be over much grieved for the consequences of the fire in their mill. They were well insured; the machinery lacked the improvements of late years, and worked but poorly in comparison with that which might now be procured. Above all, trade was very slack; cottons could find no market, and goods lay packed and piled in many a warehouse. The mills were merely worked to keep the machinery, human and metal, in some kind of order and readiness for better times. So this was an excellent time, Messrs Carson thought, for refitting their factory with first-rate improvements, for which the insurance money would amply pay. They were in no hurry about the business, however. The weekly drain of wages given for labour, useless in the present state of the market, was stopped. The partners had more leisure than they had known for years; and promised wives and daughters all manner of pleasant excursions . . .

There is another side to the picture. There were homes over which Carsons' fire threw a deep, terrible gloom; the homes of those who would fain work, and no man gave unto them – the homes of those to whom leisure was a curse. There, the family music was hungry wails, when week after week passed by, and there was no work to be had, and consequently no wages to pay for the bread the children cried aloud for in their young impatience of suffering. There was no breakfast to lounge over; their lounge was taken in bed, to try and keep warmth in them that bitter March weather, and, by being quiet, to deaden the gnawing wolf within.

Elizabeth Gaskell, *Mary Barton: a tale of Manchester life* (1848)

Crisis and consciousness

Few novels come as close as *Mary Barton* to the 'Condition of England' question. But its power – its sense of polarity – was much more than the pity of a minister's wife for the plight of the poor (although this was real enough): it was heightened by an almost palpable fear of violence. Mrs Gaskell herself recognized the tension: 'I had always felt a deep sympathy with the care-worn men, who looked as if doomed to struggle through their lives in strange alternations between work and want', she wrote, and 'I saw that they were sore and irritable against the rich, the even tenor of whose seemingly happy lives appeared to increase the anguish caused by the lottery-like nature of their own.' They were now 'left in a state, wherein lamentations and tears are thrown aside as useless, but in which the lips are compressed for curses, and the hands clenched and ready to smite'. And she believed her judgements had 'received some confirmation from the events which have so recently occurred among a similar class on the Continent'.[1]

Yet 1848 was not 'the springtime of peoples' in England. As revolutions coursed through the core of the European Continent, 'running like a brush-fire across frontiers',[2] the English working class drew back from the barricades. Its early history had been, in Nairn's words, an unmistakable 'history of revolt, covering more than half a century, from the period of the French Revolution to the climax of Chartism in the 1840s'; and yet this 'titanic social force which seemed to be unchained by the rapid development of English capitalism in the first half of the century, did not finally emerge to dominate and remake English society'.[3] In the most general terms, we may agree with Stedman Jones that this disjuncture in the trajectory of the English working class – what Anderson called this 'profound caesura'[4] – is to be explained by the divergence between the two 'moments' of 1848: 'The uneven progress of industrialisation produced a whole spectrum of differing forms of class confrontation', and while, at one extreme, the European revolutions of 1848 can be seen as 'the last general revolt of small producers subject to varying degrees of pauperisation and proletarianisation', at the other the campaigns of the Luddites almost forty years earlier – and perhaps even the whole of that 'underground tradition' unearthed by Thompson – can be seen, in their essentials, as the very *first* reactions to the same processes as they scissored through the fabric of English society.[5]

But this is only half the story. The eventual 'restabilizations' were not merely matters of the compulsive logic of the *economy*, of the transition from a purely 'formal' to a 'real' subordination of labour to capital; for the domination of the bourgeoisie resided in a conjoint *cultural* and *political* hegemony.

These are large questions, and one of the most serious responses to them is John Foster's *Class Struggle and the Industrial Revolution*. In what follows I seek to explore its analytical terrain: one which conforms to the topography which Mrs Gaskell described – and in particular to its connective imperative between crisis and consciousness – but which dissects these relations through the theoretical incisions opened up by Marx and Lenin. I do so through a comparison with Edward Thompson's *The Making of the English Working*

Class. It should be said at once that this manoeuvre is not intended to favour one discourse over the other. I regard both of them as deficient, and their inadequacies and incoherences will not be removed through a conflation of the two; but I think that each can illuminate the difficulties encountered by the other. The architecture of the two texts is strikingly different, of course, but proceeding in this way allows me to develop two interconnected claims which I take to be central to any historical geography of class struggle. First, I insist on the salience of struggle in the production and reproduction of social life. Elsewhere I have suggested that neither voluntarist nor essentialist forms of explanation can capture the 'bounded contingency' of historical structuration: the one reduces eventuation to the actions of individuals, the other to the logic of structures. But most versions of social theory which have sought to transcend this exhausted dualism continue to tremble on the edges of a functionalism and fail to explicate the ways in which outcomes (Urry's 'emergent properties') are generated *in the course of* struggles. Secondly, I argue that these various outcomes are problematic in the sense that all social practices depend on conditions and constraints which reach beyond the competence of knowledgeable human subjects. By this I mean not only that structures of social relations have definite 'fields of effectivity' but also that struggles take place within what Hindess calls 'arenas' *articulated on one another* in complex ways.[6]

I begin with a brief summary of Foster's argument.

Class struggle and the Industrial Revolution

Foster's thesis is that the emergence of industrial capitalism was accompanied by (and structurally connected to) a protracted series of economic crises which met with a parallel series of cultural and political responses. Although his analysis is, for the most part, confined to Oldham, a mill town in the heart of the Lancashire cotton industry, his writing is, I think, remarkable for its sensitivity to the simple geography of these struggles: to the space–time specificity of the new structures of production and politics. His primary purpose was to illuminate the local arena within which the confrontation between capital and labour was staged, to 'project into it the main areas of controversy' and so to 'generate questions about relationships with the wider processes of capitalist development'. These serve to define three critical phases (and here I rehearse Foster's characterizations without comment).[7]

The stability of the eighteenth century was interrupted by 'the first big crisis of industrial capitalism' when, beginning in the mid-1790s and continuing for the next twenty years, 'the incomplete mechanisation of the cotton industry' pushed the productivity of the spinning sector ahead of that of the weaving sector. This 'internal' imbalance, and in particular the constant shuttle of yarn exports, jacked up continental cloth production and subjected the hand-loom weavers to such massive competition that 'for over two decades the biggest section of the industry's labour force was exposed to an incessant downward pressure on its real wages'. These privations were aggravated by the wars with France, and if local radicalism owed its vitality more to the material deprivations imposed by the trade blockades than to any revolutionary ideologies run across them, nevertheless 'each time the radicals underlined the lesson: the war was fought on behalf of merchants and employers; the costs were passed to labour'. And this was remembered long after the peace, for 'the scale of radical influence still increased in step with the intensity of the economic crisis'. Yet its sphere was always circumscribed, because its critique sustained and informed a 'trade union' consciousness, which was concerned primarily with the sectional defence of living standards rather than with the advance of any wider political programme. It ruptured traditional authority systems and even challenged the strategies of the State itself, but its tap-roots in dislocation and distress were revealed by 'the geographical spread of radical activity. It is precisely the areas with a similar economic experience to Oldham, the ring of south Lancashire and Cheshire cotton towns – Stockport, Ashton, Rochdale, Bury, Bolton and even more the entirely weaving-based communities in the Pennine foothills – that stand out from the Home Office papers as the strongholds of anti-government organization.'

By the 1830s the cotton industry was 'well ahead of its continental rivals' and it was now 'the technological incompleteness of England's industry as a whole' which 'produced just the situation which Marx prescribed for a declining rate of profit'. This 'external' imbalance, 'the extremely narrow base of the initial breakthrough', meant that 'while there was a continual and drastic decrease in the (labour) exchange value of cotton textiles – still in the 1830s producing half the country's exports – there was no corresponding fall in the price of food or machinery. So inevitably the value of industrial output relative to the costs of labour and the increasing mass of fixed capital would tend to fall from crisis to crisis.' Factory-masters tried to stop the slide with a renewed attack on wages, and this was resisted by an escalating series of strikes which flowed from and fed back into a (revolutionary) class consciousness. This differed from previous forms of popular political practice in the depth of its critique of capitalism – in the 'organic linkage' forged between economy and politics. This was hammered out by a small group of working-class radicals, shopkeepers and publicans and petty masters, but overcame the traditional divisions between skilled artisans and labourers to bind the working community together in a new, solidary resistance to the structures of the State. And, in so far as the intensity of the crisis disclosed, with a rare and savage clarity, 'the logic of capitalist development', then its geography ensured that 'a number of towns with industries similarly exposed to a declining rate of profit in the 1830s and 40s (textiles, coal, iron) show[ed] signs of a parallel class consciousness'. This reached a peak – 'a point of culmination within the first phase of working-class organization in England' – with the strike of 1842. 'If one is looking for that act of class assertion which convinced the ruling class of the need to change course – and above all of the need to drive a wedge between legitimate trade unionism and illegitimate political action – then this vast strike, stretching from Lanarkshire and Fife [through Lancashire] to the South Midlands, must be a major candidate.'

Restabilization was under way by the end of the 'hungry forties', but although the following decades saw 'the development of a new heavy industrial technology which ultimately did much to reverse the trend to crisis' – and to pull down the price of food and machinery – 'the breakdown of the working-class movement' was more immediately the result of 'a collective *ruling class* response to a social system in crisis and integrally related to a preceding period of working-class consciousness'. Certainly, 'it seems to have been just those areas where class consciousness was previously strongest (and restabilization presumably most thoroughgoing) that eventually formed the political bases for liberalizing pressures in the country at large'. 'Liberalization' of necessity involved political concessions, and these set definite limits to 'the room for bourgeois manoeuvre', but in any substantial sense they remained peripheral to the everyday lives of most working people; what was much more central was the re-establishment of capitalist authority systems in the work-place. The mill now dominated the mental as well as the physical landscape of the Lancashire cotton industry, so that 'authority in industry was the key orienting dimension of labour sub-culture in the mid-century period'. The creation of a 'labour aristocracy' – 'a stratum of production workers exercising authority on behalf of the management' and rewarded (or 'bribed') with fatter wage-packets than their work-mates – splintered the solidarities on which effective class struggle depended. But, more than this, economy and politics were prised apart again, and the rump of the movement was reduced to a series of sectional campaigns which sought to maintain and even to extend the differentials embedded in the new labour process and written into the wage contract. This meant 'the loss of almost every institutional expression of class unity – of the whole organizational heritage developed during that extraordinarily rich period of working-class creativity which marked the earlier nineteenth century'; and 'most important of all', the loss of 'the *local* institutions of class unity'.

Milieux and space–time matrices

This recurrent emphasis on the local milieu is of immense significance. It is a necessary corrective to the abstract generalizations of purely 'theoretical' histories and to the indiscriminate empiricism of many others. And yet if, as Foster says, 'it is really not very helpful to dash about the country bringing back odd bits and pieces of information', like a spaniel at an archaeological dig, then it is equally unhelpful to rope off an arena which is so restricted that 'Oldham workers appear to fight out their own autonomous class struggle'.[8] This is because a 'de-contextualized' history of necessity fails to recover the range of determinations which affect the outcomes of social practices; and it will be part of my purpose to show that an adequate understanding of class struggle in these early years of the Industrial Revolution requires the recognition of a whole constellation of different 'process-domains' which cross-cut the local milieu in a highly complex series of engagements. These were not ordered into coherent, concentric circles, their bounds were rarely clear-cut and their interconnections were often discontinuous.

In part, of course, their identification is an empirical question, and in insisting upon its importance I do not mean to challenge the centrality of the local community and its collective response to the parochial circuits of authority which circumscribed it; neither do I wish to minimize the barriers which stood in the way of any extension of contacts and campaigns beyond its immediate confines. But the local community was part of a wider and deeper structure of social relations, and the social practices which took place within it have to be situated within the intersecting hierarchies and overlapping domains of what I shall call 'civil society'. More than this: in so far as the struggles which convulsed towns like Oldham combined and recombined 'economics' and 'politics' in various ways – this too is a leitmotiv in Foster's writings – then their formations must also be located within the sub-regional, regional, inter-regional and even international rotations of economic and political structures. These too were constantly changing and their topographies were frequently discordant, so that any 'correspondence' between them was conjunctural, and while their compound determinations were graphically revealed in the local and regional crises which disfigured the emergence of industrial capitalism, they were also registered in the generalized restructuring and recomposition of the economy and the State over the course of the nineteenth century. All this makes it impossible to provide a unitary 'map of British capitalism' during this period: the recursive motions of human history were instantiated in a human geography whose complex foliations cannot be reduced to the two-dimensional lattices of conventional spatial science. And Foster evidently knows this: thus, 'a process cutting across a number of areas – central government, economy, the local community – tends to escape systematic investigation'.[9]

But the recovery of these incisions is also a theoretical question. The milieu (or locale) is of vital importance to various formalizations of the production and reproduction of everyday life, and it is the central pivot of Hägerstrand's time geography, which represents the routinized 'intertwining' of paths and projects in time and space (on which the continuity of everyday life depends) as the skilled accomplishment of conscious human subjects. It would clearly be absurd to discount actors' own understandings of their encounters and to reduce the formation of a collective consciousness (on whatever basis) to the irreflexive compulsion of a trans-situational 'logic'. But these webs of intersubjective interactions also fold out from and fold back into sets of structural relations which are not immediately and inclusively 'present' in any one of them. These objective relations typically possess a wider 'field' than any localized system of interaction, therefore, and the skeins of structural tissue which are bound into this 'weaving dance in space and time' are limited by historically contingent constraints imposed by the reach of the knowing subject and by the spatial structure of social relations itself: what Poulantzas terms the 'spatial and temporal matrices' of capitalism. These heterogeneous inclusions cannot be understood in terms of a number of 'settings for action' ever-present within the local milieu. On the contrary, as Urry has argued, 'crucial' interventions in the directionality of specific struggles can arise through 'transformations in the temporal and spatial structure of capitalism'.[10]

I want to flesh out these skeletal abstractions by reworking Foster's materials through the *grille* contained within Thompson's account of *The Making of the English Working Class*.

The making of the English working class

Following Anderson's remarkable critique of Thompson, it is possible to identify two fundamental theses which thread their way through his narrative. In shorthand form these are 'co-determination' and 'consciousness'.[11]

Co-determination

This is the claim that the English working class 'made itself as much as it was made' in a causal parity of 'agency and conditioning'. More particularly, Thompson chose to resist the prevailing orthodoxy through which the Industrial Revolution was converted from a description into an explanation. Conventionally, 'the physical instruments of production were seen as giving rise in a direct and more-or-less compulsive way to new social relationships, institutions and cultural modes'. But, against this, the making of the English working class 'was not the spontaneous generation of the factory system' but was to be understood as 'a fact of political and cultural, as much as of economic, history'. And as such it had to be traced back to (and even identified with) the imposition of these new productive relations and working conditions and the conjoint political economy of *laissez-faire* upon a vigorous artisan culture, whose remembered rights, customary usages and jealously guarded political traditions – the birthright of 'the free-born Englishman' – formed the well-springs of a determined resistance to those deformations.

Whether the energies which they released flowed into the subterranean imprecations of the 'underground tradition' or surged to the surface in the
sudden violence of riot and insurrection, all of them were *coterminous with*
the conduct of practical life and *continuous with* the recomposition of economy
and polity between 1780 and 1832. Seen like this, of course, the new economic
landscape of mill and machine casts a short shadow over the making of the
English working class, because 'factory hands, so far from being the "eldest
children of the industrial revolution", were late arrivals'. They were not
prominent in early radical agitations and, 'except in the cotton districts',
remained on the periphery of the labour movement until, at the very earliest,
the strikes and lock-outs of the 1830s. The self-determination of the nascent
working class is thus made to reside in the political and cultural traditions
of which it is in some sense the bearer; and it is through those traditions,
instantiated and reworked in daily encounters, that a 'scanty opportunity'
is opened for working people to 'insert their own agency' and so return as
the 'subjects of their own history'. While the area of self-determination
'will not be set free from ulterior determinate pressures nor escape determinate limits' imposed ('crucially but not exclusively') by the objective
relations of overlapping modes of production, the contours of human agency
cannot be reduced to these structural templates. Class struggles are not – and
never have been – the marionette movements of the economy, and the historian's task must be to evict this 'crass economism' and recover 'the agency
of working people' by reinstating class 'as a social and cultural formation'.

Consciousness
  This is the claim that 'class happens when some men [*sic*], as a result
of common experiences, feel and articulate the identity of their interests as
between themselves, and as against other men whose interests are different
from (and usually opposed to) theirs'. More particularly, Thompson refused
to 'put "class" here and "class consciousness" there, as two separate
entities, the one sequential upon the other, since both must be taken together –
the experience of determination, and the handling of this in conscious ways'.
'Experience', therefore, becomes a 'point of junction' between 'structure
and process', as it were receiving, transcribing and relaying the impulses
'sparking across' circuits of capital and other, equally salient circuits for
which political economy 'had no terms'. The 'crucial experience' of the
Industrial Revolution for most working people – crucial because of its 'truly
catastrophic nature' – was their simultaneous experience of 'an intensification of two intolerable forms of relationship: those of economic exploitation
and political oppression'. These were not understood as independent incursions, moreover, but were constituted as parts of 'a particular complex
of human relationship' and, behind this, of a corresponding structure of
social relations. We are of course used to thinking of exploitation as

something that occurs 'at ground level, at the point of production'. In the early eighteenth century, however, 'wealth was created at this lowly level, but it rose rapidly to higher regions, accumulated in great gobbets, and the real killings were to be made in the distribution, cornering and sale of goods or raw materials (wool, grain, sugar, cloth, tea, tobacco, slaves), in the manipulation of credit and in the seizure of offices of State'. Yet by the end of the century the centre of gravity was dropping downwards, and the locus of conflict moved, decisively, towards production and the political complexions which endorsed it. Economic rationality gnawed through the bonds which bound master to man, and as the remaining threads of reciprocity which had confirmed the mutuality of the community finally snapped, so it became possible, 'for the first time, to analyse the historical process in terms of nineteenth-century notations of class'. A robust and independent working-class culture replaced the supple foliations of 'patrician society, plebeian culture', and this sea-change had its origins in the very *constancy* and *transparency* of the exploitation and oppression which skewered and encircled the labour process. Whenever and wherever working people contested the legitimacy of this new economic and political nexus, they were met 'by the forces of employer or State, and commonly of both'. The conjuncture was uniquely formative: the distancing which was set in train, part involuntary and part voluntary, ensured that 'in the heartlands of the Industrial Revolution' new cultural modes emerged which were 'designed to resist the intrusion of the magistrate, the employer, the parson or the spy. The new solidarity was not only a solidarity *with*; it was also a solidarity *against*.'

This is not the place to attempt a detailed critique of Thompson's claims, but it is possible to connect them to a set of counter-claims which can be derived from Foster's writings. The one was not a direct response to the other, of course, but by using a parallel notation we may suppose a dialogue between them and by attending to the silences in their texts start to draw out what Thrift, following Hägerstrand, terms the 'contextual' perspective: that is, the attempt 'to recapture the flow of human agency as a series of situated events in space and time'.[12] To do so, as I shall show, requires a consideration both of class relations and uneven development and of hegemony and time–space distanciation. These connect back to the distinctions drawn by Anderson, but they also feed forward as the discursive axes of an altogether different argument.

Co-determination: class relations and uneven development

The claim for co-determination is now something of a commonplace in both social theory and social history, and yet, as Abrams reminds us, if it is 'easily and endlessly formulated' it remains 'stupefyingly difficult to resolve'.[13] For all the suggestiveness of his work – and I have commented on this elsewhere[14] – I regard Thompson's account of the parity between 'agency and conditioning' as strategically incomplete, because the pivot of his inquiry is fashioned not by the structural transformations of the Industrial Revolution, but rather by what Anderson calls 'their precipitates in the subjective experience of those who lived through those "terrible years"'.[15] In particular, 'the economic as a set of objectively present relations appears in an attenuated form, *through* the cultural, *through* the "inwardness of experience"', so that 'it is the subjective, felt features of the [exploitative-cum-repressive] relationship which are really important – the cultural–psychological aspects: depersonalisation, the decline of mutuality, the destruction of custom, the forms of legitimation'.[16] A number of writers have objected to these readings,[17] but their contributions have not persuaded me that Thompson does otherwise than resolve 'the complex manifold of objective–subjective determinations whose totalization actually generated the English working class' into 'a simple dialectic between suffering and resistance whose whole movement is internal to the subjectivity of the class'. The classical Marxian dialectic, by contrast, is sprung by an objective engagement between the forces and relations of production; and Anderson insists that this continues to set such 'limits' (to use Thompson's own phrase) that the area of self-determination 'is still very much less than that of its opposite'. More particularly, he urges that 'the jagged temporal rhythms and breaks, and the uneven spatial distributions and displacements of capital accumulation between 1790 and 1832 inevitably marked the composition and character of the nascent English proletariat' and that they must therefore have a central place in any adequate account of its 'making'.[18]

This is a major lacuna in Thompson's text, and it is exactly these (objective) time–space structures traced out by the transformations of industrial capitalism that are the linch-pins of Foster's thesis. It was not so much the *constancy* of exploitation that was decisive, therefore, as 'the logic of capitalist development as expressed in particular industries': the convulsive cycle of boom and slump. This is an important advance over Thompson's problematic, and one which, in some measure, Thompson himself accepts.[19] But Foster's reconstruction of these successive crises is open to fundamental objection. Saville claims that he 'offers no serious account of the inner crisis of the cotton industry between 1830 and 1842' and that 'his understanding of the dynamics of industrial capitalism during the second quarter of the century is severely limited'.[20] I want to suggest that this is not primarily an empirical failing, and that it arises largely because Foster appears to accept without qualification a single conception of economic crisis derived directly from the 'logic' of the labour theory of value set out in Marx's *Capital*. Many different (and discrepant) readings of Marx's writings are possible, of course, but it is not necessary to legislate between these competing exegeses here: intellectual fideism is not the issue. What is important is that the concepts involved generate what one group of commentators has called 'multiple and contra-dictory interconnections' which 'cannot be resolved into the forms of hierarchy necessary to create a *general* historical process' with the falling rate of profit as an invariant 'law of motion' of the capitalist economy.[21] This is an extraordinarily difficult debate, clearly, but the crux of the matter is that, in so far as the articulation of the forces and relations of production imposes 'limits' on the forms of capital accumulation – which I accept – these are not trans-situational. Rather, as Wright has shown, 'capitalist develop-ment should be viewed as continually transforming the nature of capitalist crises' and is therefore *historically specific*. Wright has provided an exemplary summary of the chronology of these phases,[22] but these discontinuities in time are also bound in to conjoint discordances over space. Thus, for example, Harvey has demonstrated through a typology of 'partial', 'switching' and 'global' crises that the nature of capitalist crises is also *geographically specific*.[23] It is because Foster systematically occludes this time–space speci-ficity across a mosaic of different scale levels that he misses – 'and misses completely' – what Saville sees as 'the paradox of crisis and growth co-existing in the same years': that is, the process of *combined and uneven development*.[24] This foreshortens the scope of his argument, because capitalism is not only crisis-ridden – as he recognizes – but also in some sense crisis-dependent. And capital restructuring is a vital means of auto-regulation, inasmuch as the resolution of a crisis is at once quantitative *and* qualitative: 'capital accumulates through crises which become the cauldrons in which capital qualitatively reorganizes itself for future economic expansion'.[25] If this is not properly acknowledged, and a homogeneous, intractable 'trend to crisis' substituted for a heterogeneous, dialectical series of trans-formations, then, as Saville says, 'anyone using language of this kind to describe the cotton industry of the 1830s and 1840s has grave difficulties in explaining the remarkable, and relatively smooth expansion of the industry after 1850'.[26]

This immediately rebounds on Foster's representation of class responses during these periods, for the Leninist model on which his explanations depend makes what O'Connor calls a 'deterministic connection between crisis and consciousness'.[27] If this is correct, as I think it is, then it is hard to see how Saville can object to Foster's economic analysis and yet at the same time concede that its failings do not 'vitiate the general argument he is making'.[28] It is *of course* the case that class struggle is deeply imbricated in the course of capital accumulation: it partially determines the composition of capital and so enters into the determination of the rate of profit, and it is enmeshed, crucially, in the contradictions between the production of com-modities and the realization of surplus value which periodically convulse the circuits of capital.[29] But in failing to recognize the *complexity* of these internal relations – their variability and contingency, and their hierarchy of mediations – and in instead enclosing his narrative in a *unitary* model of accumulation, Foster plainly, and I think necessarily,

1 represents the constitution of working-class consciousness in the 1830s and 1840s as a movement which expresses the homogeneity of capitalist crisis, in such a way that the two form an essential unity; and
2 represents the restabilization of the 1850s and 1860s as a direct response to working-class combativity – that is, as 'liberalization' – rather than as a conjoint structural consequence of the capital restructuring which emerged from the crisis.

I now want to secure each of these claims in order to identify the incoherences which I take to be at the heart of Foster's version of 'co-determination'.

Breakdown

Whereas the episodic crises which punctuated the lives of working people in Mrs Gaskell's 'alternations between work and want' remained strange to her, and she could admit to knowing 'nothing' of political economy, Foster's argument hinges on the working class's not merely 'experiencing' these sharp vicissitudes but making determined sense of them, 'handling them in class ways', as Thompson would say, through the categories made available by a critique of political economy developed by a radical leadership or a revolutionary 'vanguard'.

In the most general terms, and echoing the changing modalities of 'exploitation' previously traced out by Thompson, Foster wants to claim that for much of the eighteenth century 'labour's main experience of crisis had been through a rapid increase in food prices' but that by the early nineteenth century 'crisis was expressed in unemployment and, even more, wage-cutting': that it was this ineluctable progression which turned popular struggles away from the middlemen and towards the masters. But these understandings were nevertheless agonizingly slow and necessarily limited, because the structures of capitalism were *not* wholly *transparent*. On the contrary, it was the very opacity of these economic formations which circumscribed the effectivity of popular political discourse. And it was here that the recurrent crises assumed their strategic importance for, like a series of lightning-flashes, they helped to illuminate an economic and political landscape whose contours were usually obscured. Thus 'the contradictions of industrial capitalist productions' were exposed with such 'unique force' in the 'deepening' series of crises which racked the Lancashire cotton industry in the first half of the nineteenth century that the radical critique, for all its imperfections, had an immediate credibility in the mill-towns and villages of the north-west, and this was readily translated into an intellectual conviction capable of a 'widening' generalization throughout the working community. 'As part of the everyday language of cotton trade unionism, one has the emergence of an economic perspective which, though still phrased in terms of the existing order, radically challenged its assumptions' and which could be fed into 'the careful, conscious process by which the radicals guided mass understanding from one level to another' and so transformed 'into a larger commitment against the system itself'. The tripartite stress on credibility, conviction and commitment is important because, as Foster's comparison of Oldham with Northampton and South Shields makes perfectly plain, immiseration is an insufficient condition for class mobilization. What is decisive is the constitution of these hardships and privations as 'exploitative' or 'oppressive', and it is here that the context counts: 'the hard, intractable *trend to crisis* into which the cotton industry became locked after 1830'.

The campaigns of the 1830s and 1840s evidently drew much of their strength from the radical traditions resurrected by Thompson. There is the same, intense experience of economic crisis, culminating in tumultuous 'festivals of the oppressed'; the same, systematic mobilization of working people, confronting exploitation by their employers and repression by the State; and the same, determined leadership, cross-cutting industrial action and insurrection to strengthen the collective challenge to industrial capitalism. But if it is impossible to ignore these continuities, Foster maintains that it is also impossible to overlook the spluttering out of every one of those early beacons of resistance. 'As soon as the objective conditions for each crisis subsided (and a few military counter-measures had been taken), people seemed to slip back into their old attitudes remarkable quickly.' And those attitudes, as Thompson acknowledged, were ones in which politics and economics were separate discursive formations. The communal vision of Tom Paine was clear-cut and still commanded widespread popular support: 'in political society every man must have equal rights as a citizen: in economic society he must naturally remain employer or employed'. In this way, as Thompson put it, *The Rights of Man* and *The Wealth of Nations* ought to 'supplement and nourish' each other. And he himself owned that the main tradition of working-class radicalism 'took its cast from Paine': although 'there were times, at the Owenite and Chartist climaxes, when other traditions became dominant'. Foster thus insists that the real difference between the 1810s and the 1830s was in the sustained rejection of the Painite orthodoxy. The old disagreements over whether to press for 'political' or 'economic' concessions were replaced by a new unanimity, in which political change was accepted as a necessary precondition for economic change. This was now the 'ultimate goal', and it was the 'organic linkage' between politics and economics, so he argues, that confirmed the solidity of class notations and that represented the climax of a class consciousness whose mutually acknowledged imperatives were strong enough for the radical movement 'to force capitalist society to the point of crisis and hold it there for a decade and a half'.[30] In sum, Foster sees the crisis of capitalist society as both reflective of and rooted in a fundamental crisis of capitalist economy.

But Thompson speaks of *England*, Foster of *Oldham*. And it is in moving between the two, in connecting up the generalization of class consciousness to the specificity of its formations, that these claims can be turned back on themselves. Morris reminds us that Foster's Oldham 'lay like some cotton-spinning Cuba in the foothills of the Pennines, plotting revolution but receiving little welcome when its delegates ventured into the wider society of Britain'. And if the logic of Foster's argument is accepted, 'it matters not that towns like South Shields and Northampton ... had little interest in such plans, for their economic structures made such a development unlikely. What matters is the lack of evidence for the same sort of behaviour in other textile towns', where the connections between crisis and consciousness should have been equally compulsive.[31]

This can be partially resolved through a reconstruction of the geography of combined and uneven development. The series of crises had a distinctive historical geography, which was tightly bound to the rhythms of the world economy. Whether or not one accepts the view that Britain did not become a fully fledged export economy until the middle of the nineteenth century, the importance of overseas markets to the cotton industry ensured that from the 1780s it was particularly vulnerable both to the secular Kondratieff cycle and to the sudden surges superimposed over these long waves of capitalist development: what Engels described as 'the perennial round' of 'prosperity–crisis–prosperity–crisis'.[32] His contemporaries knew the consequences as well as he did. Faucher, who visited Manchester at the same time as Engels, believed that 'the crises which occur in the market are more or less frequent according to the degree to which the manufacturers are dependent on foreign markets'. This goes some way towards explaining the differentiated response of the space-economy to the convulsions of the 1830s and 1840s (see Figure 1).[33] Certainly, when Faucher repeated Ashworth's claim that in the cotton industry 'we depend upon strangers for six-sevenths of our production', he recognized an important epicentre of the 'commercial hurricane'. Ashworth's figures need some nuancing, of course, especially once they stray from yarn and twist, but although the export share (C.V.) had fallen in the 1820s and 1830s from its peak earlier in the century, it remained above 50 per cent throughout the first half of the nineteenth century, and then soared still higher.[34] By the 1790s Liverpool had already eclipsed London as the major port for the cotton trade, and any dislocation of overseas markets hit Lancashire hard.[35] The same was true of the inland trade. By the 1830s Manchester had started to overtake London as the wholesaling centre for the home market, and its warehouses were piled high with bales drawn in

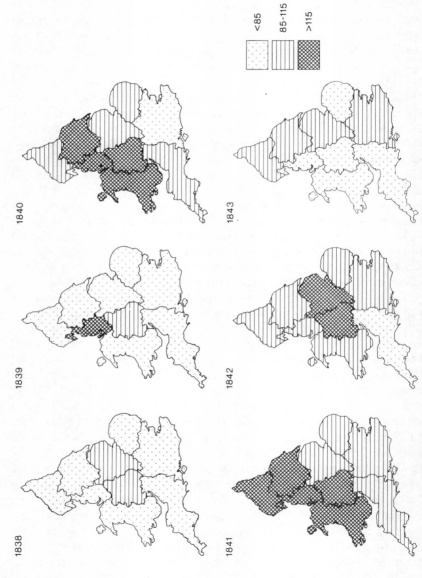

Figure 1   Standardized bankruptcy rates per annum in England and Wales, 1838–43

from the country manufacturers, to be sent out to drapers scattered throughout Britain.[36] But this too was far from stable. Here is Engels:

The home market, like all foreign ones, is glutted with English goods, which it can
only slowly absorb, the industrial movement comes to a standstill in almost every
branch, the small manufacturers and merchants who cannot survive a prolonged
inactivity of their invested capital fail, the larger ones suspend business during the
worst season, close their mills or work short time, perhaps half the day; wages fall
by reason of the competition of the unemployed, the diminution of working-time
and the lack of profitable sales; want becomes universal among the workers, the
small savings which individuals may have made are rapidly consumed, the philanthropic institutions are overburdened, the poor-rates are doubled, trebled and still
insufficient, the number of the starving increases, and the whole multitude of
'surplus' population presses in terrific numbers into the foreground.[37]

The combined effect of these 'exterior' and 'interior' crises, as Faucher
called them, was to plunge the cotton industry – confined more and more to
Lancashire – into a profound paralysis.

This was in part a simple realization crisis – Leonard Horner, the indefati-
gable Inspector of Factories, declared that 'the great depression in the trade
of the cotton mills has arisen from overproduction'[38] – but it was also
complicated by a chronic liquidity crisis. 'It was all too easy in the middle

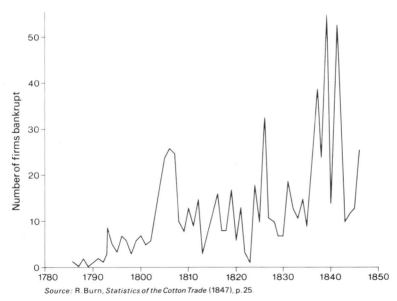

Source: R. Burn, *Statistics of the Cotton Trade* (1847), p. 25.

Figure 2 Bankruptcies in the cotton industry, 1780–1846

'thirties', says Chapman, 'for incautious firms to be flattered by the encouragement of two or three acceptance houses and more than one competing
bank' into over-extending themselves. Then, when credit contracted with the
trade cycle, 'indiscretion not infrequently ended in the bankruptcy court'.
As Figure 2 shows, this was a particularly common terminus in the late
1830s and early 1840s, as firms were forced into ever more distant markets
to find sales for their goods, most notably in the Middle East, the Orient and
South America. There, they found that the rotation time of capital increased
to such an extent that their credit networks were stretched and finally
snapped.[39]

But the sub-regional structure of these international and national impulses
was complex. Faucher drew attention to what he regarded as 'the curious
industrial topography' of Lancashire:

Manchester, like a diligent spider, is placed in the centre of the web, and sends forth
roads and railways towards its auxiliaries, formerly villages but now towns, which
serve as outposts to the grand centre of industry . . . An order sent from Liverpool
in the morning is discussed by the merchants in the Manchester Exchange at noon,
and in the evening is distributed amongst the manufacturers in the environs. In less
than eight days, the cotton spun at Manchester, Bolton, Oldham or Ashton, is
woven in the sheds of Bolton, Stalybridge or Stockport; dyed and printed at
Blackburn, Chorley or Preston, and finished, measured and packed at Manchester.[40]

It was not so very 'curious', of course, and, as this listing suggests, transmission
of price signals was mediated by an intricate mosaic of sub-regional differentiation. Rodgers has provided a detailed reconstruction of this matrix: of
the locus of cotton spinning in the centre, of the early localization of weaving
in the south and the later growth of specialized weaving sheds in the north,
and of 'a complex system of local specialisation in particular types and
qualities of work' lying beneath these divisions. 'By 1840', he concluded,
'every cotton town had acquired a distinctive industrial personality'.[41] And
Gatrell's painstaking retabulations of Horner's remarkable survey of the
cotton industry in 1841 have shown that the most marked differences in
performance at the height of the crisis continued to be defined by process.
Fine spinners were far and away the least affected, whereas the power-loom
weavers suffered the most: and the contraction of their order books squeezed
the coarse spinners who supplied them.[42] All this makes it scarcely surprising
that the crisis should have had such a distinctive sub-regional structure
(Figure 3).[43]

How does Oldham fit into this picture? Rodgers described it as 'the giant
of the coarse spinning towns' and saw its evolving specialization as in part
a result of the multiplication of small firms sharing power and premises.
'It was in this branch', so he claimed, 'that the small firm, to which hired
facilities would appeal most, stood the best chance of survival'.[44] It was not
quite so straightforward, but, whether or not there was a raising of entry

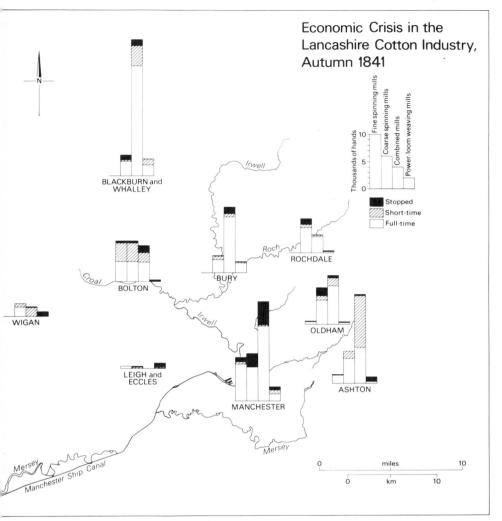

Figure 3 Economic crisis in the Lancashire cotton industry, autumn 1841

barriers in the 1830s (as Chapman has suggested), what *is* striking is Gatrell's demonstration of the ability of small businesses to keep afloat even in the depths of a long-drawn-out depression.[45] Many of these were indeed Oldham firms, but most of them were in subsidiary sectors (waste cotton and yarn doubling) rather than in the mainstream industry, so that their immediate significance is hard to determine; over 90 per cent of those working in Oldham's cotton mills were in the main sectors of the industry.[46]

Even so, some commentators have seized on these various distinctions to argue that Oldham's cotton industry 'was exceptional within the factory districts', and that 'the prevalence of small-scale industry' in general and 'the predominance of petty capitalists' in particular militated against the development of a combative class consciousness. For these reasons, Gadian flatly rejects Foster's findings: 'Class collaboration, rather than class war, between working- and middle-class groups was the key to radical success in the town. Indeed, the growth of an independent working-class conscious- ness, expressed through the Chartist movement both regionally and nationally, eventually helped to undermine, rather than to advance, the unity and thus the strength of radicalism in Oldham.'[47]

But this is a gross simplification, and one which (paradoxically) involves a tacit acceptance of the basic logic of Foster's argument: a direct progression from 'crisis' to 'consciousness'. There are two fundamental objections. First, it has been argued – I think correctly – that it is not so much the *fact* of capitalist crisis as the *form* it takes that is central to the determination of class consciousness. Two sorts of struggle can be distinguished: those, like the campaigns of the clothiers in the Yorkshire woollen industry in 1811–12, over ownership of the means of production, and those, like the battles of the spinners in the Lancashire cotton industry in the 1830s and 1840s, over control of the labour process. The distance between them is that between the purely 'formal' and the 'real' subordination of labour to capital. If they each have their own 'temporalities', as Stedman Jones has suggested, they also surely have their own geographies.[48] In an early study of concentration and specialization in the Lancashire cotton industry, Taylor identified Oldham as 'well to the fore' in the mechanization of the labour process, but we know all too little about diffusion paths during the early Industrial Revolution to make much of this.[49] One might expect some causal connection between technical change and firm size – Chapman's claims for a raising of entry barriers in the 1830s depend on just such a mechanism – but it seems clear that the spring-board for class consciousness 'lay much less in the size of the factories, than in the spinners' battle to maintain their wages and status in the face of technological innovations and sweeping piece-rate reductions'.[50] Both were common responses to crisis.[51]

By their very nature, struggles of this sort make an intersection of econo- mics and politics especially likely, and the close bonds between trade union- ism and Chartism are of considerable importance. Many of these were forged casually, in the course of everyday encounters between relatives, friends, neighbours and work-mates: thus Sykes observes that 'if the basis of Chartism lay less in [formal] organisation than in the more intangible associations of class, community, neighbourhood, workshop and mill', so too 'a great deal of small-scale industrial conflict amongst artisans arose from an instinctive defence of customary practices, founded upon an occupational consciousness which spread well beyond formal permanent trade unionism'.[52] But all these strands *could* be rapidly knit together when the occasion demanded. Sir Charles Shaw wrote to Lord Ashley in 1843:

The labouring classes are all well organized, each trade in itself and corresponding with other trades, so that whatever order may be issued by a particular trade for any agitation, it can be communicated and executed by the stewards or secretaries of the different trades in Manchester, or in the numerous towns within thirty miles distance, in twenty four hours.[53]

Reports like these were the stock-in-trade of State surveillance of radical organizations throughout the early nineteenth century, of course, and it is rarely easy to substantiate them. But there can be no doubt of the existence of such linkages during the great strikes of 1842. Involving over 500,000 workers, these were much more than spasmodic 'rebellions of the belly'.[54] If Mather is right to infer that 'no deep or premeditated nodal conspiracy underlay the disturbances' – and Jenkins has raised plausible doubts about this – he is nevertheless obliged to grant to 'conscious, creative leadership', and in particular to conferences of trade delegates, 'a larger part than is usually allowed'.[55] Contemporaries were not so reticent: in August 1842 Sir James Graham, Secretary of State for the Home Department, had warned the military commander in the north of England that 'these delegates are the directing body; they form the link between the trade unions and the Chartists'.[56] It would be wrong to exaggerate the coherence of the movement, but Sykes has confirmed that it was a trades conference, held in Manchester in the same month and attended by skilled artisans, factory workers and outworkers, engineers, metal-workers and miners, which gave 'the strongest, most coherent impetus towards making the strikes as unequivocal political move for the Charter'.[57]

This is the second objection. The strategies followed by the Chartists were constituted *within the field of politics itself* and were not autonomic responses to 'crisis'. It is of course the case that the rhetoric of Chartism subsumed a critique of political economy, and however imperfect the understandings which flowed from this corpus of assumption and assertion the Chartists' assault on an abusive capitalism – on unbridled competition, uncontrolled mechanization and unemployment – must have been compelling. It is equally true that the crisis helped hammer home the force of these arguments. 'At the onset of 1842 workmen were entering the sixth year of an apparently intractable depression, coming after many years of a violently fluctuating trade cycle, and *it was not obvious that the new industrial society could, or would, emerge relatively unscathed.*'[58] But the added stress pin-points a basic weakness in representations of Chartism as a reaction to the advance of industrial capitalism conceived as 'an objective, irreversible process'. The fragility of the new economic order needs emphasis; but it was also and at the same time a *political* order. And early nineteenth-century radicalism was less inclined to see the State as a nest of self-interest and corruption:

Instead it increasingly came to be viewed as the tyrannical harbinger of a dictatorship over the producers. As the 1830s progressed, the predominant image was no longer merely of placemen, sinecurists and fund-holders principally interested in revenues derived from taxes on consumption to secure their unearned comforts – but something more sinister and dynamic, a powerful and malevolent machine of repression, at the behest of capitalists and factory lords, essentially and actively dedicated to the lowering of the wages of the working classes through the removal of all residual protection at their command . . . As a conjunctural phenomenon, Chartism represented the rapid upsurge and gradual ebbing away of this specific vision of the state.[59]

And this was hardly confined to Oldham. The incursions of the State were felt throughout the country, especially in the wake of the Whig triumphs of 1832, and the Chartist *Northern Star* – whose influence Cooke Taylor thought 'very much underrated by the majority of people in the South' – enjoyed a wide circulation in the manufacturing districts, eventually published in London rather than Leeds, and busily spread its 'specific vision' of an aggressive capitalist State relentlessly waging war against 'the people' (Figure 4).[60] What needs re-emphasis, therefore, is that while studies of Chartism certainly require Briggs' 'proper appreciation of regional and local diversity', Chartism was nevertheless a *national* movement with a *developing* geography. And although Briggs was also right to suppose that 'refinements in the analysis of the changing structure and cyclical fluctuations of the early nineteenth-century British economy make possible a deeper understanding both of the chronology and the geography of Chartism', it makes little sense to abstract that understanding from a fuller recognition of the changing *political* geography of early industrial capitalism.[61] The 1830s were momentous years, which saw not only the enfranchisement of the middle classes and the emergence of the two-party system, but also a more or less sustained political endorsement (and enlargement) of competitive capitalism. To most working people the separate policy measures were like giant mirrors endlessly repeating against one another. Ministers had connived at the suppression of trade unions, refused the hand-loom weavers' petitions for wage regulation, abolished out-relief and extended the workhouse system. The list was a long one, but running right through it was what Richards has called the 'condensation' of the capitalist character of the State and the State apparatus. And eddying and swirling against these moves was a rising tide of popular and intrinsically *political* protest.[62]

We may conclude that it was not the *growth* of Chartism that sapped the vitality of local radicalism. On the contrary; it was the *collapse* of Chartism which signalled the end of the radical movement: and, as I will indicate shortly, these 'accommodations' owed as much to changes in the State as

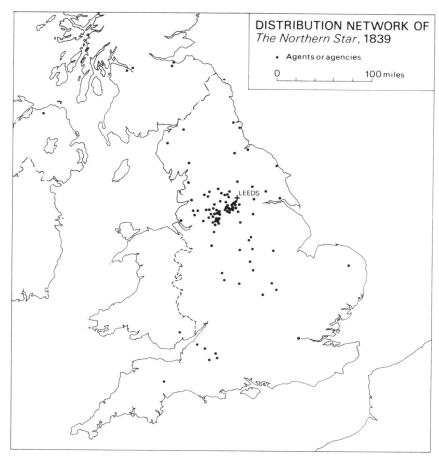

Figure 4   Distribution network of *The Northern Star*, 1839

they did to changes in the economy. In both cases the 'local' was a part of
rather than apart from the 'national'. The cross-cuts between them were
far from clean and smooth, as Foster's comparison of Northampton and
South Shields makes plain, and much more work needs to be done on the
ways in which the one dovetailed into the other. But for the present, Sykes
seems to have hit the mark: the Oldham radical movement 'did not differ
dramatically from those in other [cotton] towns', and even if its class consciousness was 'more fragile' than Foster would have us believe – and certainly more complex in its own determinations – it was still 'the most
potent force determining the configuration of Oldham's popular politics in
this period'.[63]

Repair

That 'configuration' soon shifted into new alignments. When Faucher had claimed that 'no system is more fluctuating' than that 'which seeks purchasers in foreign markets', he also acknowledged that 'to maintain its existence, it is continually forced to dissolve and re-form its interior combinations'.[64] And the logic of combined and uneven development would indeed suggest that (in the cotton industry *a fortiori*) capital restructuring *through the crisis* would have provided at least the technical basis for a reconstitution of the division of labour in the 1850s and 1860s: that the emergence of Foster's 'labour aristocracy' was part of a restabilization of the labour process on the basis of 'modern industry'.[65] Certainly, the changes were nothing short of remarkable. In the course of the 1830s and early 1840s imports of raw cotton soared and power capacity rose; the number of spindles practically doubled and the number of power-looms quadrupled (see Table 1). As Saville wryly observed, 'these are not the statistics of an industry locked in insoluble crisis'.[66]

Table 1

	Imports of raw cotton (million lb))	Spindles millions)	Power looms (thousands)
1830	331	10	55
1845	560	19.5	225

In themselves, of course, they say nothing about how the 'interaction of machines' was incorporated into interactions between workers and written into the rule-book of industrial relations: there is no *necessary* correspondence between the *technical* and the *social* division of labour. Furthermore, and connected to this, Lazonick has shown that they need *not* endorse the classical Marxian model in which 'the power of capital triumphs by virtue of the very technologies at its disposal', as 'technological development reproduces the domination of capital over labour on an ever more oppressive scale'.[67]

But one would expect Foster to take such progressions extremely seriously; yet at this point in his argument he replaces determinism by voluntarism. In so far as this entails a recognition of the asymmetries of self-determination then it too is an advance upon Thompson's problematic. For all his (proper) insistence on class as an historical relation rather than an abstract category – 'we cannot have love without lovers, nor deference without squires and labourers' – there is a sense in which Thompson's dramatic narrative substitutes Stoppard for Shakespeare. His principled rescue of 'the poor stockinger' and 'the Luddite cropper' from 'the enormous condescension of posterity' is achieved in large measure by bringing Rosencrantz and Guilden-stern downstage and banishing an anonymous Hamlet to the wings.[68] But the capacity for self-determination is not confined to the labourer and the artisan, and Foster discloses not only the effectivity of the working class, the 'agency' of working people (and the victories which he records are no less formidable than those which Thompson notes: by the 1840s the radicals in Oldham had at various times won control of the police, the Poor Law, the Select Vestry and even – through 'select dealing' – Parliamentary represen-tation); he also discloses the effectivity of the bourgeoisie, the 'agency' of the cotton manufacturers, the coal-owners, the engineering magnates and the hatters, the tradesmen and the 'little masters'. And this was no less impressive; it would have been surprising if it had been. The objection is not, therefore, that Foster demonstrates the concerted reassertion of bourgeois power, but rather that he fails to specify the basis on which this was achieved – its structural determinations.

'Liberalization' is seen as 'a collective *ruling-class* response to a social system in crisis', through which the bourgeoisie 'consciously *used* its indus-trial power' to 'split the labour force and bribe its upper layers into political acquiescence'. The creation of a 'labour aristocracy' clearly did not exhaust the resources of the bourgeoisie, whose success depended on the extension of their authority systems into the fine-grained textures of community life beyond the factory gates. But here too the stress on credibility, conviction and commitment reappears, in a fresh guise. 'Previously it had been possible to represent inequality (and capital accumulation) as the necessary price of progress', but now the bourgeoisie 'had to find other explanations for poverty and inequality that would divert attention from their own respon-sibility'. What Foster identifies as the old, 'intellectual' justification had out-lived its usefulness, therefore, and the new 'liberal' ideology thus broke with 'the dispassionate political economy of earlier generations' and embraced a set of much simpler and essentially moral arguments – in effect, a *new* 'moral economy' – founded on the sanctity (and the identity) of society and the family. Foster admits that it is difficult to characterize these new perspectives with any precision, but of this much he is certain: 'on the *deliberation* of the local bourgeois response there can be few doubts'.[69] In so far as this was 'integrally related to a preceding period of working-class consciousness', then the strategies which were pursued with such single-minded devotion and the concessions which were made, however genuine, were evidently not entirely voluntaristic; they too were bound in to the limiting structures of the mode of production. But these are *not* the limits set in the 1850s and 1860s: they derive directly from *and are closed around* the crisis of the 1830s and 1840s which had sustained the threat of working-class insurrection. Of course the struggles of the thirties and forties were important – and much more so than many historians have been prepared to admit[70] – but apart from a gestural appeal to 'an overall change in the nature of English capitalism, part of the switch to a new capital export imperialism' – which Stedman Jones in any case dismisses as 'untenable' and even, if carried through with any consistency, 'patently absurd'[71] – Foster offers no rigorous account of the *conditional* effectivity of the local bourgeois response. Instead of a delineation of the structures which bounded their actions, at once economic and political, all we are offered are the parameters set by preceding working-class actions. In short, we are given a ring-side seat at the 'boxing match' to which Gray has so forcefully objected for its 'mechanistic' view of the class struggle.[72]

Technical change entailed the subordination of labour to capital in so far as its hierarchies of skill and status depended on (and were only meaningful within) the confines of the factory system and what Marx identified as the 'dull compulsions' of its labour process. In the cotton industry the dependencies were so strong that in the depths of the depression Cooke Taylor could claim that 'the pressure of distress' had 'brought the masters and men closer together, and exhibited demonstratively their mutuality of interests'. What he called 'the equity of the relations between the employers and the employed' had been disturbed 'by the want of capital, not by the command of it'.[73]

If views like these must have seemed premature in 1842 (and they were scarcely disinterested), they were also sufficiently prescient for Thompson to commend their shrewdness and to agree that after the collapse of Chartism the very *permanence* of capitalism ensured that 'the workers had come to fear, above all, not the machine but the *loss* of the machine – the loss of employment'. It is right to give some prominence to Thompson's claims here, I think, because they denote a reversal of the emphases contained in *The Making of the English Working Class*: 'less a celebration of agency than a dwelling on necessity'.[74] And these determinations closed in still further through the reconstitution of the family within the factory. Both water-power and steam-power had been applied to common mule-spinning since the 1790s, but the spinner still had to return the carriage and wind on the yarn. The physical strength involved – and, less plausibly, the manual skill and mechanical ability – meant that men marked out mule-spinning for themselves. But the 'self-actor', developed by Richard Roberts through the late 1820s and marketed from 1830, allowed skilled artisans to be replaced by machine-minders. Roberts' company boasted that their self-actor made possible 'the saving of a spinner's wages to each pair of mules, piecers only being required, one overlooker being sufficient to manage six or eight pairs of mules or upwards', and by 1835 Andrew Ure was looking forward to the dismissal of 'the greater part of the men spinners' and the employment of less 'refractory' women and children. While younger people and a higher proportion of women were employed as minders in the 1830s and 1840s, however, men continued to fill the vast majority of jobs, even more so after 1850, and many of them seem to have recruited and supervised piecers from their own families. Some historians have argued that this retention of patriarchal authority within the working-class family 'in a period when family relations of production [had] been destroyed' was in fact 'highly functional' for the 'capitalist relations of production which took their place', because it enforced a labour discipline 'crucial to the appropriation of surplus value'.[75]

But these were not one-sided determinations, and subordination ought not to be elevated to a teleology in which, as Price puts it, the subordinated contribute nothing but the material for their subjection.[76] Kinship was more than merely functional for capital. Sometimes the family provided a means of accommodating its members to the disciplines of industrial capitalism; but just as often it functioned as a means of resisting its encroachments and of upholding a network of reciprocities which flew in the face of such a starkly economic calculus of supply and demand. And the existence of 'fictive kin' involved an extension of family ties outwards into the community, where these multi-stranded, multi-valued systems of exchange had a vital role in 'maintaining working-class integrity and autonomy' and sustaining a 'culture of consolation' rather than collaboration. On occasion, too, this could be turned into an outright rejection of subordination, for, as Foster found, 'radical allegiances tended to be inherited within families and associated with particular neighbourhoods'.[77]

Such continuities proved to be exceptionally powerful. Cotton spinning had depended on a subcontract system since the end of the eighteenth century, and the mule-spinner had been recruiting and supervising his piecers long before the introduction of the self-actor. The translation of this spinner–piecer system into a minder–piecer system in the 1830s and 1840s was thus a *continuation* of pre-existing methods of labour management and not some artful new creation of a 'labour aristocracy'. Furthermore, the *consolidation* of the minder–piecer system after mid-century was the result of struggles and strikes, certainly localized, 'disparate and uncoordinated', but none the less effective both in beating off attempts by employers to weaken the minders' control over the labour process and in establishing district wage lists through the 1850s, 1860s and early 1870s. These lists, all of which were negotiated during 'the long boom of the third quarter of the nineteenth century', institutionalized the system as the centre-piece of industrial relations in the Lancashire cotton industry.[78]

As this implies, technical change also gave a fillip to the flagging fortunes of the industry. One needs to be cautious here – economic recovery was discontinuous in space and time, and the industry, which by 1860 relied on the United States for almost 80 per cent of its raw cotton, was badly hit by the Civil War – but both productivity and output showed a remarkably rapid recovery from the crisis of the 1830s and early 1840s (Table 2). Between 1835 and 1856 total factor productivity rose by 64 per cent in spinning and 53 per cent in weaving. Between 1834 and 1873 the export trade (after 1843 dominated by cloth rather than yarn) expanded three times as fast as the home trade, and although the quality of production for the home market was always well above that for export, the value of output was pushed up to around £60 million.[79] The conversion of figures like these into profit margins and wage fractions is notoriously difficult, but Burgess considers it likely that workers 'whose strategic position enabled them to take full advantage of the widening of the investment field would receive a comparatively larger share of wages from employment that the "export economy" generated'; and this would evidently include minders in the cotton industry. At the same time, clearly, their ability to do so depended on a rough and ready acceptance of collective bargaining *within* the capitalist labour market and the capitalist labour contract.[80]

Table 2

	Labour productivity (product per man 000 lb p.a.)		Value of output (£ million)
	Spinning	Power-loom weaving	
1835	1.92	2.24	36.3
1850	3.14	3.05	41.6
1856	3.75	3.37	59.8

This was not a uniquely economic matter, of course, and has to be seen in a wider, political context. Here is E. P. Thompson again (and notice the renewed emphasis on 'determination'):

The workers, having failed to overthrow capitalist society, proceeded to warren it from end to end . . . It was part of the logic of this new direction that each advance within the framework of capitalism simultaneously involved the working class far more deeply in the status quo . . . Each assertion of working-class influence within the bourgeois–democratic state machinery simultaneously involved them as partners (even if antagonistic partners) in the running of the machine.[81]

But 'antagonistic' not 'acquiescent'. Working people were not dumb spectators at the prize-fights of high politics. They had a keen grasp of the rules which, if scarcely equivalent to those of the Marquis of Queensberry (even after 1867), nevertheless imposed definite obligations on the contestants which went far beyond the local canvas. Indeed, Nossiter has identified the 'central paradox' of provincial politics before 1868 as a delicate interleaving of the local *with the national.* In consequence, as Joyce says, politics 'permeated the daily and ostensibly non-political business of men's lives', but the allegiances which were embodied in the 'electoral fiefdoms' of the cotton kings in the 1860s and 1870s – and which he has so brilliantly reconstructed – were *not* uniquely determined by a mutely parochial 'politics of influence': they were also shaped by a definite (and far from parochial) 'politics of opinion'.[82] The two could be closely connected, of course, but both Whigs and Tories – or, as they had now come to be called, Liberals and Conservatives – continued to appeal to *public* opinion and tried to enlist *popular* support. It was this, so Gash has argued, which prevented politics from becoming a simple confrontation between the middle classes in the boroughs and the gentry in the shires.[83]

Political geography is not synonymous with electoral geography, but the pattern of Parliamentary representation summarized in Figures 5 and 6 shows something of the sea-change underway by mid-century. To represent the results in this way is to beg all sorts of questions,[84] and Nossiter has traced in much more sensitive detail the 'steady drift of support from the Liberal high water mark in 1832 to its ebb tide in 1841' and in doing so established that public opinion was shifting long before seats began to topple in 1841.[85] But the crumbling of the Whig vote is clear-cut, and substantiates Gash's claim that the Conservative revival after the Reform Act not only started earlier but also continued more effectively in the counties. An alliance between the landed gentry and the Anglican clergy, the natural constituency for Peel's revivified constitutionalism, conjoined with the agricultural interest, loud in its defence of the Corn Laws, to give the Conservatives sweeping gains throughout the English shires. The Tories were also traditionally strong in the small boroughs, many of which were estate or company towns, but Gash draws attention to the strategic importance of their 'hard-won but limited gains' in the large boroughs. Nationally, their share of the poll in 'large towns' rose from 31 per cent in 1832 to 46 per cent in 1841, and although places like Bury, Manchester, Oldham and Rochdale remained 'virtually impervious' to Conservative efforts, it is at least arguable that without the forty-four Conservative members returned for other large towns there would have been no Peelite victory in 1841.[86]

It is no easy matter to translate this emerging geography into divisions in the lobbies of the House of Commons. Aydelotte has shown that whereas votes on (say) political reform, free trade or economic policy were 'relatively simple, regular and comprehensive', party affiliations on (say) the 'Condition of England' question were almost undetectable; and these convergences are of some significance to debates over hegemony in early Victorian Britain.[87] Be that as it may, there is considerable evidence of a policy break at the national level between 1838 and 1842, which Richards sees as 'part of *a wider strategy* to contain class struggle and give cohesion to the economic and social system'. Part of the package was a series of initiatives designed to stimulate

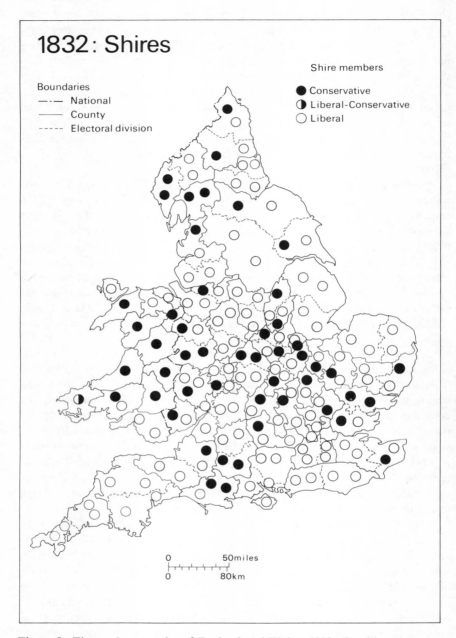

Figure 5a Electoral geography of England and Wales, 1832: the shires

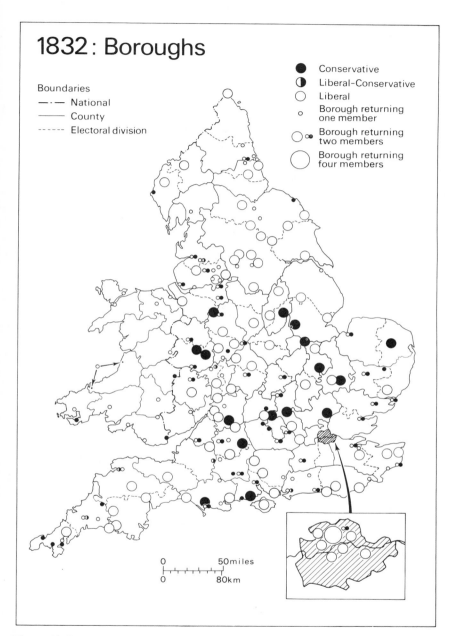

Figure 5b Electoral geography of England and Wales, 1832: the boroughs

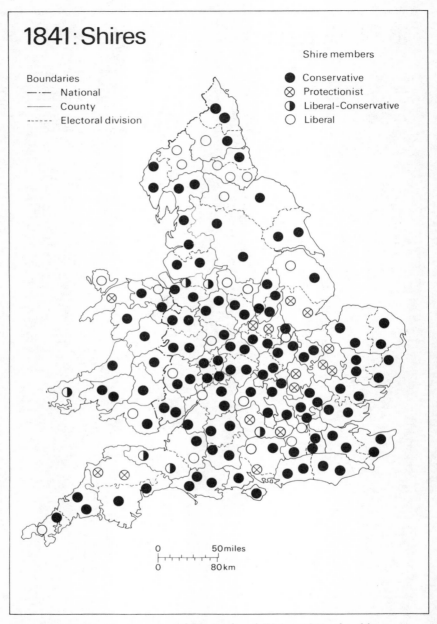

Figure 6a Electoral geography of England and Wales, 1841: the shires

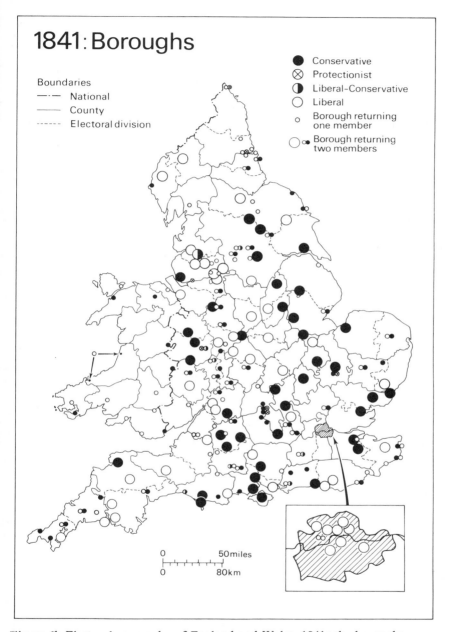

Figure 6b Electoral geography of England and Wales, 1841: the boroughs

and stabilize the economy, which was evidently helped by economic recovery; but the programme also succeeded (as it had to succeed) in directly *political* terms.[88] In abandoning the aggressive social policies of the 1830s, Peel sounded the death-knell of Chartism and its 'specific vision' of the State:

> If Chartist rhetoric was ideally suited to concert the opposition to the Whig measures of the 1830s, by the same token it was ill-equipped to modify its position in response to the changed character of state activity in the 1840s. The Chartist critique of the state was a totalising critique. It was not suited to the discrimination between one legislative measure and another, since this would be to concede that not all measures pursued by the state were for obviously malign class purposes and that beneficial reforms might be carried by a selfish legislature in an unreformed system. Peel's reduction of taxes on consumption, continued with crusading zeal by Gladstone in the mid-Victorian period, his care however unrealistic to distinguish between moral and immoral economic activity, the high moral tone of the proceedings of the government and the effective raising of the state above the dictates of particular economic interests – whether landlords, financiers or manufacturers – . . . proved fatal to the conviction and self-certainty of the language of Chartism, especially in the period after 1842, when some real measure of prosperity returned to the economy.[89]

To be sure, Foster admits 'the crucial initiatives' made during these years, but only to the margins of his analysis, and he agrees that it would be 'quite wrong' to suggest 'any simple relationship between working-class pressures on the industrial bourgeoisie and a national switch in policy'. Just so. But he also argues that 'the biggest problem' is 'to disentangle the national and the local'.[90] The *real* task, I suggest, is to specify their *articulation*.

It should now be clear that Foster's construction of 'co-determination' entails a conflation of *determinism* and *voluntarism* which is historically incoherent: working-class consciousness in the 1830s and 1840s is supposed to be determined by the geometry of capitalist crisis, and restabilization in the 1850s and 1860s is achieved through a calculated local programme of 'liberalization'. It should also be clear, more formally, that this is under-written by a *reductionist* conception of class consciousness – class responses are dictated by the structural 'logic' of capitalism – and an *instrumentalist* conception of politics – power is unilateral domination deliberately exercised by one class over another: 'one set of people controls, the rest are controlled'.[91] Separate objections can be registered against both of these, as I will show shortly, but taken together they are also theoretically incoherent. The fundamental problem in what McLennan calls this 'yoking together of arguments about the necessary logic of capitalist development with the assertion of the primacy of political design' is that it 'collapses levels of abstraction: consciousness and its effectivity are guaranteed by the necessary logic of the mode of production. Material circumstances are impregnated by political schemata, and consciousness is reciprocally given in the capital logic'.[92] Co-determination cannot be understood in this way, and the historical structuration of capitalist formations has to be explicated in a much more nuanced theoretical lexicon than Foster's Leninism can provide: one which represents society as a set of structured foliations and which reproduces what Bhaskar calls its 'ontological depth'. And this, as I have tried to show, is inseparable from an understanding of its basic *geography*.[93]

Consciousness: hegemony and time–space distanciation

So far I have conducted my discussion within the boundaries of the economy and the State, and have said little about questions of culture and consciousness. I now want to bind these into the framework of the argument. My starting-point is that Thompson's assimilation of 'class' and 'consciousness' is illegitimate. The whole thrust of *The Making of the English Working Class* is, as Anderson has shown, 'to detach class from its objective anchorage in determinate relations of production and identify it with subjective consciousness or culture'. Anderson reverses this in an elegant restatement of the classic Marxian model. He uses Cohen's defence of Marx's original writings to insist that 'it is, and must be, the dominant mode of production that confers fundamental unity on a social formation, allocating their objective positions to the classes within it, and distributing the agents within each class. The result is, typically, an objective process of class struggle' which is not 'a causal prius in the sustentiation of order, for *classes are constituted by modes of production, and not vice versa*'. This must mean that 'classes may or may not become conscious of themselves, may fail to act or behave in common, but they still remain – materially, historically – classes'.[94]

These distinctions can be elaborated in a variety of ways, of course, and there are evident difficulties in the classical formulation (some of which Cohen has since recognized),[95] but Foster draws upon an identical logic – although he strips it of any Althusserian inflection – to reinforce the distinction between class constitution and class consciousness. The Industrial Revolution 'did not involve any basic change in the social system' because 'all essential capitalist institutions were already old' and their corresponding class structures had already been constituted through the formal subordination of labour to capital (and, in particular, through the emergence of a 'reserve army' of labour). 'From the beginning of the [eighteenth] century the area's working population was mainly composed of propertyless wage-labourers: miners, hatters and (always over 50 per cent of the total) weavers. The majority were employed by no more than a couple of dozen yeoman-manufacturer families.' What was novel about *industrial* capitalism, therefore, was the inauguration of the crisis cycle and the parallel development of a 'primitive form' of class consciousness which, after all the proper hesitations have been made, 'does bear the marks of being *first*'.[96] This reinstates the significance conventionally accorded to the factory system (and Thompson's exclusion of the cotton industry from his roll-call of radicalism's rearguard is notable in this respect), but *not* as an embodiment of the new structures of capitalist production. It is the *difference* between the temporalities of constitution and consciousness that allows Foster to assign a definite, causal priority to the former.

He roundly rejects any version of the 'relative autonomy' thesis – which, in its essentials, is shared by Thompson – because it 'misses the central flywheel of class mobilization' and so 'short-circuits social consciousness'. This is an astonishing charge, but Foster insists that any notion of the irreducibility of economic, political and ideological levels, however it is formulated, cuts 'that vital cord which binds language and cultural identity to class struggle, to the system's economic law of motion and the ever-regenerated conflict over the appropriation of the product'. In Foster's view, to treat traditions and cultures 'as systems of ideas with their own relative autonomy is to destroy their social force and significance. They were carried, understood and transformed by individuals – individuals developing socially in particular and constantly changing material circumstances. It is these that need analysing.'[97] This simply repeats the priorities accorded by the *reductionist* conception of class consciousness, of course, but Foster claims that the understandings which flow from 'social being' and which are codified in 'social consciousness' are typically distorted – 'blocked' – by alienation. 'Alienation occurs in any system of society which denies part of its population equal control over social development – a denial which "alienates" their full humanity as social beings.' In a capitalist society this negation takes place within the sphere of production, but it is causally connected to the emergence of sectionalisms within the sphere of consumption, which 'serve to cancel out the most immediate expression of people's larger social irrelevance and, within these limits, allow them to find some measure of social fulfillment'. To the extent that this succeeds in maintaining 'the appearance of real social participation' then, so Foster argues, it can be described as a 'false consciousness'. It then follows that the emergence of class consciousness in the 1830s and early 1840s depended on a supercession of these sectionalisms: 'a corresponding repudiation of any system of occupational hierarchy' and 'a markedly greater degree of social closeness between working people of different backgrounds'. And the re-emergence of 'false consciousness' in the 1850s and 1860s entailed a renewal of these fragmentations and segregations, as the 'labour aristocracy' was distanced from the rest of the working-class community.[98] These distinctions were formed and re-formed in the pews of church and chapel, in the tap-rooms of the pub and the tavern, and in the tallies of the pawnbroker and the corner-shop; they were announced in the moves from one house to another – even through the symbolic respectability of curtains and a clean front step – and rounded out in the circles of friendship and marriage. And if these enunciations are not easily recovered from the deserted streets embalmed in the Census Enumerator's ledger, they nevertheless had as their backcloth the intricate mosaic of residential differentiation which played what Harvey saw as 'a vital role in the perpetuation and reproduction of the alienating social relationships of capitalist society'.[99]

Foster reinforces these progressions through a parallel typology of 'social control', which endorses the priorities accorded by the *instrumentalist* conception of politics. For most of the eighteenth century Foster considers that social controls established through the employer-dominated household, the Church and the State were 'only too effective' in securing a 'more or less direct identity with ruling-class values' and in proscribing 'any legitimate expression of separate labour interests'. He allows the (distant) prospect of a sectional 'trade union consciousness' which could, conditionally, open out into a class consciousness. But this limited vision is not acknowledged until the very end of the century, when 'a coercive occupational solidarity [extended] to all sections of the labour community' which was 'radically new, specifically illegal and in its practical application a direct challenge to state power'. Its transcendence was achieved by the efforts of a radical leadership, a 'vanguard' uniquely capable of providing a political analysis which unfolded 'in step with (and express[ed]) the system's own emerging contradictions'. This vanguard was, in effect, the 'bearer' of the authentic class consciousness which informed the popular struggles of the 1830s and early 1840s. These challenges were sufficiently strong to provoke a determined reimposition of social controls in the 1850s and 1860s. 'The *permanent* subordination of all sections of the working population to radical control' sustained a collective 'intellectual conviction' and a concerted campaign of 'revolutionary mass action' whose militancy made the local bourgeoisie keenly aware of 'the need to resume broader cultural control': to mount what Yeo calls a 'cultural counter-offensive'.

Although many of the old institutions of social control had survived (and even multiplied), however, they were much less effective in containing class consciousness by mid-century. Some, like the pubs and the friendly societies, were 'if anything still more distanced from direct control', while others, like the churches and the Sunday Schools, were controlled by small masters and tradesmen rather than by the large-scale employers. It was the new institutions – and especially the temperance movement and the Mechanics' Institutes – that were the direct beneficiaries of bourgeois patronage – that successfully 'captured' a section of the working community, those who acted as 'pacemakers and taskmasters over the rest', and brought them 'within the cultural orbit of the bourgeoisie':

Instead, therefore, of a fairly monolithic labour subculture, tied and penetrated at all its key points (pub, school, sick-club), what one seems to have are two mutually exclusive groupings with all the authority systems concentrated round the smaller one and no apparent connection between the two. While the social base of the mass subculture was the public house, it was a rejection of public house society – temperance – which was virtually a condition for entry to Sunday school teaching and adult education. While the self-educators spoke the language of their betters, the mass took pride in an aggressively opaque dialect. And while the social life of the smaller group was spent almost entirely within an intimidating complex of formal institutions, the free-and-easy friendly society remained the only – and exceptional – organizing element for the majority.

This 'cocoon of formal institutions' insulated the labour aristocracy from 'the constant ridicule reserved for bosses' men', and as such provided a vital shell for 'the process by which new forms of sectional consciousness emerged' and whose core was the labour process itself. These sectionalisms reappeared at both home and work, but their most directly political influence was on the shape of what the Webbs called the 'new model' unionism, through which 'the politics of trade unions, of the small organized elite, switch over from opposition to identity with those of the employers between 1840 and 1870'. In 'recognizing (and legitimizing) trade unions as economic bargainers' – in apparently giving ground to the radical movement – the bourgeoisie was tacitly acknowledging 'the activity of those relatively small sections whose market strength was sufficient to enable them to bargain "within the law" without having to rely – as was necessary in previous quasi-legal conditions – on the wider solidarity of the whole working class community'. This strategy thus separated 'the immediate economic interests of skilled workers from the rest of the class' and divided economy from politics so effectively that 'the sharp relapse in class solidarity was marked – not paradoxically but predictably – by a flowering of organizations and institutions meeting the sectional needs of purely economic trade unionism'.[100] Foster admits that this was not merely 'the product of bourgeois manipulation', and he also seems to be saying, as Burgess has suggested, that 'the trade unions' very ability to defend their members' "rights" and occasionally extract major concessions from employers [in a buoyant economy] meant that workers' consciousness rarely went further than a posture of sectional self-defence of the rights and privileges of the organised minority', so that the structural function of the new unionism was to confirm 'the process of working class differentiation'.[101]

These twin progressions thus appear to be reciprocally reinforcing, but they involve more than a conjunction of reductionism and instrumentalism. The first relies on an opposition between 'alienation' and 'class consciousness' which comes from Marx's early writings, particularly from the *Economic and Philosophical Manuscripts of 1844*. These were preoccupied with a critique of

Hegel's philosophical anthropology, with a clarification of the essence of what it is to be human, so that the distinction between the two was an *ontological* one. The second relies on an opposition between 'trade union consciousness' and 'class consciousness' which is derived from Lenin's *What Is To Be Done?* These arguments were a deliberate challenge to the Economistic programme of the closing decades of the nineteenth century, which circumscribed the revolutionary force of class mobilization by confining it to the union movement (Lenin insisted that 'the working class exclusively by its own efforts is able to develop only trade union consciousness' which 'means the ideological subordination of the workers to the bourgeoisie', and that, as a result, class consciousness 'can only be brought to them from without'), so that the distinction between the two was an *historical* one. Stedman Jones has argued that this disjuncture makes it

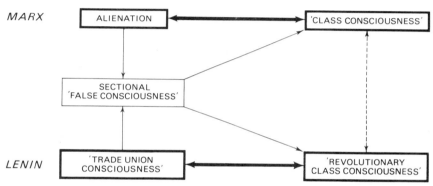

Figure 7 The genealogy of Foster's problematic

extremely difficult to connect the one to the other, but by cross-referring these couplets and switching concepts from one context to another, Foster claims that 'alienation' engenders as eries of sectionalisms which reside in a 'false consciousness', and that in so far as its supersession entails a transformation of 'trade union consciousness' then 'class consciousness' must be 'virtually synonymous with "revolutionary class consciousness"' (Figure 7).[102]

Stedman Jones is surely right to emphasize the excessive formalism of this scheme and to call for a much more discriminating problematic, but the disjuncture is not as clear-cut as he makes out. His reading of the early Marx is an Althusserian one, and several authors have refused to accept its symptomatic representation of those early writings as an 'ahistorical ontology'. That it is possible to treat alienation in historically sensitive ways, and certainly in ways much more nuanced than those provided by Althusser's appropriations of the later Marx, is now, I think, unquestionable.[103] But it is also true, rather more directly, that Lenin's own programme was, in its essentials, 'the Marxism of the early Marx',[104] and, although this is not to deny the genuine differences which remain between them – their theoretical topographies are by no means fully concordant – nevertheless, as McLennan has shown, 'for all their differences' they 'share important features. Both tend to posit a "true" or "correct" politics and consciousness arrived at in stages defined, almost, by a teleological end-point: the paradigmatic "revolution". Both thus tend to reduce ideology to a uniform condition of falsity.'[105] And it is *this*, I suggest, that is the nub of the issue.

Here I am much closer to Thompson, who strenuously repudiates the distinction between 'false consciousness' and 'class consciousness'. It is, so he claims, derived from 'a static model of capitalist productive relations' which encloses historical eventuation in an unyielding teleology, and as such provides an open endorsement of a 'politics of substitution' in which a revolutionary vanguard 'knows better than the class itself what its true interests (and consciousness) ought to be'.[106]

These are all slippery terms, of course; but that is exactly the point. Formulations of this sort fail to recognize the heterogeneity of ideology, and the result is a sharpening of contrasts between moments of class structuration. In Foster's case, the substantial achievements of the popular cultures of the eighteenth century are overlooked, and the independent integrities of 'class conscious' and 'liberal' Oldham are overdrawn. And this happens, I suggest, because both reductionism and instrumentalism stand in the closest of associations to functionalism and its systematic derogation of the knowledge-ability of human subjects. If, as Giddens proposes, ideology is fundamentally concerned with the various ways in which social actors draw upon structures of signification to legitimate sectional interests embedded in structures of domination, then it is necessarily *bounded* (that is, its effects are not purely manipulative) and it is instantiated in social practices whose interactions, however asymmetric, remain *engagements* rather than impositions (that is, its effects are not fully determined). We may say, therefore, that there are variable *separations* 'between the practices actors sustain in day-to-day reproduction and the overall symbolic orders normatively sanctioned by the dominant groups or classes in particular societies'.[107] To suppose otherwise is to exaggerate the coherence of social formations – to dramatize the sudden 'flashpoints' of conflict, to listen for the episodic choruses of corporate dissent and to mistake what Stedman Jones calls 'archival silence' for 'historical passivity'. The consequence of such elision is, often, that working people are suddenly 'marshalled, sent on manoeuvres and marched up and down' and then, when their generals are dismissed (or obliged to change sides), their revolutionary temper is enervated by opiates which the bourgeoisie 'continuously administers, and in increasingly heavy doses, to an errant but gradually domesticated proletariat'. These phrasings, and others like them, suggest a 'static metaphor of equilibrium which might be disturbed and then reasserted on a new basis', and hence reduce historical eventuation to a simple cascade of social formations through 'three successive states: a prior functioning, a period of breakdown and a renewed period of functioning'.[108] This is the same problematic as structures Foster's text, and I shall want to say, against this, that contradiction is not episodically but *continuously* present and that class struggle is not a spasmodic but a *chronic* feature of capitalist society.

We may agree, therefore, that 'social life, in all societies, contains many types of practice or aspects of practices which are sustained in and through the knowledgeability of social actors but which they do not produce as a matter of normative commitment'. Giddens suggests that this 'uncoupling' is strongly affected by the 'time–space distanciation' involved in social organization. As societies 'stretch across long time–space distances' dislocations emerge 'between the locales with which different social systems are associated', so that 'the routines sustained by practical consciousness may be in various possible ways disjoined from the normative commitments legitimised in overarching symbol systems'.[109] This is not, however, to be understood as a simple transformation of *Gemeinschaft* into *Gesellschaft*: these dichotomous categorizations usually have at their centre some model of a stable, 'traditional' society, and it is exactly this representation that is at issue. Thus, for example, Calhoun has identified 'the breakdown of the structures of hierarchical incorporation which knit local communities into the society as a whole' as a primary source of the popular radicalism of the early Industrial Revolution. These movements 'were largely based on the social foundations of local communities' and the people they mobilized 'were knit together through personal bonds'; as they reached beyond the immediate locale, so they foundered. And they 'were largely aimed at the preservation of the communities in which workers lived' and in which 'families and crafts were not distinct from communities; the social bonds with which they knit people to each other were part and parcel of community'.[110] All this may well be so: indeed, there is still no finer celebration of the mutuality and solidarity of working people than *The Making of the English Working Class*, with its impassioned requiem for 'the loss of any felt cohesion in the community, save that which the working people, in antagonism to their labour and to their masters, built for themselves'.[111] But Calhoun claims that this collective consciousness was refractory of class notations because (mirroring Durkheim) it was reflective of the *entire* social order. 'Deference and paternalism were the forms of social interaction which expressed the relationship of people at different levels in the traditional hierarchy of authority' and their formal protocols embodied distinctions between 'ranks and degrees, as opposed to classes' not as an 'arbitrary linguistic convention' but rather as an enunciation of 'bonds which bound people *across* the levels of the hierarchy, in daily interaction and both specific and diffuse obligations'. During the Industrial Revolution this skein of inter-subjective relationships was slowly unravelled. Economic integration and political rationalization gnawed through its system of parochial reciprocities, and the aggressive 'deformation of the gift' provoked a defensive, but above all a 'reactionary' radicalism.[112]

But, paradoxically, this thesis is vitiated by the same conflation of class structure and class consciousness that Calhoun finds in Thompson and by the same 'arbitrary assumption of order' that he finds in Foster.[113] Even if artisans and labourers endorsed a 'traditional' conception of community – and we know remarkably little about the various 'planes' and 'levels' which composed their cognitive worlds – it is still possible to locate their shifting structural coalitions within the modes of production of Georgian and early Victorian society: to see their actions as moments of class structuration. And it is necessary to do so, I shall say, because the disengagement of social integration from system integration – the variable separations introduced through time–space distanciation – was by no means confined to the incursions of the Industrial Revolution. It is, in some measure, characteristic of *all* class-divided societies and is given renewed impetus by the uneven development of capitalism as a whole.[114]

I now want to secure these claims through a re-examination of the two periods of 'passivity' which Foster equates with 'false consciousness'.

The eighteenth century

By the early seventeenth century, Wrightson has argued, England had already developed a series of 'superimposed cultures' through time–space distanciation:

> The mechanisms of the market, the influence of a more aggressive state and church, the expansion of education and of participation in a literate culture went far towards the integration of diverse provincial economies and societies into those of the nation. Yet the benefits of economic development, participation in expanded local government, active involvement in the political, religious and cultural currents of the day were largely confined to the upper and middling ranks of provincial society. For those below these levels, the period saw the emergence of the poor as a permanent class, increased social regulation, alienation from a church which had lost much of its colour and ritual yet which made new and unreasonable demands upon its members, and effective exclusion from an elite culture which was not only novel, but aggressive.

The mechanisms are much the same as those which Calhoun sees in motion a hundred years later, but the difference between them is not primarily one of chronology. Wrightson suggests that external integration produced internal differentiation: that 'the culture of the gentleman, the yeoman farmer, the artisan or the labourer, was to a large degree the same across the nation' –

this requires caution and may bear some qualification – but, more important, that within local communities 'significant differences had emerged between the cultures of these different groups. These might be dampened by deference and social imitation, and overlaid by vertical ties of clientage and patronage; they were none the less real'. These polarities culminated in a 'radical dis-association' between 'the polite culture of the rulers of eighteenth-century England and the plebeian culture of the labouring people'.[115]

The phrase is, of course, Thompson's. He describes eighteenth-century society as a 'field of force' and its logic of paternalism as embodied in an ideology whose precepts were not confined to an adamantine deference. Indeed, in the course of the eighteenth century

a substantial proportion of the labour force actually became more free from discipline in their daily work, more free to choose between employers and between work and leisure, less situated in a position of dependence in their whole way of life than they had been before or than they were to be in the first decades of the discipline of the factory and the clock.

The moral economy was scarcely an enforced culture of collaboration, therefore, and its usages worked in both directions to define social protocols and practices through a grid of intersecting obligations which informed routine interactions between the squire, the parson, the master-manufacturer and the skilled artisan. But, as Giddens emphasizes, the 'taken-for-granted' is not immediately conformable with the 'accepted-as-legitimate': Thompson finds that although 'on the surface all is consensus, deference, accommodation', suddenly, 'from an anonymous and obscure level, there leaps to view for a moment violent Jacobite or Levelling abuse'. And he insists that we can take *neither* the obeisances *nor* the imprecations 'as indications of final truth; both could flow from the same mind, as circumstances and calculation of advantage allowed'. Once we start 'turning over the bland concepts of the ruling authorities and looking at their undersides' in this way, then 'even "liberality" and "charity" may be seen as calculated acts of class appease-ment in times of dearth and calculated extortions (under threat of riot) by the crowd: what is (from above) an "act of giving" is (from below) an "act of getting"'. The distinction of most importance, therefore, is between those historians who envision a 'traditional' society in terms which compel them to reconstruct social relationships largely *as they were meant to be seen*, and those who refuse to be nudged 'towards a view of society as a self-regulating social order' in this way and depend upon a properly dialectical representa-tion of social reproduction.[116]

Yet to speak of 'calculation' is not to suggest that paternalism and de-ference were merely tactical – convenient fictions. As Thompson reminds us, 'the rhetoric and the rules of a society are something a great deal more than sham. In the same moment they may modify, in profound ways, the behaviour of the powerful and mystify the powerless. They may disguise the true realities of power but, at the same time, they may curb that power and check its intrusions'.[117] But these capacities, together with those of calculation, necessarily depend upon the knowledgeability of human subjects, and while this was scarcely undifferentiated – Thrift speaks of geographies of 'knowing' and 'unknowing'[118] – a recognition of its central importance can help us to see that the web of eighteenth-century social relations was *not* 'supine' (as Foster claims) and that artisans and labourers were *not* cowed or 'controlled' into 'political passivity'. On the contrary, Porter reports that travellers from abroad found the English 'extraordinarily politically well-informed and assertive, from peers down to shoe-blacks and the millions in between, clamouring around the outworks of the official political nation'. Theirs was a ragged but robust group of overlapping, jostling and competing cultures, but in so far as the political fabric – 'pulled, torn, tattered and patched' – was reknit so readily, this was less a matter of coercion and repression than of concession and representation. The 'river of violence' which coursed through the political landscape was never far from the surface, certainly, but it was contained by a series of customary codes which, if not quite the liturgy envisaged by Porter, nevertheless established the terms on which the social order was to be endorsed.[119] These discursive formations were strengthened throughout the eighteenth century by the mushroom growth of the provincial press and the efflorescence of coffee-houses and taverns. And in the wake of each fresh political crisis, rippling out through these networks of formal and informal association, the scope and scale of what Brewer calls the 'alternative political nation' was enlarged and the circles of its heterogeneous political cultures widened until, by the 1770s, it was as much a part of the political process as the House of Commons itself.[120] There is no space here to trace its developing geography,[121] but we can agree that if it was not, perhaps, a fully *radical* culture, it was most certainly not a *reactionary* one. Thompson concedes that it was neither proletarian nor proto-revolutionary; but it was an unmistakably *rebellious* culture, and it was given direction through its imbrication in the wider processes of class structuration.[122]

These distinctions may not count for much in narratives which are enclosed by a compulsive 'logic of capital' whose successive transformations have to be represented as a double-edged contest for 'control'; but they are not quibbles. Thompson dismisses the absolutist protocols of both reductionism and instrumentalism with the single concept of *hegemony*. At its simplest, this is little more than a recognition that class domination rarely resides exclusively in the exercise of coercive force and that it is not confined to the press of economic and political power: that it more usually depends upon a sustained series of negotiations within 'civil society' which establish a (precarious) culture of (conditional) consent. In its original, Gramscian form the concept is open to a number of objections. Perhaps most serious are its

remarkable distanciation from the conditions of production and its derogation of the effectivity of political institutions. There have been several attempts
to extend Gramsci's fragmentary notes, of course, and to reinstate culture as
what Thompson once called the 'missing term' in conventional analysis,
without simultaneously eclipsing the orbits of economic and political practice.[123] I shall not be concerned to discuss these in any detail here, but it is
necessary to emphasize that any more developed form will have to avoid a
new absolution. Here is Thompson again:

> But while such cultural hegemony may define the limits of what is possible, and
> inhibit the growth of alternative horizons and expectations, there is nothing deter-
> mined or automatic about this process. Such hegemony can be sustained by the
> rulers only by the constant exercise of skill, of theatre, of concession. Second, such
> hegemony, even when imposed successfully, does not impose an all-embracing
> view of life; rather, it imposes blinkers, which inhibit vision in certain directions
> while leaving it clear in others. It can co-exist (as it did co-exist in eighteenth-
> century England) with a very vigorous self-activating culture of the people, derived
> from their own experience and resources . . .
>
> It follows that I cannot accept the view . . . that hegemony imposes an all-
> embracing domination upon the ruled – or upon all those who are not intellectuals –
> reaching down to the very threshold of their experience and implanting within their
> minds at birth categories which they are powerless to shed and which their experience
> is powerless to correct.[124]

These capabilities were not the exclusive preserve of the eighteenth century,
with its studied 'theatre' and 'counter-theatre': and Thompson's restrictions
on hegemony must be applied with equal vigilance to its conceptual admission
to the social dramas of the nineteenth century.

The nineteenth century

In an early exchange with Thompson, Anderson identified an alliance
between the aristocracy and the bourgeoisie which, although racked by bitter
disputes in the first decades of the nineteenth century (and which even tottered
on the brink of collapse from time to time), had nevertheless recovered
sufficiently by the 1850s to constitute a 'single hegemonic class': one which
'imposes its own ends and its own vision on society as a whole'. Thompson,
in contrast, while conceding the continued cultural significance of the aristocracy, argued that 'a new, and entirely different predatory complex' had
emerged, spearheaded by the bourgeoisie in an altogether more decisive
and triumphant posture. The historical geography of these configurations is
of the utmost importance, but this is deeply imbricated in the *whole* process
of class structuration and, more particularly therefore, in Anderson's description of the working class of the later nineteenth century as a 'corporate
class' – one which 'seeks to defend and improve its own position within a
social order accepted as given'.[125] Whatever the merits of these specific

designations, other historians have been quick to draw upon the same general notions. Thus, for example, Gray argues that 'the crisis which Foster rightly locates in the second quarter of the nineteenth century' – and which he situated within the 'suicidal' economics of the cotton industry – was 'above all a crisis of hegemony, of the political relations between classes and fractions of classes'. It then follows that its resolution 'cannot be reduced to a single, dramatic moment of transition, or to the conspiratorial imposition of bourgeois schemes to bribe and indoctrinate the working class'. For 'it would be equally true to say that relations of hegemony involved the impo- sition *on the bourgeoisie* of some form of representation, at all levels of social practice, of working-class interests (especially, but not exclusively, those of the labour aristocracy)'.[126] This implies, and is in turn impelled by, a con- ception of ideology which is common to all these writers, whatever their empirical disagreements. Politics is not, as Gramsci repeatedly stressed, a *marché de dupes*. Its constitutive ideologies have to make some sort of sense of the world in which the people who share in them live, and they cannot be collapsed into unidimensional discursive planes. Restabilization, as Joyce reminds us, is therefore 'not reducible to mere social control. Rather than unilateral imposition of cultural uniformity from above, such situations always involve mutual constraints, boundaries beyond which neither side can trespass if the social relationship in question is to remain viable; and the hegemony of the northern employer class was no exception.'[127] This sets definite *limits* to 'incorporation'. Even the neo-Durkheimian constructions of hegemony advanced by Tholfsen to account for the 'unifying and stabilising function of liberalism' in the later nineteenth century acknow- ledge that working people 'did not passively acquiesce in middle-class hegemony. A robust working-class subculture, cradled in the traditions of early Victorian radicalism, encouraged resistance and independence' and asserted 'the worth and dignity of working men' in terms which denied 'the middle-class claim to social, intellectual and moral superiority'.[128]

But these limits can be challenged. Anderson sees in the 'distinct, hermetic culture' of the working class 'an extreme disjunction between an intense consciousness of separate identity and a permanent failure to set and impose goals for society as a whole'. Nairn presses this even further, to argue that the very 'apartness' of working-class consciousness implied a kind of de- ference; 'for it resigns everything else, the power and secret of society at large, to others, to the "estates" possessing authority or wealth'. Withdrawal is the very essence of a 'corporative' consciousness, and its distortions marked a 'fundamental victory for the ruling orders' of late Victorian Britain.[129]

'Deference' is rather more complex than this, however, as I have already indicated, and Joyce is especially sensitive to its myriad ambiguities: the affective, the calculative and the coerced. But he too insists on the spectacular *success* of bourgeois hegemony, 'the overweening confidence of the employer class at mid-century', and chooses to emphasize what he calls the *rootedness* of deference rather than the qualifications that hedged it about. The organic metaphor conveys the sense in which deference was propagated through a revivified paternalism, a new moral economy, which 'grew out of the centre of people's lives and was not something imposed from without'. Its epicentre was *work*, simultaneously 'the source of defensive forms of class solidarity and of a culture of subordination', and its experiences spiralled out into and were amplified within the circles of the local community. Works dinners and outings, libraries and reading rooms, sports clubs and baths, chapels and elementary schools, almshouses and orphanages: all these institutions beat the bounds of a public and essentially *parochial* paternalism. This 'sense of place' was central to the success of paternalism, so Joyce argues, because it allowed the employers to define and delimit the horizons of their employees in such a way that their influence 'over the ordinary business of people's lives' was felt both inside and outside the factory. And in sharp contrast to Foster he finds that this was a matter for 'the great majority of the factory workforce' rather than a privileged minority, because 'so much of what was an integral part of daily life – a smoke, the reading of a news-paper, playing in a brass band, rather than a lesson in elocution – took place within the territory of the factory'.[130] And it was these informal, 'inward' experiences that were the most decisive. Some commentators have jibed at the employers' public displays and good works: 'treats and trips, probably the most common expression of their mutual regard, were also the least profound. Sympathy and concern were occasionally embodied in the bricks and mortar of schools, chapels and libraries, but not often.'[131]

Yet Joyce not only shows that these became much more frequent after mid-century, but also argues that they were confirmations of a primary and pervasive paternalism 'largely unknown to the historical record'. Its social disciplines and distinctions were rarely given formal expression – they were part of what Giddens calls 'practical' rather than 'discursive' consciousness – but they were nonetheless supremely effective. And Joyce claims that they were mediated, crucially, by the recomposition of the family economy, which reproduced the hierarchy of patriarchal authority and enforced its protocols of mutuality and reciprocity not only within the factory but throughout the local milieu.[132] We might conclude, therefore, that

Despite the fluidity of its composition over time, the locality was sufficiently stable to constitute a relatively complete social situation in which the prescribed norms of neighbourliness, paternalism and deference appeared to work for the most part, and from which alternative definitions of the social order could be effectively excluded. The most vital of social relationships were established and maintained within a specific local context and it was in this context that the hegemonic activity of the national ruling class, their domination of the social consciousness of their inferiors, was most successful.

But this is not Joyce on the nineteenth century: it is Wrightson on the seventeenth.[133]

The bounds of paternalism

The ease of substitution is arresting, but I intend it to be rather more than a *jeu d'esprit*. I want to argue that most of these discussions of hegemony are inculpated in the same failings as the formulations which they claim to supersede, and that it is for this reason that the modalities of class struggle are so attenuated in narratives enclosed by their theoretical categories. To contrapose Wrightson to Joyce is, in a sense, arbitrary: clearly, neither of them proposes an identity between hegemony in the seventeenth century and hegemony in the nineteenth century. *But there is nothing in this system of concepts which enables us to specify the distinctions.* It is not simply that the terms are 'too large for discriminating analysis', as Thompson once owned;[134] it is, rather, that the couplet of paternalism-cum-deference allows historical eventuation to be locked into a circular chain of effectivity which reproduces an endless stasis instead of the contingent and contradictory relations of historical transformation. And this is not a uniquely empirical matter. Stedman Jones has warned that although concepts like hegemony 'may register some moral distance from the apologetic complacency of functionalist theory, they in no way break from its theoretical linkages'.[135] These can be connected back to Foster's problematic in a fairly direct way, let me say, because Gramsci's theoretical innovations also owed much to a critical appropriation of Lenin's writings. The intellectual genealogy is a complex one; Gramsci did much to clarify (and qualify) Lenin's instrumentalism through the incorporation of a genuinely 'popular' political culture, and a number of authors have made considerable advances in the formalization of its heterogeneous compositions. But the underlying difficulty can be simply stated: if the success of hegemony is signalled by stability and its collapse by crisis, then this can only rephrase the question rather than resolve it. To suggest otherwise is to confine analysis to the closed and empty circle of functionalism: outside its perimeter hegemony remains as much an *explanandum* as an *explanans*.

Its historical explication depends upon its being prised away from functionalism in two, closely connected senses. First, the 'uncoupling' of social integration from system integration requires the systems of intersubjective interaction within the local milieu to be understood in non-functionalist terms. By this, I mean that Gray is right to identify 'the most important aspect of hegemony over the working class' as 'their forced habituation to the relations of industrial wage-labour, and the ideological practices involved in this process', just as Joyce is right to underscore the significance of a 'sense of place', of an ideology of localism, in maintaining and extending the relationships of paternalism and deference instantiated in these time–space relations. But habituation is not legitimation, any more than (as Joyce supposes) deference necessarily 'converts power relations into moral ones'.[136] The separations which can (conditionally) interpose themselves are not incidental. The social reproduction of 'the capitalist as capitalist and the wage-labourer as wage-labour' to which Gray draws attention is a *contingent* accomplishment achieved through *struggle*. Hegemony is always partial and provisional, therefore, and class tensions constantly threaten to break through its rhetoric. It would be misleading to confine these to dichotomous relations of domination and subordination. 'Hegemonic ideology had differentiated versions and interpretations, and was constantly argued out and reformulated within the ruling class' which was itself 'constantly re-constituted, modified, strengthened or undermined in party struggles'.[137] But, as I have been at pains to establish, this was not independent of the constitution of working-class struggles and their cross-cutting of the local and the national. It may well be that Joyce's 'undifferentiated local patriotism' owed as much to the pickings of prosperity as it did to the gewgaws of 'treats and trips'. Indeed, Dutton and King regard these conventional expressions of paternalism as at best peripheral to the central concerns of most working people: 'wages and hours of work were far more important'.[138] And to see their movements as the mirrors of continuous struggle is not the prerogative of Marxism: even Musson thinks Joyce 'has exaggerated the degree of acquiescent subordination'.[139] But we must not make the opposite mistake and read a coherent class consciousness into all confrontations of this sort. Although 'the buying and selling of labour power according to market calculation necessarily implied conflict between workers and capitalists', Burgess reminds us that 'both capitalist and worker had to observe the rules of the game otherwise it would become unplayable'.[140] It is exactly this 'framing' of conflict *within* the boundaries of the established order that prompted Foster to speak of 'liberalisation', of course, but, as I have shown, the retention of a division of labour which maintained hierarchies of skill and status, and the eventual introduction of wage-lists which institutionalized those distinctions, remained the contingent outcomes of struggle rather than the necessary consequence of subordination. And in so far as these campaigns depended on a hard-nosed recognition of 'rules' which ensured that, as Joyce concedes, 'the failure to deliver the economic promise of paternalism could very quickly result in the disintegration of deference',[141] then hegemony *could have no independent effectivity*.

Secondly, therefore, conflicts could never be completely contained precisely because work *was* at the centre of people's lives: because, as Joyce says, 'it got under the skin of everyday life'. If Lancashire factory masters engineered consent, they also manufactured cotton. The two were intricately interlaced. To be sure, Joyce acknowledges that 'deference is not to be understood without a consideration of the dependence that was its seed-ground';[142] and Reid had agreed that working people were not only 'depen-dent on the capitalist system in a general sense for their means of subsistence . . . [but] the competition for work, the division of labour and the structures of authority in the work place gave their subordination a specific content deeply and daily ingrained in working-class culture and organization'.[143] We can surely accept these recommendations. It is plainly necessary to show 'what it is that workers are being forced to cope *with* and to defend *against*': but this does *not* mean endorsing an enclosing circle of determinations which marks out the 'limits of labour' without at the same time establishing the conjoint 'limits of capital'.[144] To do so would be to follow Marx too closely in his portrayal of the labour process in which, as Lazonick notes, 'capital triumphs by virtue of the very technologies at its disposal' and in which the capitalists 'get their way'.[145] This is in effect a double reduction. The economy secures its cultural and political conditions of existence through auto-genesis – the domination of capital over labour is replicated in 'corresponding' cultural and political dominations – and the social formation is articulated by a 'class subject' (the bourgeoisie) which imposes its 'will' on historical eventuation. This is the same 'circular and unilinear' functionalism which was the object of Poulantzas' critique of the Anderson–Nairn thesis; and, whatever one thinks of his own prescriptions, his intervention clearly spells out the limitations of a concept of hegemony cut free from the disjunctures and discordances of the social formation.[146] For the 'promise' of paternalism depended on more than a fulfilment of the protocols of negotiation, a staking out of what some authors have identified as a 'terrain of compromise'. *It was also dependent upon the structural dynamics of capital accumulation and the structural compositions of the capitalist state.* These were uncertain and unstable. The labour process was riven by contradictions, whose multiple determinations skewered the social formation in complex ways and whose heterogeneous historical geographies could provide no guarantees of either an articulate working-class consciousness or a cohesive bourgeois hegemony. We can agree with Gray on the salience of 'the *local* nature of struggle, and its relative inco-herence at a national or even a regional level: its great strength, derived from deep roots within local communities, was also in this sense a weakness'.[147]

But we must also admit similar bounds to the hegemonic process. Pater-nalist strategies are inherently limited within capitalist societies because their 'field of effectivity' is necessarily the local 'arena of capital'; yet they neces-sarily depend upon economic and political structures whose time–space distanciation transcends the local milieu.

Conclusion

It cannot be stressed too strongly that these discussions are no more than sketches. My debt to the work of others is obvious from the notes and references, and in any exploration there is a trade-off between the strength and security which such bibliographic equipment can provide and the burden which it imposes on the traveller. But some conclusions stand out. First, the 'historical geography' of class struggle is not delimited by the conventional cartographic representation of strikes, riots and rebellions. My objection to such an approach is not (especially) that it trembles on the edges of a 'spatial fetishism': indeed, part of my purpose has been to demonstrate the *salience* of spatial structures for the production and reproduction of everyday life. The real problem is that such a perspective can easily under-value the significance of day-to-day struggles inside (and outside) the work-place. These are not the spectacular confrontations which set the pulse racing; but the transformations which have so long eluded traditional historical geographies lie as much in the ebb and flow of such seemingly mundane conflicts as in the episodic 'revolutions' which excite our con-temporary imaginations and sensitivities. Secondly, and connected to this, historical geography cannot afford to be a synonym for local history. This is not to minimize the genuine contributions made by local studies, and neither is it to exaggerate the difference which a formal theoretical apparatus can make to the refractory historical archive (although here I would insist on the importance of careful abstraction rather than indiscriminate generali-zation). What I wish to underscore, rather, is the need for a fully *contex-tualized* historical geography: one which spells out the intersections between the local, the regional, the national and the international. All the agencies which have featured in these pages had definite 'conditions of existence' and 'fields of effectivity', and their changing geographies were not incidental to the sequence of historical eventuation. Finally, class struggle cannot be dis-sected inside 'economic' *or* 'political' *or* 'cultural' laboratories; forensic investigations which confine themselves to these arbitrary enclosures cannot expect to reconstruct the changing anatomies of capitalist societies with any fidelity. Too much effort has been expended on the search for such reductive explanations and on the policing of the boundaries which have grown up around them. Any serious exploration will have to transcend these limits, for they lie not in the past but in ourselves.

Acknowledgements
I am very grateful to John Langton and Richard Walker for their comments on this essay.

University of Cambridge

4

Agricultural revolution?
Development of the agrarian
economy in early modern England

MARK OVERTON

The term 'agricultural revolution' is firmly entrenched in the literature of agrarian change in England from the sixteenth century to the nineteenth century. Since it is now adopted as a label for at least five periods when various changes in agricultural production are held to be significant, it should preferably be qualified by reference to a particular period and a specific series of changes, or at least by the name of the agricultural historian responsible for applying the term in a particular context. If it is not so qualified, then perhaps it is best restricted to the historiography of a particular debate, rather than to a collection of events during some period in the past.[1] This essay is concerned with both uses of the term: that is, with the way in which the debate has been conducted, and with the agricultural changes to which the debate has been directed. Briefly, the argument to be put forward is that although the agricultural revolution debate is now moribund, an exploration of its historiography reveals some reasons for its demise, which in turn suggest how the debate might be revitalized, so providing the means towards a clearer understanding of the agrarian economy of early modern England. Although this might seem ambitious enough, the discussion has three other aims. The first is simply to sketch a path through the agricultural revolution debate for those who may not be familiar with it,[2] thus setting the scene for the critique that follows. The critique itself provides an opportunity to discuss, in the context of a particular historical debate, some of the general philosophical and methodological issues that have tended to preoccupy historical geographers for the last decade, in order to emphasize the importance and relevance of those discussions to the practice of historical geography.[3] Finally, the essay has a specific contribution to make at the empirical level by presenting some new data on yields, output and innovation.

   The main thrust of the argument is that the debate over the agricultural revolution is moribund for two reasons. First, the empirical methods employed

118

by agricultural historians have produced neither convincing generalizations about the course of change nor the data necessary to measure the phenomena to which they are referring. The dearth of information about some of the most important indicators of agricultural change is as much due to the practices of agricultural historians as it is to an absence of primary source material. A more systematic approach to historical documents could provide both sounder generalizations and the data on which to base them. Secondly, most agricultural historians have managed to avoid direct confrontation with theories of agrarian change. This is partly responsible for the weakness, or in some cases the absence, of explanations of agricultural revolutions, and, perhaps more importantly, has severely narrowed the range of questions asked of the past. The existing accounts of agricultural revolutions owe more to the writings of Arthur Young than they do to contemporary theories employed in the social sciences. It is with these accounts that we need to begin.

Accounts of revolutions

The word 'revolution' has been applied to particular periods of agricultural change held to be 'significant' since at least the eighteenth century, and the phrase 'agricultural revolution' was probably first used by Marx.[4] But it is those writers who followed R. L. Prothero (later Lord Ernle) who bear the responsibility for popularizing the term. Ernle's concept of the revolution was set out in his book *Pioneers and Progress in English Farming*, published in 1888, and elaborated in his major work, *English Farming Past and Present*, published in 1912. Still in print, this book remains the major textbook covering the development of English agriculture from the Middle Ages to the nineteenth century, although the comments by Fussell and McGregor in the modern introductions to the sixth edition clearly demonstrate how outdated the book is.[5]

Ernle placed the revolution firmly in the period 1760–1840, and characterized it as the introduction of new techniques of production made possible by the replacement of a rigid agrarian structure. The technical innovations were new crops (turnips and clover) and their associated crop rotations which increased the supply of fodder and therefore manure, so raising grain output per acre. Equally dramatic advances came in the sphere of livestock production by advances in the practice of selective breeding which increased the killing weights of both cattle and sheep. These technical changes were facilitated by Parliamentary enclosure, which swept away the open common fields and allowed the creation of large capitalist farms. According to Ernle these changes were allegedly responsible for transforming English agriculture within a few years from an almost peasant subsistence economy into a thriving capitalist agricultural system capable of feeding the teeming millions in the new industrial cities.[6]

New fodder crops are seen as important because they enabled English agriculture to break out of a 'closed circuit' which prevented increases in output except by extension of the cultivated area. Under a three-course system of wheat, barley and fallow (assuming the cultivated area to be fixed), any increase in the proportion of land under grain would reduce the proportion of fallow, so reducing fertility and therefore yields. Thus the increase in grain output accruing from an increase in the area under grain crops would be offset by a fall in yields per acre as a result of the reduction in fallow. This vicious circle was broken by replacing fallows with fodder crops. Turnips acted as a cleaning crop by smothering weeds, and provided winter fodder for animals. Clover was also a source of fodder but in addition had the valuable property of fixing atmospheric nitrogen into the soil. More fodder meant more manure, which in turn increased the fertility of the land. The way was thus open for an ascending spiral of progress, in as much as more food could be produced from the same area of land.[7]

Ernle held that innovations of this kind were only possible with the removal of common property rights, for the right of farmers in a community to graze their animals on other farmers' lands after the grain harvest would have prevented turnips being sown on the stubble. Enclosure was also considered a prerequisite for selective animal breeding, in that it prevented the promiscuous mingling of livestock on the commons.[8] Ernle considered the role of individual enterprise to be most important; in common with late nineteenth-century views of the Industrial Revolution, his agricultural revolution was brought about by the heroic achievements of a small group of innovators – by, as Curtler puts it, 'a band of men whose names are, or ought to be, household words with English farmers: Jethro Tull, Lord Townshend, Arthur Young, Bakewell, Coke of Holkham and the Collings'.[9] In so far as Ernle considered these changes had a particular geographical distribution he paid particular attention to the areas of the country with light soils (for allegedly these were the most suitable for growing turnips), particularly west Norfolk – the home of two of his great men.[10]

As Kerridge has demonstrated, the 'myths' that sprang from Ernle's work, promulgated by Curtler and Mantoux in particular, have proved remarkably persistent; for while some have been eradicated from textbooks for an undergraduate readership, they are still entrenched in popular histories.[11] Three years after *English Farming Past and Present* was published an article had shown that 'Turnip' Townshend was a boy when turnips were grown on his estates, long before Ernle said he introduced them.[12] In 1925 Marshall considered Jethro Tull, the inventor of a seed drill, something of a crank.[13] It also seems that the great animal breeders of the eighteenth century made little impact on cattle sizes.[14] In at least two cases the source of these myths can be traced back to the 'great men' themselves. The idea that Townshend introduced turnips into Norfolk after seeing them grown in Hanover comes from the *General View* written by Kent, who in turn took it from a report of an interview between Arthur Young and the Townshend family.[15] The reputation of Coke of Holkham has been most thoroughly deflated, to the extent that some of his activities so praised by Ernle seem to have been positively harmful. The Norfolk folk-course rotation of wheat, turnips, barley and clover, for example, was 'carried to excess' according to Coke's steward, and it is to Coke's great uncle, Lord Leicester, that we must look for some of the revolutionary improvements described by Ernle. Some of the most exaggerated claims for Coke's achievements seem to have come from Coke himself.[16]

Many similar criticisms and revisions of Ernle's views have been made: in short, he telescoped the pace of change, he was in error in ascribing innovation to his 'great men', and he overemphasized the rigidities of common fields as a barrier to innovation.[17] However, although most agricultural historians would agree that Ernle's account is 'hopelessly out of focus'[18] the essential ingredients of his revolution, technical change and institutional change, still constitute the main themes in most general accounts of the period.[19] There is controversy over the chronology of these changes and over their impact on total agricultural output, rather than over whether these particular changes are the ones that deserve the attention of historians.

The most vigorous onslaught on Ernle's revolution has come from Kerridge. After preliminary offensives, in 1955 citing examples of turnips being grown in seventeenth-century Suffolk, and in 1959 extolling the virtues of convertible husbandry, the main attack was launched in 1967 when Kerridge defiantly announced in the opening paragraph of his *Agricultural Revolution*: 'This book argues that the agricultural revolution took place in England in the sixteenth and seventeenth centuries and not in the eighteenth and nineteenth.' More specifically, he argued that the revolution was between 1560 and 1767 with most achieved before 1673.[20] Kerridge had three lines of attack on the elements of Ernle's revolution. First he argued that some of them did not occur at all – the mechanization of farming for example. Secondly, he put forward the view that other elements were 'irrelevant' or not as important as Ernle stated. In this category he placed Parliamentary enclosure, the replacement of bare fallows, the Norfolk four-course rotation, sheep and cattle breeding, and the replacement of oxen by horses for draught power. Thirdly, he maintained that some of the improvements Ernle stressed occurred much earlier: namely, the introduction of fodder crops, new crop rotations and field drainage. The seven criteria of Kerridge's revolution form the chapter headings for his book: up and down husbandry, fen drainage, fertilizers, floating the watermeadows, new crops, new systems and new stock.

These criteria are 'agricultural' and very much in the Ernle tradition of technical change – the 'cows and ploughs' tradition – though the chronology of their introduction is altered. In this sense the book contrasts with the

Agrarian History of England and Wales, Volume IV,[21] published at the same time but giving a much more rounded picture of rural society. It also differs in the emphasis placed on up and down husbandry (or ley farming), as opposed to an expansion of the cultivated acreage, as the means to raising agricultural output. One reviewer has called Kerridge's interpretation 'perverse'.[22] Indeed his exaggerated claims and occasionally cavalier use of sources make some of his conclusions hard to accept. For despite the volume of his footnotes he relies heavily on late eighteenth-century writers and has insufficient specific evidence on the incidence of convertible husbandry.[23] Kerridge lays great emphasis on the early adopters of an innovation; it seems that a few precocious farmers growing new crops, or dabbling in some new husbandry practice, provide sufficient grounds for claiming a revolution.

Chambers and Mingay, who identified a third agricultural revolution, followed Ernle more closely in that they emphasized the period after 1750 as the truly revolutionary era; a period when new husbandry practices became common amongst a majority of farmers. Published in 1966, their book *The Agricultural Revolution 1750–1880* elaborates upon an earlier survey of the field by Mingay.[24] They acknowledge that Ernle's picture of a sudden and rapid transformation in the eighteenth century is mistaken, and that the improvements which they emphasize for the eighteenth century had long antecedents; yet, as the title of their book suggests, their revolution is firmly placed in the period proposed by Ernle. Their criteria too are similar to Ernle's. Heading the list are new fodder crops and crop rotations, convertible husbandry and Parliamentary enclosure, with a group of less important elements following: animal breeding, field drainage, and new machinery and implements. Although their book reaches forward to the 1870s, the revolutionary period is seen as the eighteenth century.[25]

The two other claims that have been made for a set of agricultural changes worthy of the term 'revolution' are more restricted in scope. The first, put forward by F. M. L. Thompson, argues that the importation products, such as oilcake and guano, during the nineteenth century enabled agricultural output to rise to unprecedented levels and so merits the title of a 'second agricultural revolution'.[26] This is a technical revolution and is seen (despite its title) as the third step in the transition to a modern agriculture. Like the first agricultural revolution as described by Ernle, its significance lies in breaking a 'closed circuit', only this time by importing inputs to the agricultural system from abroad. On the other hand, the pattern of farming, the mix of crops and stock, and the nature of farm output remained similar in their essentials to the pattern of the late eighteenth century. The other claim for a nineteenth-century 'agricultural revolution' has been suggested by Sturgess, who took up a theme introduced by Darby in arguing for a revolution based on the underdraining of the clay-lands,[27] thus allowing the first agricultural revolution to spread from light soils to heavier ones.

The work reviewed so far as been concerned with establishing or justifying a claim that an 'agricultural revolution' of a particular character took place in a particular period. Other agricultural historians have been content to accept the fact that a revolution occurred during the period after 1750 as given and unproblematic.[28] Some others ignore it altogether, although they write about farming practice, usually using probate inventories as their principal source material.[29] In a different category, the work of Arthur John and Eric Jones, by suggesting the processes by which new farming methods were introduced, and providing a fairly sophisticated explanation of their introduction, almost amounts to a claim for a revolution in the century after 1660.[30] Four general surveys of the agriculture of early modern England, for example, all stress the late seventeenth century as a period of particularly significant change.[31] Yet this period lies outside the bounds of any of the five 'revolutions' discussed above, and Jones is at pains to point out that he is not claiming any sort of 'revolutionary' significance for the changes he discusses.[32]

This is further proof, if any more were needed, that the phrase 'agricultural revolution' is thoroughly confusing and is best dispensed with as a term referring to a series of specific historical events. But in addition to disagreeing over content and chronology, authors differ over the meaning of the phrase itself. Mingay, for example, says a revolution need not be rapid; Fussell considers it should be; van Bath says it must be preceded by stagnation; Woodward considers that agricultural change consists of too many elements to be encompassed under the one heading; while Kerridge thinks that, 'something must revolve: the top must become bottom and the bottom top' (presumably a reference to 'up and down' husbandry).[33]

Explanations of revolutions

Before abandoning the term as meaningless, however, we should consider the attempts that have been made to provide some explanations of these various 'revolutions' (including the John–Jones 'non-revolution' of 1660–1750). Not surprisingly, different authors have different conceptions of what constitutes an adequate 'explanation', although these remain implicit in their work. Gras, for example, equates explanation with narrative description.[34] Kerridge, however, does speak explicitly of 'causes'; he states: 'In short the real cause of the agricultural revolution is that the improvers were given a chance. Human nature saw to the rest.' At his most explicit he concludes: 'Improvement of this kind is what creative and able people will set their hands to in the ordinary course of things, providing only that the rights of private property are assured and they have sound money with which to carry on their trade.' This appeal to what Kerridge calls 'intuition' and 'common sense' is both too trivial and too general to constitute an adequate explanation.[35]

Much more worthy of serious consideration are the views of John and Jones. Published in a series of articles from 1960 onwards, their work amounts to an explanation of the introduction of new crops and farming systems from the 1660s onwards which was to bring about the crucial transformation in output. The four elements of this explanation were most conveniently summarized by Jones in 1965, although they had already been discussed in print by John a few years earlier.[36]

After 1660, they argue, there was an increase in the output of animal products in response to a swing in price relatives towards livestock and away from grain.[37] Associated with this came an increase in the cultivation of new fodder crops (principally turnips and clover). However, grain output also increased, which Jones regards as a 'perverse' response to the adverse price relatives for grain.[38] This came about because those farmers who were unable or unwilling to switch over to livestock production, or who were unwilling to reduce their grain acreage, strove to offset a fall in their incomes by cutting costs. Costs were cut by raising grain yields per acre through the innovation of fodder crops. Thus the innovation of fodder crops was a means to expanding grain output.[39] These changes in farming enterprises had a spatial expression in that grain farming came to dominate lightlands (principally the chalk downlands) because the new fodder crops were more suitable for these environments.[40] Finally, apart from the stimuli of prices and the market, tenant farmers were assisted in making these changes by their landlords who, anxious to avoid the expense of farms falling into hand, helped their tenants make capital improvements to their farms.[41]

Although these arguments are not backed up by any reliable figures for prices, output or innovation, they do constitute an attractive hypothesis, accounting for the timing of innovation, the increase in grain output (witnessed by rising grain exports) and a change in the geography of farm enterprises. In at least one respect, however, John and Jones fall into the same trap as most other agricultural historians in their analysis of the innovation process. As well as being functionalist, their explanation of innovation is, strictly speaking, an *a posteriori* one, moving from effect to cause. They look at the long-term effects of turnips and clover in raising yields within a cropping pattern based on the principles of a Norfolk four-course and assume that farmers introduced these crops in the mid-seventeenth century with this end in mind. Seventeenth-century farmers could not see into the future and may not have foreseen, at least initially, that the new crops they were growing could eventually transform agricultural production into a system of 'high farming'.[42] Perhaps one explanation of why agricultural historians seem to adopt this assumption is that the relationship between fodder crops and output is accepted uncritically from late eighteenth-century agricultural writers. As William Marshall put it in 1795, 'No dung, – no turnips, – no bullocks, – no barley, – no clover, – nor tathe upon the second-years ley for wheat.'[43] The actual processes by which new crops were introduced and their initial impact on husbandry systems have not been studied. Thus, the evidence for fodder crops being grown in the late seventeenth or early eighteenth century is supposed to be symptomatic of a revolution because it is assumed that the cultivation of fodder crops is an indication of higher grain yields. While this might have been the case in the late eighteenth or early nineteenth century we have no clear evidence that it was so a hundred years earlier.

On reflection it seems most unlikely that farmers would introduce fodder crops specifically to raise grain output through an increase in yields. The reason for this is very simple. While a classic four-course raises the yields of grain, compared with a three-course, less grain is grown. Thus, unless farmers increased the total area cultivated, they would have needed great faith that

Table 1. *Yields and output of wheat, barley, clover and turnips under different conditions of cultivation* (in lb per acre of dry matter)

Rotation	Manure	Wheat	Barley	Turnips	Clover
A. Yields per acre					
Continuous cropping	No	647	875	285	Fails
Wheat, turnips, barley, fallow	No	1516	1396	415	
Wheat, turnips, barley, clover	No	1368	1489	277	3245
Wheat, turnips, barley, clover	Yes	1740	1987	3483	6740
B. Output per acre over four years					
Continuous cropping	No	2588	3500	944	
Wheat, barley, fallow	No	2021	1816	359	
Wheat, turnips, barley, clover	Yes	1740	1987	3483	6740

an increase in yields would not be offset by a fall in the area of grain. Further, the biological processes whereby clover fixed nitrogen from the air were not properly understood until the nineteenth century, although some contemporary commentators did recognize the benefits of clover in making land fit for corn.[44]

We can shed some light on the relationship between yields, cultivated area and total output by using data derived from the Rothamsted experiments. These have been underway since the 1840s and were initiated to discover ways in which soil fertility could be maintained and improved during the course of crop production. The experiments have yielded an overwhelming mass of facts and figures which agricultural historians have been surprisingly slow to utilize.[45] Table 1 gives some results that are particularly relevant to our purposes, and shows the increases in the yields of crops in a classic Norfolk four-course rotation of wheat, turnips, barley and clover when the conditions of their growth are changed from continuous cropping without manure to a full-blown manured Norfolk four-course. It also gives some estimates of the total output of each crop over a four-year period under three different rotations.[46] Making the extreme (and unrealistic) jump from a wheat, barley, fallow rotation with no manure to a Norfolk four-course with manure leads to a *fall* in wheat output and only a very slight increase in the total output of barley.[47] It is also noticeable that there is little point in growing turnips unless they are manured, yet one of the reasons for growing turnips was to produce an increase in supplies of manure.

This is not to deny the importance of the Norfolk four-course. Total output of grain *and* fodder increased, so farm incomes should have risen. Fodder crops enabled light land to be more easily cultivated and provided a valuable addition to supplies of fodder.[48] The point at issue is that the rotation is unlikely to have been introduced specifically to increase grain output by cutting costs through increased yields alone, without more land being cultivated. Thus, the increases in output which accompanied the agricultural revolutions described by Kerridge and Chambers and Mingay must have derived from increases in the cultivated area as well as from increases in yields per acre. Skipp has shown how the adoption of convertible husbandry in Arden was associated with increases in the cultivated area, as was agricultural advance in the eighteenth century – notwithstanding Kerridge's assertions to the contrary.[49] This was the opinion of an anonymous author writing about Norfolk agriculture in the *Gentleman's Magazine* for 1752: 'We sow on these improved farms five times as many acres of wheat, twice as many of barley.'[50]

Increasing the area cultivated might, in the long run, have reduced unit costs, but in the short term at least it would have involved increased expenditure in ploughing land previously uncultivated, or in buying or renting more land. Other costs were increasing too. Rents, for example, were probably rising,[51] and what evidence we have suggests that labour costs were also increasing.[52] It seems very strange that farmers should introduce new crops that are supposed to have been labour intensive at a time when labour costs were rising.

Finally the dichotomy between light and heavy land needs some qualification. In so far as there is a geography of the 'agricultural revolution' it is based on this light soil/heavy soil dichotomy, and (again like other agricultural historians) Jones and John follow in Ernle's footsteps.[53] It is certainly true that turnips were unsuited to cold, heavy clays because 'root' formation would be inhibited, animals would puddle the land when feeding in the field and it would be difficult to produce the fine seed-bed that turnips require.[54] At the other end of the scale, turnips are not necessarily suited to the lightest soils, especially if rainfall is low. 'On a close clayey soil saturated with rain turnips will not grow, and on a light sandy soil, without moisture, they cannot.'[55] Indeed the early turnip cultivation in Norfolk was centred on the loamy soils of the centre and south-east of the county rather than on the very light land to the west.[56]

Unfortunately, the John–Jones hypotheses are little more than speculations since they are not supported by any data that can confirm them. Of course the criticisms of their views put forward here are equally speculative for the same reason. An obvious way forward out of this impasse is by examining the empirical methods employed by agricultural historians.

Empirical problems

Like most historians, agricultural historians have occasionally expressed concern about the ways in which empirical evidence is employed in their research. This concern is manifest in articles discussing particular sources and either suggesting that they have been neglected[57] or criticizing the ways in which they have been used.[58] In the context of the agricultural revolution debate a more general criticism has been raised against historians who have relied too heavily on published literary evidence as opposed to unpublished primary documents. Ernle, for example, has been castigated by Kerridge for reading books and not documents. This partly explains why, according to Kerridge, Ernle's picture of the past was so 'distorted', since, 'by itself literary evidence cannot be other than inconclusive, ambiguous, and, often, contradictory'.[59] Later writers, including Kerridge himself, also seem content to base some generalizations on the words of a few contemporary authors. Kerridge's assertions about yields seem to be based on Marshall, Plot and Norden,[60] while Deane and Cole's eighteenth-century yield statistics depend on the comments of a few contemporaries reported by Fussell in an article in the *History Teacher's Miscellany*.[61] To take another example, the John–Jones thesis seems unduly influenced by the writings of William Ellis, particularly in its stress on the encroachment of turnips onto the downlands. Ellis described himself as a 'Chilturn farmer' and his understandable local bias is reflected in accounts of agricultural change based on his writings.[62]

Obviously it is in the nature of historical source material that some information is simply not available, and that it is often impossible to substantiate a particular speculation other than by using the opinion of a contemporary author. Yet when they supplement books with documents some historians fail to make as much use as they could of the evidence that is available to them, in that it could be persuaded to yield more information than is actually extracted. One reason for this might lie in the mode of argument that some historians adopt when using their evidence. Statements are accompanied by references to documents and contemporary literature, which are intended to illustrate the point being made. More generally we are invited to accept or reject a statement or set of statements about the past by the force of literary persuasion and appeals to selected documents. The 'instances' in the evidence referred to can often be matched by 'counter-instances' which can be used to contradict the point being made. For this reason we can label this mode of argument the 'instance/counter-instance' approach.

Such an approach may be criticized on a number of grounds,[63] but the particular objection here is that it has militated against the production of more reliable series of data with which agricultural change can be measured. As Mingay has lamented, 'we do not know with accuracy just when clover or turnips were grown by a substantial number of farmers',[64] and the agricultural revolution debate has been conducted without systematic quantitative data on innovation, yields, output, or the extent of the area cultivated. Perhaps agricultural historians have not felt the need for such data because they have been satisfied by the conclusions they have drawn about the past using arguments based on instance and counter-instance which have no need of such data. Indeed Kerridge has gone so far as to assert that 'we have no need whatsoever to refer to net yields or to gross volumes of production', in attempting to prove that his agricultural revolution took place.[65]

It could also be suggested that the mode of argument is adopted because of the absence of quantitative estimates of the parameters of agricultural change, rather than because historians see no need for them; in any event such estimates should furnish us with the data necessary to provide a firmer foundation for generalizations about the past. Of course, quantification can only be used with evidence that is amenable to measurement, but at the same time it can provide answers, albeit perhaps limited ones, to some questions that previously were unanswerable.[66]

Agricultural historians have not eschewed quantification entirely. Many of the generalizations they make are quantitative in character, and their discussions frequently refer to snippets of quantitative data. More systematic attempts at deriving series of numbers were associated with early work on probate inventories, although the degree of statistical sophistication in presenting data was rather limited.[67] Building on this tradition, it is possible, by introducing a little statistical theory and working systematically through a large number of probate inventories, to produce a great deal more information, including the kind of data to which Mingay referred as missing. Thus, using very simple quantitative techniques, it is possible to answer some hitherto unanswerable questions which have been central to the agricultural revolution debate.

The innovation of fodder crops has been discussed generally in the literature for over eighty years; yet only recently has it been measured, though admittedly only for the period 1580–1740 and for two English counties – Norfolk and Suffolk.[68] Kerridge stresses that an 'agricultural revolution' occurred in north-east Suffolk, because turnips became established between 1646 and 1660.[69] While he certainly produces a great body of evidence, it represents a partial selection of available material presented unsystematically. A systematic analysis of the same probate inventories as he himself used answers his basic question in a more precise manner and produces a different answer. By looking at every available inventory systematically, instead of making a partial selection, the 'revolutionary' period (to use Kerridge's definition) moves to the 1620s and the 'revolutionary' area switches to central Norfolk. By the 1630s at least seven farmers were cultivating turnips in fields for fodder.[70] More importantly, the quantitative part of the exercise, which simply involves counting the frequency of turnips in inventories, provides the data to chart the diffusion of the crop.[71]

Table 2. *Fodder crops in Norfolk and Suffolk inventories, 1587–1729*

	Root crops						Grass substitutes					
	(1)	N	(2)	N	(3)	N	(1)	N	(2)	N	(3)	N
1587–96	0.8	674	*	211	*	521	0.0	674		156		280
1629–38	0.9	713	*	180	0.06	584	0.0	713		146		304
1660–69	1.6	416	*	119	0.19	318	0.7	416	*	98	*	173
1670–79	9.3	362	0.63	100	0.45	236	3.7	363	*	86	*	133
1680–89	19.1	240	0.74	63	0.46	154	4.3	240	*	55	*	105
1690–99	29.4	153	2.23	37	1.29	92	6.3	153	*	39	0.24	75
1700–09	40.2	272	1.27	71	1.25	173	11.7	272	0.10	78	0.32	140
1710–19	47.4	334	2.15	99	1.52	217	17.4	334	1.01	95	0.32	125
1720–29	52.7	380	2.21	120	1.81	242	23.6	380	1.49	97	1.04	171

Notes:
(1) Percentage of inventories mentioning the crop   (2) Mean acreage
(3) Mean value   N Number of inventories used   * Insufficient data

As Table 2 shows, using some 4,000 inventories for Norfolk and Suffolk, under 10 per cent of farmers in those counties with an extant inventory were growing turnips between the 1580s and the 1680s, but by 1700 some 50 per cent were. Kerridge therefore emphasized the importance of the early adopters (to use Rogers' terminology)[72] while Mingay stressed the period after 1750 by which time the late majority were adopting. Apart from the efforts of historical geographers, particularly Walton and Yelling, there have been very few attempts to measure agricultural change in this way, with the exception of some recent work on the nineteenth century.[73]

In fact the definition of the innovation needs to be more subtle than this in that it should take account of how the crops were incorporated into husbandry systems. Before about 1630 turnips seem to have been grown not as fodder crops, but as vegetables for human consumption.[74] Until the middle decades of the eighteenth century neither turnips nor clover seem to have been an essential part of crop rotations on the majority of farms. They were not grown in sufficient quantity to have had much effect on overall fertility and thus do not appear in crop combination indices calculated from acreages of individual crops recorded in inventories.[75] By the 1720s for example, the proportion of the cropped acreage under turnips in the two counties was only about 9 per cent and under clover 3.5 per cent.[76]

Table 3. *Prices, output, yields and acreages derived from Norfolk and Suffolk inventories, 1587–1729*

	(1)	(2)	Wheat			Barley			(6)	(7)
			(3)	(4)	(5)	(3)	(4)	(5)		
1587–97	56	97	58	45	73	73	111	134	93	80
1629–38	62	74	81	44	57	91	86	100	84	93
1660–69	100	100	100	100	100	100	100	100	100	100
1670–79	107	99	96	100	104	127	242	190	97	117
1680–89	141	106	89	71	79	118	129	110	121	172
1690–99	112	100	104	82	79	104	294	284	104	136
1700–09	121	100	98	93	107	116	275	233	124	77
1710–19	142	108	104	115	110	125	326	261	116	70
1720–29	148	121	101	169	160	141	542	383	151	137

Notes: (1) Bullock/barley price ratio (5) Acreage per farm
(2) Sheep/barley price ratio (6) Number of bullocks per farm
(3) Yield (bushels per acre) (7) Number of sheep per farm
(4) Output (bushels per farm)
All figures are means expressed as index numbers (1660–69 = 100)

Inventories can also yield information about prices, crop yields and output, though not without making both mathematical and statistical manipulations of the data and assumptions about the valuations recorded in inventories. The price ratios in Table 3 assume that inventory valuations can be equated with market prices, and while there is some controversy over this it does seem that trends of inventory valuations closely follow trends in market prices.[77] A method for calculating grain yields has been discussed in a previous paper,[78] and will not be elaborated here. By relating average yields to average acreages it is possible to give a rough estimate of the average output of grain per farm. This is not an ideal measure, for if average farm sizes changed over time we should be wary of using the trend of average output per farm as a direct indication of the trend in grain output as a whole.

Unfortunately it is impossible to provide information on the output of livestock. We do not know the weights of animals, the age at which they were killed, or the yields of various animal products like meat, tallow, hides and wool. All we have from inventories are the numbers of animals.[79]

When these data are put together the most significant feature of husbandry developments after 1660 seems to have been not the introduction of new crops, but a dramatic increase in the output of barley (as Table 3 demonstrates), despite the fact that relative prices were moving towards livestock. Although barley yields rose slightly the main contribution to this increased output came from an increase in the area cultivated with barley, due partly to a rise in the total area cultivated and partly to a decline in the acreage of rye.[80]

All this presents a considerable puzzle as far as the John–Jones hypotheses are concerned. The output of grain went up in the face of falling price relatives as they suggest, yet it seems that this was due more to an increase in the area of land sown with barley than to cost-cutting increases in yields. On the other hand, while fodder crops were introduced quite rapidly, the number of animals did not show such a dramatic increase.

A possible explanation is, briefly, as follows. Despite unfavourable prices farmers expanded their barley output to meet a growing demand for malt, both from home and overseas. From 1697 malt exports received a rebate of some 14 per cent of their value and English merchants were able to gain reasonably secure overseas markets during the early decades of the eighteenth century.[81] Secondly, farmers could have been feeding barley to their animals, and so responding in a rational way to the swing in price relatives towards livestock. An animal fed on barley can reach maturity more rapidly than one fed on grass, so while the number of animals did not rise very much the turnover of animals and the output of meat could have increased.[82] New fodder crops had two roles to play in this process. First, they would have provided a higher-yielding supply of green fodder when areas of pasture were reduced as the cultivated area expanded; and, secondly, they would have reduced the necessity of some (but not all) bare fallows.

A complementary explanation of their introduction is based on farmers' attitudes towards risk. The period from 1500 to 1700 is described as the 'Little Ice Age', characterized by a fall in average temperatures and an increase in precipitation.[83] New sources of fodder, particularly turnips, provided some insurance against the failure of a hay crop. If a grass crop was inadequate then turnips could be sown as late as August to provide some winter fodder.[84] Thus, innovation of fodder crops could be interpreted as a form of risk aversion, as indeed could the increasing proportion of land under barley, a crop which could be used both as a cash crop to be malted, or, if it failed to reach sufficient quality, as a fodder crop.

It is evident from these speculations that the application of quantitative techniques is a beginning rather than an end. Far from stifling debate or leaving matters cut and dried, these methods open up new areas of research. The data considered here deserve a much fuller discussion,[85] and the intention in presenting them is not to produce yet another version of the 'agricultural revolution' but to demonstrate that the quantitative analysis of historical documents, producing generalizations based on the systematic analysis of a large body of evidence, can provide some of the essential data that have been missing from existing accounts of agricultural change and so resolve questions that have remained unresolved for a considerable time, as well as suggesting further avenues for research.

A final point about the application of quantitative techniques is more general, and perhaps more fundamental for the study of history or historical geography: namely, that the acceptance of quantitative techniques does not imply acceptance of particular theories, still less of particular philosophies. Early writing in the geographers' 'quantitative revolution' tended to introduce quantitative techniques hand in hand with neoclassical economic theory and the philosophy of logical positivism, implying that the acceptance of the technique meant that the theory and philosophy must also be accepted.[86] Economic historians fall into the same trap. Murphy, for example, launches a critique of the 'old' (non-quantitative) economic history from the standpoint of a positivist philosophy firmly allied to the theories of neoclassical economics.[87] However, although statistical methods do have their own philosophical assumptions, about the nature of inference for example,[88] in themselves they do not necessarily entail any assumptions about the world, in the sense of social, economic or political theories. It is to these that we now turn.

Theoretical problems

Agricultural historians, like most historians, have tended to avoid direct entanglements with theory,[89] and certainly the agricultural revolution debate has been conducted at an empirical level of inquiry. The question of what does or does not constitute an 'agricultural revolution' is not, however, an empirical question; it is a conceptual one. No matter how many historical facts are accumulated, no matter how many new historical data we can produce, the question of the existence or otherwise of some 'agricultural revolution' cannot be determined solely by examining empirical evidence.

The essential significance of the agricultural revolutions both of Kerridge and of Chambers and Mingay lies in the capability of an increased agricultural output to accommodate a growing population. As Outhwaite has pointed out, during Kerridge's revolution (1540–1700) some three million natives and some 3,000 foreigners were fed by the increase in agricultural production. During Chambers and Mingay's revolution (1750–1850) some seven million extra people were fed by English agriculture.[90] Which then is the more 'revolutionary' era? In absolute terms clearly the revolution identified by Chambers and Mingay is more significant, yet in both periods agricultural output increased to permit a doubling of the population. But how was this increase in output achieved?

According to Grigg, 'If the phrase "agricultural revolution" is to have any meaning, it must surely apply not simply to an increase in agricultural output by expanding the agricultural area or to the experiments of a few farmers but to a general and rapid increase in productivity of the area under consideration.'[91] Yields increased during both the 'revolutionary' periods we are considering. For wheat the increase was from some eight bushels per acre in the 1580s to about fourteen bushels in the early eighteenth century.[92] From 1750 there was probably a rise from about sixteen bushels per acre to about thirty bushels per acre in the 1830s.[93] In each case there was an approximate doubling. Which period was the more 'revolutionary'? Couched in these terms the question seems rather a trivial one. At this conceptual level at least the criteria deciding whether an agricultural revolution took place seem almost arbitrarily defined. There is not a great deal to choose between the two periods, and no obvious criteria for making the decision, or for deciding which 'revolution' is the more 'significant'.

The way round this problem lies at a higher and more theoretical level of inquiry. The debate about the role of theory in history is an extensive one,[94] although the extreme positions can be categorized fairly simply. On the one hand a strong empiricist tradition eschews theory and considers that history should be concerned with collecting historical facts which can then be constituted into some 'historical truth'.[95] On the other hand, as Carr puts it, 'It used to be said that the facts speak for themselves. This is of course untrue. The facts speak only when the historian calls on them.'[96] Taken perhaps to an extreme, 'In effect history is theory.'[97] The attitude towards 'theory' taken in this chapter is in broad agreement with a recent editorial in the *History Workshop Journal*: 'Theory-building cannot be an alternative to the attempt to explain real world phenomena, but is, rather, a way of self-consciously defining the field of enquiry, classifying and exposing to self-criticism the explanatory concepts used, and marking the limits of empirical investigation.'[98] Theory therefore has two roles to play; first, in questioning the questions asked of the past, and, secondly, in providing the framework for an explanation of agrarian change.

Thus a central concern of the agricultural revolution debate lies in the relationship between population growth and agricultural change mediated through technical changes in farming practice.[99] This general relationship has, of course, been discussed from the time of Malthus onwards, and formed the basis for Slicher van Bath's overview of Western European agriculture.[100] Yet only recently have contributions begun to develop the theme within the period when the 'agricultural revolution' supposedly occurred in England, though without explicit reference to that debate. On a local scale, for example, Skipp used an 'ecological' model as a framework for analysing agricultural change in the Forest of Arden between 1570 and 1674, where he identified both positive and negative agrarian responses to the pressure of population.[101] More generally, Wilkinson and Grigg have applied various 'ecological' or 'population–resource' models to the development of English agriculture as a whole;[102] while Schofield and Wrigley have chosen a series of Malthusian models as their basis for an interpretation of the data compiled in their *Population History of England*.[103]

It is not possible within the confines of this chapter to set out these approaches in any detail. It is, however, worth stressing that they do constitute a very loose body of theory[104] in the sense defined above, and can serve both to recast some of the questions already alluded to in the agricultural revolution debate, and to provide some explanatory framework for the answers. It is now up to agricultural historians to provide some agricultural statistics to match the new demographic data generated by the Cambridge Group for the History of Population and Social Structure. Why, for example, does the relationship between the rate of population growth and the rate of change in prices alter so dramatically between 1781 and 1806 when it had remained virtually constant for over 200 years?[105]

One limitation of such approaches is that despite the fact that demography is about people, they reduce agricultural history to a narrow 'technicism' in which demographic and agricultural trends are correlated at a macro-level. Once the specific relationships between population pressure and agricultural change begin to be explored the issues are not so much 'ecological' but rather are about prices, landholding and employment – in other words, about the concerns of social and economic theory.[106] The economic theories which seem to underlie discussions within this 'population–resource' paradigm are not usually made explicit but seem to derive from classical and neo-classical economics. Harvey has demonstrated, for example, how Malthus' ideas assume private property arrangements and a particular class structure.[107]

At a more specific level, therefore, accounts of agricultural change have been couched in terms of the contribution of 'factors of production'; land, labour and capital, which, together with technological change, are held responsible for increases in output.[108] Despite the popularity of this approach, historical geographers have been critical of attempts at historical explanation that derive from neoclassical economics. Most of these criticisms need to be taken very seriously, particularly the charge that the theory is fundamentally ahistorical, and essentially static.[109] Nevertheless, in terms of the elegance of their models, the rigour of their arguments, and, more importantly, the new light they can shed on some aspects of agricultural change, some recent contributions by economic historians should not be dismissed out of hand. Crafts, in particular, has produced new insights into old problems, albeit by the use of simple macro-economic models applied to extremely weak data. In a series of recent papers he has suggested that the Malthusian trap was in fact rather shallow,[110] that agriculture did release labour to industry in the eighteenth century,[111] and that there was a small positive association between the Parliamentary enclosure of common fields and outmigration.[112] The first of these conclusions has obvious implications for the argument that the essential feature of an agricultural revolution must be expanding output to meet a rising population.[113] The second and third may give some comfort to those historians who view the past in a radically different way from those adopting a neoclassical perspective.

As an alternative to the 'technicism' of the population–resource models and the philosophical and methodological assumptions behind neoclassical models, some historians are turning to Marxian theory as a framework within which to study the agricultural history of the period covered by the agricultural revolution debate.[114] Marxian theory is attractive for a number of reasons. It is primarily about people (or groups of people) rather than impersonal 'factors of production' and treats economic life and social life as one and the same. Thus, it is concerned with relationship between people in the process of production, and recognizes that not all individuals (or groups) have equal power in determining the allocation of resources. The theory is also historically specific; it assumes different forms and makes different assumptions for particular historical periods.[115]

While the material available on Marxist economic and social theories is voluminous,[116] there has been comparatively little work which applies this theory to the specific study of agricultural change. Some of this literature is not particularly distinguished. Lazonick, for example, seems concerned to vindicate Marx's every statement about Parliamentary enclosure, ignoring those which subsequent research has shown to be incorrect.[117] Collins goes to the opposite extreme in an attempt to 'falsify' Marx's views by applying a Popperian methodology to statements in *Capital*, in order to undermine the entire theory.[118] More successful applications of Marxian ideas to English agriculture have come from Saville, Carter and Tribe. Saville provides a series of rather stark generalizations about the course of agrarian history from a Marxian perspective,[119] charting the rise of capitalist farmers, the disappearance of the peasantry, the growth of a rural proletariat and the increase in the concentration of landownership. Tribe gives a more comprehensive survey of agrarian developments in eighteenth-century England,[120] while Carter's monograph represents one of the first attempts to employ an explicitly Marxian framework as the basis for a detailed local study – a case study of nineteenth-century north-east Scotland.[121]

An example of a more specific issue raised by a Marxian approach is Tribe's novel analysis of the agrarian literature published between 1500 and 1800. He uses this to demonstrate convincingly how the idea of the farmer as 'husbandman', an individual working with nature, gives way to the idea of the 'farmer' as manager of a capitalist undertaking.[122] In the specific sphere of agricultural marketing Thompson demonstrates the penetration of market exchange into farming, leading to a change from a paternalistic 'moral' economy to a 'political economy' characterized by the capitalist ethos.[123]

But the issue that has received most attention from Marxist and non-Marxist historians alike is the one most central to Marx's account of the transition from a feudal to a capitalist mode of production.[124] A distinctive feature of capitalism is that labour is 'free', in the sense that the labourer is not tied to the land by owning property and so must sell his labour power in the market-place in order to survive. A second essential feature is the establishment of private property rights in land and the dissolution of common rights;[125] this, taken with the first, contributed to the development of the three-tiered structure of landlord, capitalist tenant farmer and labourer.[126] For Marx, Parliamentary enclosure provided the mechanism for this process. It eliminated the class of small farmers who by owning land had managed to avoid complete entanglement in capitalist production relations, and also eradicated common rights through the force of statute law,[127] thus paving the way for the creation of large capitalist farms.

The debate over the role of enclosure still continues, and while it seems likely that Marx overemphasized its importance, for our purposes the details of the empirical arguments[128] are less important than the manner in which the debate has been conducted. Those who argue against Marx usually choose to ignore his theoretical formulation of the problem and concentrate their arguments at the empirical level alone. Thus, while Mingay, for example, recognizes the existence of the theoretical level, he chooses to dismiss it out of hand by suggesting that the term 'peasantry' is charged with 'romanticism and sentimental overtones'. He prefers to talk about the fate of a class of 'small farmers' which he arbitrarily defines as a group including tenant farmers who farmed between twenty and one hundred acres.[129] The terms of reference have now been changed, so that, while Marx, and those who follow him, are considering the issue of the decline of a peasant class which was independent of capitalist production, Mingay is discussing the fate of a group of farmers arbitrarily defined by the acreage they held. These theoretical differences must be made explicit before the debate can be understood at the empirical level.

In contrast to the arguments over the fate of the peasant, there has been little controversy over the establishment of capitalist property relations. Private property rights became firmly established in the eighteenth century and were completely dominant by the middle of the nineteenth century when Parliamentary enclosure had run its course. This changing attitude to property is documented by Macpherson, who charts the confirmation of private property rights, the treatment of property as a commodity, and property as the incentive to necessary labour.[130] Property rights, however, are also seen as crucial to the development of agriculture by those who adopt radically different theoretical positions. North and Thomas, for example, base their theory of the rise of the Western world, couched in terms of neoclassical economics, on the development of property relations, and Kerridge also considers these an essential prerequisite for his agricultural revolution.[131] This provides a good example of how the 'facts' are not 'speaking for themselves'; the 'facts' of changing property relations can only be given meaning by recourse to some theoretical structure.

Accepting or rejecting a particular theory of agricultural change does not, therefore, simply depend on an appeal to historical evidence. The choice must in part depend on the presuppositions of the historian. Collingwood argues that people hold two sets of presuppositions: those which he calls 'relative presuppositions' which are amenable to modification in the light of experience, and also a set of more deep-seated 'absolute presuppositions' which cannot be so challenged.[132] These absolute presuppositions could be said to constitute the 'ideology' of the historian, in the sense that they determine his system of values or beliefs and his manner of thinking. No theory, except the most low-level or trivial, can be value-free. Joan Robinson, for example, shows how various economic theories rest soundly on what she calls 'metaphysical' statements which derive from particular 'ideologies'.[133] The claim to be value-free is itself an ideological claim;[134] or, put another way, 'ethical neutrality is meaningless, for indifference is itself a moral position'.[135]

Ideology, defined simply for the moment as a system of beliefs, inevitably underpins interpretations of agricultural history. McGregor has demonstrated that Ernle was closely identified with the ideals of the late Victorian aristocracy, and wrote his book as a deliberate piece of propaganda, emphasizing the virtues of leadership, self-help and individualism.[136] Kerridge has made his position very clear. He accuses Tawney, for example, of seeing 'the world past and present in terms of socialist dogma', which led to his 'wholly untrue picture of early capitalism as cruel and greedy'. Kerridge believes he can 'restore the historical truth'.[137] Quite clearly therefore he expresses his commitment to some anti-socialist view of agrarian change and to a philosophy that admits of some specific truth to be discovered about the past. If not exactly serving as a warning, at least these views give a guide to his ideology of agrarian change. Likewise Mingay's complaint that the Hammonds 'had the advantage of knowing at the outset what the conclusion was likely to be' in their study of enclosure,[138] suggests that it is desirable, and therefore possible, for the historian to approach his work with his mind empty of assumptions, values or presuppositions about the world.

'Ideology', however, is frequently assigned specific meanings other than the simple one given here.[139] Unfortunately it is often used loosely as a pejorative term to imply distortion or bias, caused by the intrusion of values, moral judgements or even deliberate lies into what should be 'objective', value-free or 'scientific' inquiry. When Eric Jones complains of the intrusions of politics and 'ideology' into agrarian history, claiming that the historian can work at some level of dispassionate investigation approaching objectivity, he seems to be using 'ideology' in this sense. Walsh has commented that historians 'take their own value judgements so much for granted';[140] and indeed Jones' writing, inevitably, reflects his system of values: 'There is already too much dispute in academic life without adding the dimension of ideology. To return to the particular case, if the total return to farm labour as a factor of production did not rise over the 1850s and 1860s, let this be demonstrated from the evidence.'[141] The dispute to which he refers is in fact at heart ideological; to call the farm labourer a 'factor of production' is not to adopt some value-free label, but to adopt the terminology of neoclassical economics with its ideological overtones. 'Factor of production' has just as many ideological implications as 'proletariat'.

It is futile therefore to pretend that value judgements do not exist, and to brand certain approaches to the past 'ideological' as an excuse for ignoring ideas we dislike.[142] On the other hand, if Jones is using ideological to mean 'dishonest', we must agree with this part of his complaint, for by claiming that historians cannot be truly objective we are not claiming that they cannot be honest. Forcing empirical evidence into some rigid and dogmatic theoretical framework could be termed dishonest if it involved ignoring contradictory evidence (as Lazonick does for example).[143] However, when theories become more general, more abstract, and closer to the philosophies from which they derive, it is increasingly difficult to modify them by empirical evidence alone, and debate must be conducted at a higher level. This is the difficulty with Collins' criticisms of Marx.[144] Empirical evidence can modify Marx's original account of the process of proletarianization, but it cannot invalidate the concept of the proletariat, or any other of Marx's general theoretical propositions.

Conclusion

Although the central concern of this essay has been with the historiography of a rather narrow debate about agricultural change in England, it has proved impossible to discuss that debate without considering the wider issues of quantification, theory and ideology which have concerned historical geographers for some considerable time. It has not been the intention to make a particular contribution in these fields; indeed, in contrast to some recent writing which has tended towards obfuscation, the level of discussion has been deliberately kept at a fairly simple level. Rather, the intention has been to apply some of these rather general methodological arguments to the specific debate about the 'agricultural revolution', as a means both for understanding that debate and for suggesting how our understanding of agricultural change in England might improve.

There can be no doubt that much of the writing on the 'agricultural revolutions' discussed here has acted as a deterrent to the understanding of the past, particularly for those approaching the subject for the first time. Subsequent work has studiously avoided becoming entangled in the debate so that the 'new orthodoxy' about technical change in English agriculture explicitly dissociates itself from it. The debate is also ignored by those who have attempted to analyse agricultural change from a more explicitly theoretical stance, whatever their theory might be. Thus, for over a decade, since the late 1960s when discussion degenerated into personal abuse,[145] the specific debate has been allowed to die.

In resurrecting it I am not attempting to redefine a set of 'revolutionary' events, or to vindicate a particular view of an 'agricultural revolution'. (That phrase is now beyond redemption as it is surely meaningless, except as a pejorative label for a most unfortunate historiographical episode.) Rather I have attempted to demonstrate that the reasons for the demise of the debate, which lie in the mode of argument at an empirical level and in the theoretical level at which it has been conducted, provide the paths towards its revitalization. Explorations of historical data using statistical techniques give new insights into old problems and effectively provide new evidence from existing sources. Explorations of theories of agrarian change are perhaps even more rewarding, since they lead to the re-evaluation of both old and new evidence and so produce a stream of questions about the past – the lifeblood of historical inquiry. The first step along this path is to make implicit theories explicit, and then to apply, modify and develop our theories so that we may progress towards a deeper understanding of agricultural change in early modern England.

University of Newcastle upon Tyne

5

'Modernization' and the corporate medieval village community in England: some sceptical reflections

RICHARD M. SMITH

In the last decade and a half a theme has emerged to become markedly prominent in the work of certain early modern English historians. It relates to the manner in which 'the tight institutionalised nature of society was loosened and with it the concept of the mediaeval community'.[1] A medievalist cannot but be greatly intrigued by these preoccupations on the part of early modernists insofar as they are based on a particular characterization of rural society in the Middle Ages and especially founded on belief in the existence of a specific patterning to social intercourse in the medieval village. In this debate the emphasis has been on the notion of a 'moral community' rather than on the physical, more overtly tangible, features of rural society – such as village morphology or field arrangements and functions – which have traditionally constituted the prime foci of the historical geographer's research in this area. I shall introduce this essay by reviewing the principal features of early modern English society that historians of this research school have isolated, especially those that carry broad historico-geographical implications. I then proceed to consider the extent to which these arguments find a readily detectable position within a long-established paradigm of societal change. In other words, I attempt to assess the novelty of these recent interpretations in the light of the historiography of writings on social development, paying particular attention to the nineteenth-century debates on social evolution. I conclude my discussion by exploring the need for, and potential of, a more serious commitment by historical geographers to the study of the law, its institutions and its administrative functions on behalf of the Crown to further our understanding both of centre–periphery and community–state relations in medieval England.

The social correlates of the medieval/early modern divide

There is irony in the fact that some of the most forthright statements concerning the character of social relations within the medieval English village have been made by Tudor and Stuart historians. Christopher Hill eloquently states the feelings of this school of thought when he reflects upon the changes that he believes were occurring in the sixteenth-century communities:

> The old geographical communities with their rough and ready but effective hierarchical subordination, their traditional ceremonies, their succession of popular seasonal festivals, with a nominated priest in theory directing the spiritual life of the community: these were passing. The communities of the sects which eventually emerged were voluntary, electing and paying their own minister, relieving their own poor, . . . [using the words of Sir Henry Maine or indeed Tönnies] *contract* communities had succeeded *status* communities.[2]

Hill reflects on two by-products of this development; first, the decline of the tradition whereby the medieval lay and ecclesiastical aristocracy felt a duty-bound obligation to be hospitable to the poor. Indeed, the existence of vagabondage and a mobile poor in late sixteenth-century England are seen as obvious examples of the breakdown of the local community as a unit of employment or of social security. Stress is therefore placed on developments that supposedly led to the dissolution of redistributive mechanisms believed to have been highly specific to a peculiarly medieval moral economy. Secondly, Hill points to the process whereby society was becoming atomized: 'Economic processes were atomizing society, converting it from a hierarchy of communities to the agglomeration of equal competing individuals depicted in *Leviathan*.'[3] The change, Hill argues, was from patriarchal families functioning in corporate communities, towards much more introspective, smaller households. This latter theme is also emphasized by Thirsk when, writing presumably about the medieval family, she states that 'sociability was forced upon the individual. His home was so cold that he had to move about and visit his neighbours to keep warm.'[4] Furthermore, a recent interpretation of the history of the family by Stone has drawn heavily upon the ideas above in arguing for the transition from 'the open lineage family of the middle ages' and the emergence of the nuclear family during the course of the sixteenth and seventeenth centuries.[5]

Closely allied views of the medieval village community, stressing its contrasts to the sixteenth-century village, loom large in the writings of Keith Thomas. Thomas, in his mammoth attempt to explain the rise, incidence and subsequent decline of witchcraft practices and beliefs in the sixteenth and early seventeenth centuries, claims that it is necessary to study the 'weak points in the social structure'.[6] In other words, 'The great bulk of witchcraft accusations thus reflected an unresolved conflict between the *neighbourly* conduct required by the ethical code of the old village community and the increasingly *individualistic* form of behaviour which accompanied the economic changes of the sixteenth and seventeenth centuries.'[7] (My italics.)

We must assume that in referring to the 'old village community' Thomas has in mind a social entity that predominated in the Middle Ages. Citing examples from the tenants of the Abbot of Ramsey in Huntingdonshire, the Abbot of Crowland in Cambridgeshire, and manors in the Chiltern Hills, he claims that the medieval manorial system did much to cater for the needs of the elderly, especially widows, by means of the customs of free bench – namely, a right to inherit from a quarter to the whole of her late husband's holding. This, combined with various local customs such as gleaning the stubble before the period of common grazing and the right to sleep in the church if homeless, served to provide the basis for a stable social system. The decline of the manorial system, Thomas maintains, combined with increased pressure of population on land, inflation, the growth of towns and commercial values, enclosure and the engrossing of commons, served to precipitate a crisis among the poor and those who in their turn were in danger of becoming impoverished. Seen in this light, it is understandable why for Thomas and an 'unreformed' Macfarlane also, accused witches should invariably be found not only as the very poorest in the community but certainly among those groups that had fallen in social and economic status and their accusers should be located among their village neighbours of a slightly higher social standing.[8] These more materially fortunate individuals were those who in some way failed to meet old 'customary' expectations of charity and support and, in the event of misfortunes arising in their families, were prepared to accuse the unfortunate person they had recently turned away from their door, or to whom they had refused employment, of spiritual malpractices.[9]

The intellectual roots of Thomas' arguments are clearly located in the writings of his teacher, Christopher Hill. Indeed that line can be followed further back to R. H. Tawney. The Protestant Reformation is argued to have brought fundamental changes to the community ethos. At the heart of these changes were Puritan desires to eradicate the ceremonial functions of the syncretic medieval Church. These ceremonial functions are, it is argued, supposed to have bound the community together in a way that was absent from the reformed Church's emphasis on the individual; the removal of secular business transactions from the Church, this school would suggest, made the church building less of a community centre in the sixteenth than it had been in the fifteenth century and earlier. The sixteenth century, according to this view, sees the emergence of a 'contradiction between the church as the whole community and the church in a different sense as the community of believers only'.[10] Indeed, the Church changes its role from an agency promoting social integration to one furthering social differentiation.

With this paradigm clearly implanted in their consciousness a group of younger and currently highly active social historians has refined and elaborated this line of argument with very detailed empirical research. It is perfectly exemplified in a recent attempt to summarize some of the wider social and cultural changes believed to have occurred in early modern England. The problem is couched in terms of bridging the gap between a late medieval English society as described by R. H. Hilton and an eighteenth-century English society as so vividly portrayed for us by E. P. Thompson.[11] It is necessary, therefore, briefly to elaborate the 'before' and 'after' linked by the social changes that are argued to have taken place in the sixteenth and seventeenth centuries.

Hilton, in a series of writings, has depicted late medieval rural society as one in which internal differentiation of the peasantry was little advanced and in which distinctions between husbandmen and landless labourers were described as of little social significance. Conflict is seen by Hilton as being between individuals and families within villages, rather than between social groups – a lack of differentiation, it is claimed, owing much to the relative cultural homogeneity of the peasantry and even more to the fact that the gap between landlord and peasant was still much more significant than that between peasant and labourer.[12]

Thompson writes of a situation in which the old 'peasant' society had been largely dissolved and replaced by the classic pattern of squire, tenant-farmers and agricultural labourers.[13] He sees a radical dissociation between the polite culture of the rulers of eighteenth-century England and the plebeian culture of the labouring people. In the absence of a highly structured class organization, however, he characterizes the relationships between 'patriciate' and 'plebs' as fluid and manipulative. In these circumstances the maintenance of the cultural hegemony of the gentry is seen as crucial and is upheld, Thompson claims, by various means. An overwhelmingly significant factor is that while the position of the gentleman as paternalistic patron is *highly visible*, gentry control and exploitation of the common people are of *low visibility*. Such control is argued to have been imposed indirectly through the upper echelons of the tenantry.

The view of the school of thought that has been, perhaps, rather curtly summarized is that the passage from Hilton's to Thompson's world is characterized by the rise of the *parish notable*.[14] The parish notable would have been the person well endowed with land, indeed the rising yeoman-farmer of the fifteenth century. He would have become the respectable tenant-farmer of the eighteenth century. The fundamental process in this change is seen to be that which causes the individual to lose his identification and solidarity with his neighbours, to become more closely and more consistently associated with the values and interests of the ruling classes. In the terms provided by Robert Redfield, the higher echelons of village society are drawn out of the morass of undifferentiated village culture of the 'Little Tradition' to align themselves unambiguously with the 'Great Tradition' whose values they now find it in their own interests to extol.[15]

It is without doubt Keith Wrightson who appears as the most eloquent, and indeed most convincing, advocate of these interpretations. For Wrightson what the later sixteenth and the seventeenth centuries experienced was 'an intensified interaction between the locality and the larger society, which both drew together provincial communities into a more closely integrated national society and at the same time introduced a new depth and complexity to their local patterns of social stratification'.[16] In Wrightson's opinion it is important to see developments in terms of a conjunctural situation in which national demographic, economic, administrative and above all ideological changes both coincide and interact in a manner which (significantly) is most frequently confined to and observable within *local* social relations. Indeed, Wrightson's own research has been based on an intensive study of an Essex rural community which provided him with a framework within which to apply ideas worked out microcosmically to the macrocosm of the English nation.[17] Furthermore, it is in large part Wrightson's ability and willingness to relate his research in small-scale societies to developments at a higher level that has been widely acclaimed by reviewers of his work who, with considerable justification, saw so much earlier research on local communities as particularistic, introverted and atheoretical.[18]

The economic and demographic processes against which the character of village-based social relationships were supposedly reorientated are well known and have very recently been made even more certain. Many indicators could be utilized to support the view that the period between 1500 and 1700 witnessed the enhancement of market integration and increasing regional specialization. The emphasis in recent work by social historians is on explaining how, at the level of the community, these forces created serious dislocations with increasing social differentiation; for yeomen and husbandmen well endowed with land prospered largely at the expense of their cottager or wage labouring neighbours who were periodically shaken from their tenuous hold on land by insolvencies brought about by the harvest failures that became ever more frequent in the later years of the Tudor and early years of the Stuart regime.[19] The polarization of wealth locally is therefore seen as a concomitant of national economic integration and as requiring increasing national responses such as legislative moves (in the Tudor Poor Laws) to deal with a 'new' problem of poverty and regulative controls through the Book of Orders.[20]

Superimposed upon these 'underlying forces' and certainly not detached from them, a massive reshaping of the forms and processes of both national and local government has been propounded by early modernists. Although not denying the existence of at least the semblance of a framework of centralized royal power in the Middle Ages, these Tudor and Stuart historians would stress rather the administrative disintegration of the mid-fifteenth century, singling out for emphasis the inability of the Crown to acquire the service and loyalty of the powerful among the nobility and their clients in the county gentry. Effective political control at the centre is seen as proven largely through the work of Professor Elton and his pupils, who have been for the most part concerned with arguing the case for a Tudor revolution in government which was reflected in, among other things, the use of royal patronage whereby powerful territorial magnates were bound more closely to the Crown and the control of rebellion.[21] Both these developments were cemented by the proliferation in local administrative systems of the justices of the peace, whose role became increasingly concerned with ensuring that regulative legislation was implemented in the peripheries. Through these procedures, associated with a widening of the base of Parliamentary representation, the nationalization of the Church and the emergence of royal court councils to deal with the government of the north and the Welsh marches, the political geography of the country is seen to have been welded into a more solid substructure.[22]

Greater solidification in the upper tiers of government, if to be ultimately effective, would need the support of efficient agents of local administration. The principal agents in this 'increase of governance' were the upper tiers of county society – so-called 'county communities', of which there has been much discussion since Peter Laslett first sketched out the bare details of this social entity in 1948 and Professor Everitt put flesh on those bones in 1966.[23] It was from these groups within county communities that the deputy lieutenants, sheriffs and especially justices of the peace came. But of even greater significance in the opinion of the most recent writing were the activities of the upper ranks of the 'peasantry' who increasingly, in the early seventeenth century in particular, are believed to have filled the presentment juries in local courts or occupied such offices created by the Tudor statutes as those of overseers of the poor or village constables.[24] However, their foci of activity moved from the village-based manorial courts, which are seen as having been essentially introspective in the Middle Ages, to the externally located quarter sessions and petty sessions of the King's justices. It is argued too that these 'workhorses of central government' were not just recipients and implementers of orders but could take initiatives in the formulation both of policy and of statutes helping to give Parliament a 'national' representativeness as the 'provinces' became ever more clearly integrated into the nation-state.[25]

The pump generating the energy needed for both greater market integration and political cohesiveness was primed by the so-called penetration of the provinces by Protestantism. I have already referred to Hill's interpretation of these developments; this has been modified mainly through the identification of those groups in society most responsive to, and most ready to

146   Richard M. Smith

absorb, the changes. Once again, the mediatory group – the 'village notables' – has pride of place in these processes.[26] This group had participated in the other great cultural change – the so-called 'educational revolution' – and was ripe for appreciating the significance of theological niceties and the contrast between biblical precepts and popular customs.[27] What occurred, it is argued, was the emergence of a cultural schism that irreparably split local communities, and was reflected in such matters as literacy levels, utilization of growing educational resources and a visible culture specific to the 'middle class' or 'better sort', who now stood apart from a 'culture of poverty' which intransigently characterized those left behind in these social changes.

My comments so far have the appearance of a somewhat breathless journey through a detailed and complex set of arguments, in an attempt to sketch the case of those who would argue for the presence in late sixteenth- and early seventeenth-century England of the simultaneous processes of national integration and local differentiation. There may well be differences within this group of historians, who have been perhaps too readily lumped together. Hill, for instance, appears to have seen the processes of change much more in terms of a model of society originally possessing organic coherence within which cellular fragmentation proceeded to create communities of inward-looking, privatized households having increasingly marked social stratification. Wrightson, for his part, acknowledges a pre-existing stratification but presents an image of local society as a layer cake whose parts become sharply distinguished one from the other as the uppermost tier bears down more heavily upon an expanding lowermost level, whose access to the outside world is increasingly possible only through the 'better sort' whose interests come to be served by aligning themselves with forces external to the cake itself.

Incorporating the village: interpretations from political science

Early modern historians expounding views such as those of Wrightson discussed above, although perhaps not conscious of it, are writing about the medieval English village community as if it were isolated from – or, in the words of the political scientist, were unincorporated in – the nation-state.[28] What they appear to describe is the process whereby isolated communities in the course of the sixteenth century became progressively incorporated as a result of a combination of economic innovations, legislative reform and administrative initiatives in the matter of centre–periphery relations.

It is important in this discussion to review certain features of the writings of those social scientists who have constructed arguments which particularly concern the mobilization of groups, strata and individuals in rural communities into a larger national polity: i.e. how at the village level outward-orientated forces triumph over inward-orientated forces. Most of these discussions have been undertaken in relation to rural populations in non-European areas of the world, although very often European historical experiences have been introduced as supposedly providing precedents for present-day developments. Some of the most valuable work has resulted from a dissatisfaction with the future of 'modernization' and cultural diffusion theory to explain why some rural societies exhibit change but others do not.[29] It has been loudly critical of social science paradigms which view the individual or the community as though they existed *in vacuo*.[30] It has emphasized the need to consider peasants as a subordinate or subservient group or class to dominant power-holders (whether landlords or centralized states) who have controlled their essential resources; it has cautioned against an overeagerness to dismiss Marx, through the relegation of economic constraints and class pressures as causal factors, to a secondary position, with undue attention placed consequently on the individual, culture, values and norms;[31] it has criticized the use of naive anthropological analogy in that much of such work in that discipline as is based or focused on the community involves 'primitive' communities rather than peasants living in complex societies whose behaviour patterns can only be understood in terms of the way they relate to the outside world.[32] In effect, work in this field constitutes a body of criticism highly damaging to an earlier style of community analysis often practised by historians; examples of such analysis will be discussed later.

With certain qualifications the arguments concerning incorporation are based on a linear view of change. Emphasis is placed upon understanding the conditions that promote inward-looking behaviour in village communities. In particular, a prime role in the creation of village introspection is given to exploitative conditions that promote withdrawal; in political systems where power is shown to have been dispersed both socially and geographically (i.e. feudal or patrimonial domains) lords would wish their dependent tenants to limit their involvement with outsiders; in systems where landlords were absent or of limited significance, peasants would need to adapt their behaviour to powerful persons far removed from the village (i.e. in highly bureaucratized states).[33]

Where lords were powerful and controlled vital resources, it is argued, it was they who enforced their peasants' inward orientation, because it was outside the community that peasants might have found alternatives to the services they (the lords) provided. Peasants consequently could not risk over-involvement with the outside world for fear of losing what the lord supplied. Of course, the extent of the lords' effective control would depend upon the scope of their hold on, and their degree of monopoly of, the resources and upon the primacy of those resources in the villages' economy. Villages would vary according to whether there was total landlord dominance, total absence thereof, or competing lords with no one possessing an overall monopoly.

The persistence of the lords' dominance is interpreted as reflecting the lack of visible alternatives open to the peasants themselves. In a regime of dispersed power the 'State' would not exist as a repository of resources for those in the lower level of the social order, for the government would be either unable or unwilling to penetrate the lord's domain with its rudimentary bureaucratic tools. In fact, it would most frequently be found that the State had an implicit alliance with the landlords.

Villages dominated by freeholders (allodial) might be equally inward-orientated, although this behaviour has to be seen for the most part as an adaptive response to their relationship with those socially and spatially removed classes which controlled the State and to the insecurities of outside market participation. The traditional State often had neither the bureaucratic capabilities nor the will to perform a variety of services within villages, and tended therefore to have a limited, indeed single-stranded, relationship with individual villages mainly through its representative in the form of the tax collector.[34] 'Diagrammatically the villages are small circles representing organic functioning communities. The state is the centre, linked to each village by a line representing imperium.'[35] Villagers in this situation are then supposed to have seen the State as essentially exploitative and consequently to have withdrawn from any participation other than that which was absolutely necessary. When this introspective *mentalité* obtains (and in this allodial and landlord-dominated villages are believed not to differ from one another), minimax solutions, maximizing control over the environment with a minimum of risk, are believed to predominate and consequently create a barren soil for the absorption of innovative modes of behaviour.[36]

Both the freeholding and the landlord-dominated, inward-looking communities are supposedly characterized by a range of behavioural practices that restrain individual freedoms. Land may in a corporate community be available only to those born there and marriage may be highly endogamous. Great stress will be placed on the household economy as a self-sufficient enterprise, so that the risk of dependence upon others is minimized.[37] Alliances with kin or fictive kin (i.e. godparents) would be given priority for mobilization in the event, for instance, of intra-village disputes.[38] Prestige within the village will be enhanced by expenditure on ceremonial occasions, weddings, burials or events associated with a local religious cult. However, in dissipating surpluses to gain internal status few resources are left to the wealthy to forge outside alliances. Limitations on work (i.e. backward-bending supply curves of labour) are another means of ensuring that social differentiation is contained within strictly defined limits. Behaviour patterns which superficially have the appearance of reflecting perpetual internal conflict – gossip, slander and criticism – may fundamentally be serving to maintain conformity to internal, inward-orientated norms. However, these behaviour patterns themselves coexist with others that help to promote tranquillity and cohesion –

such as godparentage, endogamy and reciprocal gift-giving. Likewise, recourse to outside law-enforcing and dispute-resolving agencies is rare, and internal village mechanisms are used. Even in the matter of external relations such as the meeting of tax payments, the village as a whole is taxed so that the wealthy can take a disproportionate share in relation to their poorer neighbours. Indeed, we have in listing the above parameters presented most of the essential traits regarded as highly characteristic of the closed corporate community.[39]

Movement from inward to outward orientation is most likely to occur when there are forces at hand which consistently and systematically make it impossible for a large number of the village's households to balance their accounts. Imperialism and neo-colonialism have been seen, in much current work, as forces promoting such changes; however, any development that enables the centres to transfer wealth with growing efficiency from the peripheries would be likely to produce similar results.[40] Demographic growth – so characteristic of many non-European areas in the last century, creating pressure on resources and disturbing the balanced relationship of heirs to vacant properties along with the withdrawal of landlord patrons, who themselves become more enmeshed in the wider status system and no longer undertake paternalistic services, thereby hitting hard at the peasant's household balance sheet – is proposed as a major factor helping to destabilize intra-village social relations.[41] Increasing dominance of the centre in the form of tax demands – which may indeed promote greater market involvement of the peasant agriculturalist, this in turn tending to increase the penetration of villages by urban-based wholesalers – helps to create the essential preconditions for ultimate incorporation of the village.[42] Stress can be relieved by out-migration, changes in the land tenure system and a decline in neighbourly commitments as the upwardly mobile, outward-orientated begin to see the village moral economy as oppressive and stifling. Severe economic crises (i.e. harvest failures) lead to greater social and economic differentiation and a reduced ability on the part of the disadvantaged to apply sanctions against the village elites' outside involvements.[43] Consequently, the latter individuals experience an increased security from their greater participation in an alternative, externally located status system.[44] Inevitably the outward-orientated – or, as Wolf terms them, the 'nation-oriented' – are drawn from these groups which have traditionally produced the brokers mediating between the village and the outside world: those which are familiar with the channels of communication and patterns of outside behaviour, so that they can operate effectively in the new milieu.[45]

A stylized presentation of these patterns and processes is attempted in Figure 1.[46] At either extreme in the differential allocation of power where the degree of external relations is low, a community is likely to stifle the emergence of outward-orientated individuals or groups. It is in the middle range of the spectrum of the allocation of power – that is, where there is a somewhat unequal distribution of power – that some peasants may have sufficient resources, given proper opportunities, to establish links with groups or institutions outside the village. It is in the middle range that some villagers can withstand the weakened sanctions of both peers and patrons. Indeed it would not be too great an oversimplification or generalization to state that the early modern English historians to whom we have referred would see many English villages at the beginning of the seventeenth century within that same middle range exhibited in Figure 1 by area X. Of course, it is vital for these arguments of early modernists that proof can be marshalled to show that in the preceding centuries English villages were disproportionately encountered in the categories exhibited by types Y and Z in Figure 1. I shall

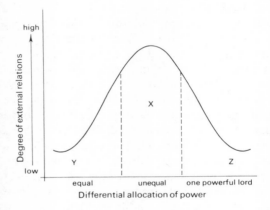

Figure 1

return later to a consideration of the evidence bearing on this fundamental question, but before I do so it is necessary to reflect on certain issues raised by this account and analysis of incorporation which rests on seeing change as a linear and evolutionary process.

The nineteenth-century shadow on the 'community debate'

Eric Stokes once wrote that 'the science of history proceeds no doubt as the detailed criticism of sociological generalisations, but of generalisations so rudimentary and so little analysed that they constitute primitive archetypal images lurking in the background of the historian's consciousness rather than a formed system.'[47] These words, written admittedly in a quite different context from my present discussion, nonetheless alert us to the way in which the stark dichotomies of nineteenth-century sociological thought continue to haunt the recesses of our own thinking. Perhaps no debate reflects these issues better than that conducted during the nineteenth century on the village community in terms of unilinear evolutionary schemes and supported by the reckless use of the comparative method – a debate with a remarkable capacity to recur up to the present day and with only superficial differences to distinguish it from its nineteenth-century predecessor. As Clive Dewey notes, in the nineteenth century the concept of the village community 'played shuttlecock to radical and conservative battledores'[48] and, possibly because of its very vagueness, it 'could be many things to many men', depending for instance 'whether one emphasises its economic or its political aspect', for 'in historiography there was a liberal ancient village and a socialist one'.[49]

For what have been termed 'romantic conservatives' the village community's ability to resist change stemmed from its high degree of internal cohesion allowing it to present a bold front to any threat from the outside. For as long as it was hierarchically organized division did not generate conflict between classes, for a mutual dependence founded on both economic necessity and ideology continually reknit the threads torn by any such discord as was only a natural product of close residential propinquity. As Dewey puts it, 'An equal yet stable and harmonious society: what could be more attractive to the conservative mentality?'[50] Furthermore we should note just how similar, at least in its surface appearances, the conservative's image of community was to the unincorporated village I have discussed above.

A diametrically opposed interpretation of the village community emerged in the writings of the utilitarians, who were interested in 'progress' not in 'order', and especially not in order founded on stifling individual enterprise by communal restraint. The maintenance of social stability, for this school, could be provided by the State and above all by the market and needed no suppression of individuality in the claustrophobic atmosphere of the village.[51] How close once again does the incorporated village appear to the utilitarian world, where individual ownership and separate cultivation are founded upon a common legal code, and the provision of goods and services is provided by the market.

This over-simple categorization of views was anyway not to survive the comings and goings of ideological fashions in the nineteenth century. First of all the rather neat dichotomy I have sketched above was complicated by the intervention, if not overtly intentional, of the 'Germanist' historians, E. A. Freeman, W. Stubbs and J. R. Green. Freeman portrays the village community in essentially political terms as a 'face-to-face democratic society' – an ethos that had little to do with its being a producer's cooperative.[52] Indeed Stubbs saw co-ownership as a drag on progress and, by beginning his *Constitutional History* with Tacitus' remarks about the Germanic peoples, asserted that liberty was rooted in the soil from which those people emerged.[53] Green took this even further, referring to the assertion of independence in the Germanic spirit by quoting Tacitus' reference to their separate houses:

'they live apart, each by himself . . . each dweller within the settlement was jealous of his own isolation and independence . . .'.[54]

As John Burrows notes, the entry of Sir George Gomme to this debate with the publication in 1890 of *The Village Community*, in which he is contemptuously sceptical of the Germanist ideas and promotes a view of societal development that has continued to possess irrepressible power and influence over men's minds, brings us sharply into the sphere of influence associated with later nineteenth-century theories of evolution. For, according to Gomme, in early times 'individual ownership in land is not recognised' and social change is essentially founded upon the disentangling of individual from communal property.[55] Gomme's ideas form part of an interpretation of societal development which is most usually associated with H. S. Maine. The study of the village community consequently became an integral part of the debate that was concerned with the differences between so-called 'progressive' and 'unprogressive' peoples.[56] Maine was a prominent Victorian critic of democracy and he saw his work on village communities as instrumental in showing how democratic and socialist communities were inherently repressive and stagnant.[57] In attempting to show that mankind had no natural claim to individualism, he portrayed the latter as a state or stage achieved only by those progressive nations within which creative minorities and free competition had been able to thrive. A central thesis of *Ancient Law* was that early society begins with the group (in particular the family) and that the early law is concerned not with individuals but with the family; the family in early law is synonymous with its head, whose authority subsumes each of its members, whose dependence is never lost except on the patriarch's death. As Peter Stein notes, this theory had for Maine the advantage of explaining certain features of early Roman law, on which Maine was a leading authority: for example, the preference for agnation, the tracing of descent exclusively through males, rather than cognation and the practice of adopting sons from another family. In regard to property Maine denied that early law recognized individual ownership, for in early Rome, he argued, there is evidence of a 'family' ownership before the law acknowledged the proprietary rights of the *pater familias*.[58] But for the bulk of his evidence on early property law Maine had recourse to Indian village communities which he considered exemplified the expansion of the family into a large group of co-owners holding the village land in common. He wrote: 'the village community of India is at once an organised patriarchal society and an assemblage of co-proprietors', and in an interesting, and for his time perfectly acceptable, use of analogy he was prepared to see Europe's past (and by definition England's) preserved in the Indian present.[59] Likewise, Maine stated that the Russian village appeared to be very nearly an exact repetition of the Indian community.[60]

We are offered in Maine's work a simple but powerful and enduring set of dichotomies which as polarities are linked by processes of irreversible, sequential change: for instance, from patriarchy to liberty, from political organization based upon kinship to territorial propinquity, from collective property to individual property, and above all from societies founded upon status to those founded on contract.

We should not forget that Maine was ostensibly concerned to establish general principles in the development of early law. Yet it was in this area that we observe the most effective and perhaps highly damaging criticisms of his scheme. F. W. Maitland argued that some of Maine's most famous and oft-quoted theses were not justified when applied to the earliest English law of which we have knowledge. Referring most definitely to Maine, Maitland wrote: 'it has been a commonplace amongst English writers that the family rather than the individual was the "unit" of ancient law'. On the matter of the absence of the agnatic principle in early English kinship Maitland is quite clear. He writes: 'so soon as we begin to get rules about inheritance and blood-feud, the dead man's kinsfolk, consist in part of persons related to him through his mother'. The same person in Maitland's view could have belonged to different kinship groups. 'If the law were to treat the clan as an unit for any purposes whatever, this would surely be the purpose of *wer* and blood-feud', but it does not do so.[61] Anglo-Saxon society was not therefore composed of patriarchal clans founded upon agnation.[62]

Maitland's views on the applicability of Maine's ideas on communal ownership to the early English village community were equally dismissive. Referring to early medieval English village landholdings he wrote: 'Great pains had been taken to make the division equitable . . . it does not point to a communistic division of the fruits . . . the individual's hold upon his strips developed very rapidly into an inheritable and partible ownership . . .'[63]

Not content to deny the proprietary ideals that sustained Maine's theories of the village community, Maitland argued for a social patterning in early English village society that dismissed the possibility of villages' having been closely knit bodies of agnatically related kinsmen. Marital exogamy and inheritance ensured that relationships (presumably involving kin) between members of different villages would have been closer than those between co-habitants of the same village. Furthermore, he believed it wrong to view the village as a self-governing unit, for the village court was dominated by oligarchic peasant proprietors below whom were to be found a mass of cottars, artisans and servants.[64]

By the end of the nineteenth century, when Maitland appeared to have dealt a deathly blow to Maine's ideas, the ideological meanings of individualism and collectivism and their political concomitants had changed sides in a highly dramatic manner. The harmonious village ideal of the earlier conservatives had now been grasped by radicals who saw it as a lost Utopia. For conservatives were now to be seen as proponents of the sanctity of property and freedom of contracts. Individualism and its accepted inequalities took on for them the hallmarks of progress. These changing viewpoints were corollaries of much broader changes in late Victorian society and economy. For as soon as *laissez-faire* became the established economic system conservatives and radicals, in Dewey's words, were 'forced to exchange labels: proponents of laissez faire became conservative apologists of the status quo: critics of laissez faire became radical malcontents'.[65] For late Victorian utilitarians every institution was simply an agglomeration of individuals, and we must at the very least see the rigour, length and repetitiveness of Maitland's attempts to expunge communalism from early English law as a reflection, even in this 'virtuous' historian, of the dominant ideologies of his time.

We should note too the considerable hostility in the late nineteenth century that historians (including eminent historians of the law) then displayed in their attitudes to the developing school of British sociology. They associated sociology with biological reductionism, inaccuracy (both criticisms that Maitland addressed to Maine) and Spencer. Maitland indeed had much to contribute to a sociological history but was reluctant to venture beyond the insular confines of English legal history. It has been suggested that Sidgwick had been responsible for warning Maitland off sociological idealism, particularly its insistence on the social group (whether the community or the State was seen as the primary unit) as the appropriate level for the understanding of man and his history and its tradition of speaking of the institutions of the social and cultural world as the objectification of 'spirit' without the need to reduce human actions and beliefs to purposeful acts of human will.[66]

Maitland's triumph over Maine, however, was primarily confined to the rather circumscribed arena of legal history. Dewey may be correct in asserting that public interest declined in these debates and that the village community was assigned to the 'arcane preserves of the professional historian and anthropologist', but it did not become a more neutral or a more ideologically sterile construct in the hands of these disciplines.[67] Certain of Maine's views lived on outside England in the ideas developed by Tönnies, whom some regard as his most ardent admirer. In his work *Gemeinschaft und Gesellschaft*, published in 1887, Tönnies developed his argument from Maine's treatment of progressive societies and portrayed a conflict that arose from the co-existence of two distinctive forms of social grouping.[68] One such grouping, *Gemeinschaft*, is a community or fellowship of those sharing, to some degree, a common way of life: for example, a family or guild. The other, *Gesellschaft*, is a limited relationship based on rational will and the desire of the parties through 'contracts' to achieve a specific purpose. They provide a tool for characterizing relationships supposed to predominate in two quite opposite categories of society. Some of these views were preserved and further developed by Tönnies' younger contemporary, Max Weber, and may have re-entered English historical scholarship from that particular locus. They are certainly apparent in the approach to social change encountered in the writings of R. H. Tawney and of a line of historians upon whom his influence was great and to whom we have already referred. Indeed we have in this pedigree an important link connecting much recent work in English economic and social history of the Tudor and Stuart periods with issues which were current in late nineteenth-century discourse involving history and sociology and which, though then disappearing in England, continued to hold a prominent place in the mainstream of continental European debates in social theory.

It is not correct, however, to assume that nineteenth-century influences on the approach to medieval English village society waned, since the latter century's flame was rekindled by a Harvard sociologist, G. C. Homans, who was much influenced by certain models of the relationship between family forms and village social structure that had strong connections with the ideas of the French social engineer, Frédéric Le Play.[69] It would be no easy task to connect Le Play with issues we have so far discussed, though we may note his distaste for the individualistic legislation of post-Revolutionary governments in France and the disturbance of old values produced by rapid industrialization. He combined the attributes of both the romantic radical and the conservative in his work but, like Maine, he did see a necessary connection between social change and its reflection in family forms. He saw both the patriarchal and the stem family as older and more stable than the nuclear and simple families which he believed to be growing in importance and which he viewed as symptomatic of a general moral decay. Unlike Maine, however, he appears not to have regarded individualism as the hallmark of a progressive society, considering it a force detrimental to authority in the family and to stability in social relationships.[70]

What Homans did, in his turn, was to give research in medieval village society a much firmer grounding, basing his views on original sources that had been produced in the villages or, more specifically, in the manors of the time. His geographical coverage of village societies was somewhat lop-sided, being concerned almost entirely with 'champion' England where manor and vill were more likely to have been coterminous and where open-field farming was more fully developed. It was an account which sought to analyse the family forms of full-, half- and quarter-virgaters in terms of Le Play's concept of the stem family, and to understand that family form through the application of a structural–functional anthropological framework to the village community. Homans, in his interpretation of social relations in the medieval English village community, described an ethos in which individualistic actions were seen to have been dominated by collective ideals or communal behaviour, designed to maintain the closely woven fabric of society in a state of social balance. Private initiative, interests and responsibility were seen to have been subordinated to the rights, privileges and interests of the group of village residents. He states:

In illustrating the theory of the social system from what we know about English villages of the thirteenth century, the factor of mutual dependence will be considered at an obvious level, that is, the mutual dependence of the institutions which make up the society. For one thing, each of the dispositions of the champion husbandry was intricately dependent on all the others. If we are describing the common herd we are at once forced to speak of the hayward elected by the community of the village, of the hedges set up around the open field, of the common fields themselves, of the rotation of crops practised on them and so forth. In the same way, each of the customs of the village family; the descent of land to one son, the marriage of that son, the fate of his children not inheriting and the provision made for widows and widowers – each was adapted to all the others so as to form a consistent whole.[71]

Indeed he sees peasant sentiment concerning the rights of all family members in land embedded deeply in the tenets of customary law which were monitored in the local tribunals of the hall-moot as well as reflecting the notion of village society as a collection of shareholders.[72] Although he was aware of evidence indicating differences in wealth, he believed that neighbourliness consistently ironed out potential division. His portrayal of village society is not, however, based upon a detailed analysis of any one community but is essentially eclectic, utilizing numerous cases from manor court rolls to weave an idealized picture of the peasant group.

It can be said that it was left to a group of historians now known as the 'Toronto School' and associated in particular with J. A. Raftis, to recreate and indeed extend Homans' work with an enthusiasm for data manipulation not previously seen.[73] This more detailed work on individual villages has resulted in a series of publications dating back to 1964, all of which are founded on a specific methodology designed to produce an intensive reconstruction of the activities of individuals and family groups as witnessed in the proceedings of the manorial court. However, the 'Toronto School' has also espoused a conceptual approach to the nature of village society which, certainly in its earlier work, has given great emphasis to the community's harmonious and organic qualities – much in the style of Homan's original contribution. All the published work of this school has been focused upon a group of Huntingdonshire manors whose medieval archives have survived in large measure because they formed the manorial records of the Abbots of Ramsey. Two individual studies from this group are worthy of further consideration insofar as they indicate the range, and indeed the markedly different interpretative options, presented by data which are remarkable mainly for their similarities. In the two studies of E. B. DeWindt and E. Britton on the villages of Holywell-cum-Needingworth and Broughton respectively a common methodology, which is far from unproblematic, is adopted whereby individuals are placed into families that are ranked principally by their degree of

involvement in communal affairs: 'A' families were those that regularly produced village office holders; 'B' families only occasionally produced such
officers, while 'C' families never did so; a final category, 'D', was used for
isolated individuals and known outsiders mentioned in the records. In their
analysis of the social relations between these family groups DeWindt and
Britton use common indicators of which the most important is the personal
pledge, a system of providing surety for the fulfilment of a court-imposed
obligation. A person required to appear in court, pay a fine, repay a debt or
perform such other obligations would be required to provide pledges who,
on pain of a financial penalty, would ensure the fulfilment of the obligation.
Critical in this analysis is the assumption that the choice of pledge was a
decision in the hands of the individual concerned.

DeWindt discovered very little pledging between kin and a predominance
of pledging within the strata in which individuals had been placed. When
pledging occurred outside or across these groupings it was discovered that
leading families (A-type) pledged for families of lower status. DeWindt was
inclined to play down any suggestion that within-group pledging indicated a
stratified or class-based structuring of village society, and emphasized instead
the dependence of lower on higher status pledges. This finding was given
greater stress in as much as it denoted, in DeWindt's view, the presence of
'networks of co-operation arising from and in service of common needs'.
DeWindt clearly chooses an interpretative option firmly within the tradition
exemplified by Homans when he adopts a 'harmony model of social organisation' – property transactions, even debts are thought in his interpretation
to reflect a 'spirit of co-operation'. Furthermore, he takes the curious view
that A-type families are prominent not because of their better economic
resources but because their members have a 'competence to take responsibility
and assume leadership in the village'.[74]

Britton's study of Broughton is structured around an account of social
behaviour where rank and hierarchy are given pride of place. By observing
social interactions involving in particular pledges, debts and land-exchanges,
Britton finds a degree of cohesion in A-type families so intense as to suggest
to him a class consciousness. He also draws considerable attention to conflict
between these families and individuals in C-type families (between the 'haves'
and the 'have-nots') which reached a high pitch in years of dearth and harvest
failure. We would appear to have in these two geographically close villages
within the same monastic estate two communities that represent, if we care
so to label them, Tönnies' *Gemeinschaft* (Holywell) and *Gesellschaft* (Broughton) – polar opposites in the matter of their social relationships.[75]

Both these studies, in common with all those emanating from the Toronto
School, are characterized by an absence, indeed a deliberate omission, from
their analysis of forces external to the village and/or manorial society. This
is not to suggest that they treat the village as a closed system, for they have

been loudly insistent upon the importance of migration between villages and from village to town as facts of life in the medieval English countryside. However, they have incurred the pointed criticisms of, in particular, Hilton and his students, for a reluctance to incorporate into their arguments a consideration of the fact that village communities were units within a larger feudal mode of production and as a consequence had to contend with the very real pressures exerted upon them by landlords.[76]

It is perhaps symptomatic of Hilton's approach to these issues that he has never undertaken a specific community study himself. Furthermore the wide-ranging nature of his interests makes it difficult to categorize his arguments. Nonetheless in his writings, extending over the period since the Second World War, certain themes recur with sufficient regularity to indicate a specific position on the medieval English village community. Indeed it is not a difficult task to identify in Hilton's writings on village society and economy a penchant for presenting them very much in the style of the political scientist's portrayal of an inward-orientated community, the product of the village's existence in a world of politically powerful lordship and a relative weakness or indeed deliberate lack of involvement on the part of the Crown and central government in the landlord/tenant relationship. However, Hilton would doubtless resist any attempt to have his work used as part of any general theory of the peasantry and the village community, as he has always been careful to highlight what he regards as the historically specific conditions of European feudalism.[77] For instance, unlike views encountered in much of the literature of the 'incorporationist' school he would certainly see 'collective action' (a euphemism for the class struggle) on the part of the villagers as an important factor in the promotion of change as the penetration of these villages by central government or larger national or international markets.

Hilton is prepared to admit that the medieval village was by no means invariably a community of equals and he is not inclined to disregard discord. But, he states, 'there was social conflict during the period but it was first of all conflict between tenants and lords, secondly between tenants and officials'.[78] He insists on emphasizing the collective element in agriculture, particularly where manor court and village coincided, and feels that the court imposed common rather than individual pursuits. His views are understandable given the Midland England context with which so much of his research career has been concerned. He insists on the primacy of the peasant household as the fundamental unit of economic activity;[79] he emphasizes the way both the lord and what he terms 'conservative elements' in the village community worked to prevent the concentration of properties in the hands of the few, using the courts to break up engrossed holdings.[80] Wage labour he regards as socially diffuse with a strong preference on the part of villagers for the trading of 'use' values through inter-household contracts.[81] He notes the presence of a self-conscious sense of community in the use in the documents of expressions such as *communitas villae* or *vicini* and in the promulgation of by-laws produced *cum assensu omnium tenentium liberorum et nativorum.*[82] He sees further evidence for a collective mentality in instances in the sources from the eleventh to the end of the fourteenth centuries of whole villages or groups of villagers taking demesnes at farm from estate landlords.[83] He notes how the community could 'crystallize' through the external demands imposed upon it by the Crown for tax payments.[84] Indeed, in Hilton's view, the *villata* were fiscal units where, although the tax-gathering responsibility may have rested in an individual county with the sheriff, there is little doubt that local responsibility for collection fell upon the leaders of the village community (who, after 1334, had the exclusive responsibility for raising the fixed sums in the lay subsidies). But, for Hilton, a far greater force in promoting a sense of community came through constant collective resistance to seigneurial authority, and especially to increased seigneurial pressures in the thirteenth century, in what he refers to as an ongoing 'guerilla war'.[85] Of course for Hilton this collective sense reaches its apogee in the events of 1381. Indeed Hilton would see his work and that of others who write about the matters on which villagers took common action as 'reacting against earlier theories of peasant individualism which had in their turn been reactions against unsupported nineteenth century theories about village communism'.[86]

Hilton has been aware of certain problems that these displays of collective resistance pose for the student of the medieval village community. For instance, the potential leaders of collective resistance were most likely represented by village notables – those whom Hilton would call 'the elite of the well-to-do husbandmen' – without whose cooperation the lordship was unmanageable. These individuals were potentially capable at any moment in time of being pulled in more than one direction.[87] They were mediators insofar as they staffed the juries of inquest which would decide upon custom and adjudicate in disputes. When on presentment juries they would decide who would be indictable for offences against the seigneur, and as tithing men they had responsibility – albeit refracted through their own and the wider community's interest – to the sheriff's tourn. The conflicts that these various obligations might bring about were on occasion considerable. It is not clear whether this group saw their interests served at all times in promoting the cause of the wider community, which is somewhat difficult to envisage as a coherently structured group.

Hilton's sensitivity to these difficulties is displayed in his reflections on what he sees as a decline in the cohesive force of the village. While he admits that the demise of the manor as a functioning institution in the fifteenth century can be easily exaggerated, he remarks that one 'cannot fail to be struck by the relative lack of life in the institution after the middle of the century'.[88] In part he sees this as having to do with a diminution in the power of landlords in a land-abundant situation with smaller and more mobile populations which had become more differentiated by the growth of yeoman graziers and demense farmers holding by leasehold tenure. Certain processes thereby removed the 'kulak' peasant family from the scene either as a mediator or as a potential leader of resistance. For Hilton, then, the village community was clearly declining a full century before the later sixteenth-century decay attributed to it by other scholars though a century *after* the date preferred by the 'Toronto School'.[89] One wonders, however, whether the community's decay (like its resilience, in Hilton's interpretation) is heavily dependent upon its social reification as a unit for the waging of the medieval rural class struggle. For in Hilton's Marxisant analysis, which is founded (laudably) on an attempt to view the village community in a wider social and economic system, there appears to be, as in so many of the interpretations that find their origins in nineteenth-century theoretical discussions, a notion of change as a once and for all affair: first we have communities and then we do not. We may argue that Hilton's conclusions to some extent derive from the partial nature of his approach, which is nonetheless more holistic in character than the detached treatment of rural communities in the work of the 'Toronto School'.

We come finally to a very recent contribution to this debate which, for all its self-proclaimed intention to break away from the social theories of the nineteenth century and their approaches to change, is still firmly ensconced within those paradigms. Macfarlane's 'audacious' book *The Origins of English Individualism*, in which he portrays the inhabitants of the English medieval countryside as self-assertive individualists, is founded upon the thesis that the economic individualism we associate with the modern world is to be found in England at least as far back as the thirteenth century.[90] He draws heavily, although far from exclusively, upon the history of English tenurial law and common law and, occasionally with disarming modesty, says that in all this he is only following the paths broken by Maitland and Stubbs, who argued a case for the English legal and constitutional systems being firmly in place by 1283 and 1307 respectively. Insofar as an important part of Macfarlane's notion of 'Englishness' derives from the uniqueness of the common law, he is promoting an avowedly 'Maitlandian' argument, part of which, as I suggested above, needs to be more fully assessed with due attention to the context within which it was fashioned. Furthermore there are times when Macfarlane, like the nineteenth-century Germanists, becomes heavily dependent upon the comments of Tacitus to find some origin for 'the peculiarities of the English'.[91] This is not the place to conduct a detailed assessment of this book beyond reflecting on the incompatibility of its arguments with the notion of a medieval community which was to be wholly dismantled in the course of what has been termed the 'parturition of "modernization"'.[92]

We can, however, pose again a question that has been asked of a very basic assumption in Macfarlane's general thesis. His concept of individualism encompasses a view of human beings both as economically autonomous entities and as persons possessing a perception of themselves as autonomous units within the social world. For, as Mark Goldie neatly demonstrates, although Macfarlane is concerned with demolishing the Marxian model of a great transformation, he ironically accepts one fundamental element of it: that the ideological superstructure follows the pattern of the economic substructure.[93] Should it necessarily be accepted that, if economic individualism dates from the thirteenth century, political and philosophical individualism also formed an integral part of the package? Indeed Macfarlane supposes that if the law and the litigation revealed in the sources are individualistic then the economy must also have been; he thereby assumes that the superstructure reflects the substructure and only the substructure.

In this discussion so far I have remarked upon the degree to which arguments have tended to be couched in terms of oscillation between extreme viewpoints. For certain proponents of the syndicalist position had exalted the community and had minimized the importance of both the individual and the relationship between the community and the State if not of lordship. All four elements coexisted and affected each other to the extent that it becomes a positive distortion to discuss them separately. From all flanks the autonomy of the community was subject to pressures; from the independence of its constituent parts and from the intervention of the State at the various levels at which it crystallized in the administrative hierarchy connecting the village to the king's court.

Institutional autonomy in medieval England: some geographical issues

When I referred, as I did above, to the distortions brought about by the compartmentalization introduced into so many of the discussions, I had no intention of underestimating the very great difficulties in the adoption of a deliberately holistic approach. In part the nature of the sources makes for a high degree of segmentation in the investigation of institutions. For instance, it is very easy to see why the views of Maitland should be so firmly insistent on the presence of a legal code in the twelfth century that was noteworthy for the prominence in it of individual rights, given that his career as a legal historian was so preoccupied with the 'common law' of the freeholding population with access to the *curia regis*. Likewise, Hilton has approached these problems using evidence originating for the most part in the records of 'customary law', which concerned customary tenants in their relations with their landlords. Unlike their early modern counterparts, who are now used to mobilizing a range of records from the various levels in the administrative hierarchy, medieval historians of village communities have often been lulled misguidedly into a one-source approach to the behaviour of individuals.[94] One reason often given to account for this is that a manor court of the thirteenth or fourteenth century subsumed within its purview administrative functions that were devolved in the sixteenth century upon a variety of ecclesiastical, secular, parochial, county and State agencies. This is a highly debatable viewpoint, and it is interesting that historians of Anglo-Saxon England, with a far less segmented body of evidence (and more importantly, far less of it), have tended in many instances to produce an account of that society and its component parts which appears more integrated than any that emerges from accounts produced of later centuries.[95]

Indeed it will eventually be worth our while to extend our thoughts back to Anglo-Saxon England as part of a longer-term consideration of the process of 'incorporation' depicted by students of early modern English communities. We have already noted the crucial role believed by this school to have been played by the 'middling sort' who acted as brokers between communities and the larger society. Wrightson, for instance, believes that because of the positions they held they were automatically provided with the task of 'defining the terms on which external influences were incorporated into the fabric of the local social system'.[96]

It is in considering their role as local administrators, law enforcers and managers of social morality that the argument about the 'middling sort' has been most thoroughly elaborated. To understand this we need to specify the ways in which individuals and groups related to the law and its processes in later Tudor and early Stuart periods. Prosecutions, for instance, could be initiated in a number of ways: by individual indictments made by private members of the community; by public presentment by a hundredal presentment jury; by a jury of substantial freeholders – the grand jury – sworn to present all such 'crimes' committed in their county as were listed in their charge; by certain individuals, such as petty constables or surveyors of highways, who could initiate presentments, although compared with private plaints and the various forms of jury presentment these accounted for a small proportion of all prosecutions. In fact, in overseeing this system the Justices of the Peace operated at a noticeably far remove from the sites of the infringements of the innumerable statutes that then rained down upon the provincial localities from central government. The Justices would require high constables of the county hundreds to order the petty constables and presentment juries of townships (leets) and villages to present offenders, thereby leaving final responsibility to 'officers' in the lower levels of the system – a feature of the system noted and only slightly exaggerated in J. H. Baker's statement that the responsibility for prosecution fell on the 'public at large'.[97] For the system to work with reasonable efficiency required a high level of participation (i.e. an innate refusal to bureaucratize the law and its operation), and, primarily because of this distinctive feature, the legal processes displayed a highly discretionary character. As Wrightson notes, constables and jurymen were placed in a difficult mediating position between their 'own communities' and the law.[98]

The flexibility implicit in a system of indictment operating in a society without an organized police force, county prosecuting solicitors or a Director of Public Prosecutions extended to and was repeated in the mode of trial. Under the common law, trial by jury implied a public inquest by twelve persons sworn to find the truth, before whom the accuser and the accused pleaded their respective cases and provided evidence. In theory these jurors, as judges of both 'fact' and 'law', could place their own interpretation on unpopular law and could engage in the kind of 'pious perjury' that would produce false acquittals quite contrary to the evidence.[99] Of course, there is another side to this insofar as a jury, whether of presentment or of trial, could equally well reflect interests in society contrary to those of the person indicted or accused.

It has been amply demonstrated through a comparison of prosecutions handled by J.P.s in seventeenth-century Essex and Lancashire that presentment juries could either operate mainly as passive instruments for the settling of disputes arising in their localities or fulfil a more aggressively regulative role in attempting social control. In the early seventeenth century both the overall prosecution rate and the level of regulative prosecutions were far higher in the Essex than in the Lancashire quarter sessions.[100] In Lancashire, because of the geographically fragmented nature of its quarter sessions (i.e. there were four distinct courts of quarter sessions), the hundredal presentment juries were also the grand juries and were composed of minor gentry rather than villagers, whereas in Essex hundredal juries were for the most part dominated by village notables. In consequence the Lancashire juries were far less likely to take initiatives of their own or respond to government directives than were their Essex counterparts. To operate effectively in the community, therefore, in matters to do with alehouse offences, vagrants and the illegal erection of cottages, central government needed both the means and the willingness of persons in the peripheries to present offenders. Differences in the degrees to which the institutions of presentment extended deeply into the localities themselves largely determined the composition of offences appearing in the quarter sessions, producing statistics which constitute a set of data highly ambiguous for any meaningful geographical study of village 'petty' crime.

Wrightson's argument gives great stress, as we have seen, to the growth of a willingness on the part of the upper echelons and outward-orientated inhabitants of seventeenth-century villages to deal with local behaviour they found to be threatening or contravening the moral values they now shared with those who had influenced them from outside their communities.

8888

8888888

164   Richard M. Smith

However, he realizes that, given the pressures needed and the countervailing tensions set up, local jurors and petty constables would have had to exercise their roles with great caution and a not inconsiderable reluctance. Indeed this points to a large role for an informal resolution of disputes at a local level to avoid the actual involvement of more formal legal measures. Studies pointing to a growth in 'crime' in years of economic difficulty – particularly those concentrated in the period stretching approximately from 1590 to 1630 – do not interpret these developments as indicating an explosion of lawlessness.[101] Rather, they are seen as indicating a greater willingness of people to prosecute or to interpret what were once customary norms (such as the right to remove wood or food from another's property) in good times as an act of theft in years of economic difficulty. Indeed they indicate once again the extent to which willingness to present or to prosecute was important in determining the nature of the evidence at the historian's disposal.

In fact such evidence is highly suggestive of the extent to which the village displayed the characteristics of a 'moral community'. For Ingram has effectively argued that in seventeenth-century Wiltshire arbitration mechanisms in both civil suits and cases of criminal misdemeanour helped to restrain a quick resort to litigation and were not necessarily dependent upon judicial initiatives.[102] For example, gentlemen or ministers figured prominently in this role and were in a position to expose an individual who was not willing to accept a reasonable settlement to the rigours of neighbourly disapproval. What is of particular concern to our discussion of the moral community is that not all categories of criminal were equally able to take advantage of the informal means of extra-curial settlement. Ingram presents interesting evidence to suggest that informal dispute resolution worked in favour of local people and against outsiders. For instance, because of a geographically specific definition of 'crime' local people who were short of necessities had at their disposal certain means of acquiring food or fuel which were unlikely to lead to felony prosecutions. Over half of those indicted for theft at Wiltshire quarter sessions in the three sample years from the first quarter of the seventeenth century were people apprehended at some distance from their permanent residence, and of those parties living within a six-mile radius of the location of the crime only one in every six was from the same parish as his indicter. Furthermore the conviction rate of those indicted persons in the sample reflected the impact of geographical propinquity in a striking manner; 93 per cent of the 'outsiders' were convicted but almost a third of the cases involving 'neighbours' ended in an acquittal. Neighbourliness was both a factor restricting an individual's willingness to prosecute a case and also clearly a factor influencing a jury's judgement of guilt.[103]

In this deliberately brief consideration of the operation of legal processes involving early modern English villagers within the secular courts where they appeared both as litigants and as offenders, I have drawn attention to certain findings from recent work. First, I have noted the high level of participation of the populace as a whole both as prosecutors and officers of law-enforcement at the level of the village, hundred and quarter and petty sessions. Secondly, it should be noted that the initiative to implement a prosecution rested very much with persons outside the legal professions – presentment by local groups or juries was a major factor. Thirdly, the same dependence upon the unpaid amateur in the form of the trial jury characterized the procedures of judgement in both civil and criminal cases. Fourthly, a considerable part of the local court's work and that of its officers concerned the enforcing of regulative measures issued by central government. Fifthly, and perhaps of greatest significance, there was tremendous selectivity in applying the law at various levels in the hierarchy of local courts. This was an important factor making for abundant highly localized means of conflict resolution outside the courts and helping to promote a noticeably xeno-phobic pattern to indictments and convictions on the part of the villagers. Sixthly, and something of a paradox in the light of this apparent autonomy on the part of villagers and their own definition of crime, was the high degree of curial integration that characterized the system as a whole as it resounded to the beats sent out from its centre.

Can these features that we have isolated in the matter of the law and its perception and use by English village societies in the sixteenth and seventeenth centuries in any sense be seen as specific to that phase in English history? In asking this question we are obliged to consider certain fundamental features of the English legal system and to reflect on both their age and their mutability over time. In particular we should reflect on the comment made by Alan Harding that 'one of the perennial problems of government is geographical'.[104] Whether we discuss the eleventh or the sixteenth century we might ask how the King's wishes are transmitted to the localities without losing impetus on the way? How indeed is the King to oversee the enforce-ment of his orders from a distance? Historical geographers have by and large not perceived this particular problem to be worthy of attention beyond an occasional nod of recognition to the development of medieval administrative patterns in general accounts of the period or, more particularly, worrying about the niceties of change in that pattern as a niggling difficulty complicat-ing the straightforward mapping of data within the framework provided by these administrative units.

It would not be difficult to assemble a veritable host of historians who would argue passionately for England in the last two centuries of the Anglo-Saxon era as the most efficiently organized state in Europe – in V. H. Gal-braith's words 'a "national" state in the making'.[105] The growing strength of royal authority, especially in the phase of national unification under the West Saxon kings, is associated with such fundamental features of social development as the decline of the feud and of the functional significance of the wider kin group, both seen as incompatible with strong kingship.[106] Be this as it may, our interest in this discussion lies in the means by which the centralized unification was achieved. It would appear that one secret of this royal success rested in the ways in which Saxon monarchs were able to 'institutionalize' local communities in their own service.

Medieval archaeologists and historical geographers, by natural inclination, would note the tangible manifestations of the elaborate system of Saxon government in the remarkable forts of the 'Burghal Hidage';[107] numismatists would draw our attention to these centres as places where the astoundingly sophisticated coinage (with its frequent demonetizations) was produced.[108] However, these burghs served also as centres of royal administration where dues and services owed to the King from the surrounding shires were collected by the shire 'reeve' and where the ealdormen presided over the meetings of the local landholders in the shire-courts at which important announcements concerning royal proclamations and ordinances were made. It was in these shire courts that cases (usually to do with land held by the King's book) sent down from the witan were considered and judgements given. Edward the Confessor used a written and sealed declaration to these courts; this suggests that one of the most fundamental elements of the legal system – a form of action begun by a writ obtained from the King – was in existence if far from fully elaborated in the early eleventh century.[109] It was there, too, that evidence suggesting a rudimentary inquest jury was being employed, where the thegns of the shire would be asked by the King 'to pronounce for me the judgement' concerning persons who had infringed protected rights.[110]

At a lower level in the administrative hierarchy the hundreds or wapentakes fulfilled an equally important role in the operation of royal government. When information is first available from Wessex in the tenth century the hundreds appear as fiscal units dependent upon a royal manor where the King's taxes were collected, but during the reconquest of areas from the Norsemen were imposed artificially over very large tracts of country.[111] However, it was these units that were used by the English kings for the preservation of peace and the prevention of theft. In the tenth century we have a royal ordinance requiring that hundreds were to meet every four weeks for 'each man to do justice to another . . .'.[112] It was also ordered that the men of the hundred, under their leaders, were to pursue thieves, and that strange cattle could not be kept without the knowledge of 'the man in charge of the hundred or the man over the tithing'.[113] Furthermore each male member of the hundred over the age of twelve was expected to belong to a tithing, members of which were mutually responsible for their good behaviour and, if necessary, for accusing, arresting and producing any of their number found guilty of a crime.[114] Again, two features are apparent in the operation of the hundredal system; the strong emphasis on communical responsibility for presenting offenders against the King's peace and the mobilization of all men of the hundred and the tithing as agents of the Crown.

In many respects the phenomenon of Domesday Book itself remains ample testimony to the coherence given to Anglo-Saxon society by this administrative structure. As Galbraith noted, 'on almost every page of Domesday Book evidence of the vitality of the shire is to be found'.[115] For it was there that the Domesday Survey was put together and 'hammered out' in sessions of each county court, reinforced by the testimony of the relevant hundreds and representatives of each village (i.e. the reeve, the priest and six men) in the hundred. The evidence in the *Inquisitio Comitatus Cantabrigiensis* – the single, unique survival of the procedure followed in the Cambridgeshire part of 'circuit III' – indicates the information (and the form in which it was offered) provided by each of the sworn jurors from each of the hundreds of the county. In Galbraith's opinion, it indicates the required attendance of all the village representatives at the meetings of the county courts and brings out the true complexity of the task undertaken by the commissioners.[116] It suggests furthermore, although the point is incapable of absolute proof, that village representatives were thoroughly familiar with the procedures utilized by the commissioners; and this in turn has led some historians to believe that there were indeed Anglo-Saxon predecessors to William's great survey.[117] What we are suggesting is that many of the elements we singled out as characteristic of local government in sixteenth- and seventeenth-century England had crystallized by the second half of the eleventh century into something more developed than embryo-form. Without the survival of Domesday Book we would know relatively little of the likely structure and functioning of Anglo-Saxon local government. Indeed, that document's existence is in no sense fortuitous as its very construction depended fundamentally on the pre-existence of this striking Anglo-Saxon organizational system.

It is, however, something of a convention in the writings on legal developments in England to regard the late twelfth century as a phase of major innovation and indeed as the period within which the historical foundations of the common law can be located. Nonetheless powerful voices can be heard reminding us of the remarkable dependence of many of the so-called 'novelties of procedure' upon precedents set by the Anglo-Saxons.[118] There is much to recommend this view, given that William showed no wish to dismantle the administrative system he received at the Conquest. Indeed the units of government (from vill through hundred to county) which William employed in the construction of the Domesday Survey remained intact with only minor modifications until 1974.[119] What the Angevin reforms of Henry II did promote was a noticeable impetus towards greater centralization and a larger role in the nation's legal machinery for the *curia regis*.[120] Henry II may have done no more than invigorate the law, but the difference between what came after and what had been there before him was that he succeeded in giving the legal system a fixed identity. This was achieved by establishing set procedures: sending out the general eyre, the use of the returnable writ, and the employment of the jury both as a policing and as a judging agent on behalf of the Crown.[121]

Henry II built up a core of judges based on the *curia regis*, but the principle of the eyre revolved around the King sending his justices to the county and ordering the sheriff to have the county court summoned before them. The eyre commission was the highest and most comprehensive of the commissions given to itinerant justices, literally for all pleas, *ad omnia placita*. Undoubtedly the greatest contribution of the eyre to the administration of justice lay in the unifying influence exerted over the country at large by commissioners learned in the ways of central courts of justice, since they imposed the standards of the common law on the communities of the shire on their travels. Indeed this was the likely outcome of all forms of itinerant justice, of which the general eyre was only one.

Another major procedural refinement by Henry II was the writ ordering the sheriff to summon the defendant in any dispute over free land to come before the justices. On that writ were the words 'and have there the summoners and this writ' – a phrase which legal historians regard as of great importance, for it was through this device that the return link from the county to the Crown was established. The new 'returnable' writs were folded and sealed; they contained orders from the King to the sheriff and involved instructions to summon juries and parties and to inspect the disputed property, and they reminded him of the need to return the writ to the justices with details of the action he had taken.

Henry II also laid down the terms of authority given to commissions of assize – which in theory stood below the eyres and other itinerant commissions in the rank order of authority – setting out a classification of the types of business. These initially concerned civil matters only: for instance, the establishment of an opportunity for a dispossessed tenant to seek judgement on the question of his recent dispossession (novel disseisin) or wrongful exclusion from entry into his inheritance (mort d'ancestor). The sheriff's instructions in the Writ of Novel Disseisin included the summoning of a jury of recognition to answer narrowly specific questions about the recent history of the land in dispute, and in the Assize of Mort d'Ancestor the jury would be asked whether the ancestor died seized of a fee, whether it was since the King's coronation, and whether the claimant was the 'next' or nearest heir.

Indeed Henry's administration largely depended on the use of local juries both to decide property cases and to identify criminals. Here a crucial choice was made which affected the whole future course of English law and, we may suggest, centre–periphery relations.[122] The jury of presentment, although by no means a new concept, was stressed in all its essentials by the Assize of Clarendon (1166) and provided in its first clause that

for the preservation of the peace and the maintenance of justice inquiries be made through each county and hundred by twelve of the more lawful men of the hundred and four of the more lawful men of each vill, under oath they will say truly whether in their hundred or vill there be any man who is assumed or generally suspected of being a robber or murderer or thief or any man who is receiver of robbers or murderers or thieves since the lord king was king.[123]

Presentments of such offenders by juries were to be made to the twice-yearly sheriff's 'tourn' through the hundreds – occasions when in theory he was also to review the frankpledge lists of men in tithing, each tithing being represented by its chief pledge. Indeed the chief pledgers constituted the presentment juries at the levels of the vill and the hundred (see Figure 2).

It remains an interesting question why the English Crown laid upon local neighbourhoods so onerous a set of duties. One historian has argued that at the outset the Crown had no choice, and has suggested that when large-scale use of juries began in 1166 there were scarcely enough experienced men even to direct the new Crown court system.[124] In this interpretation the early common law juries are seen as the essential means of conserving trained manpower in a government that had taken on tasks of such immense scope and complexity. However, the possibility might be entertained that the Angevin reforms like the Domesday Inquest were exploiting pre-existing traditions of group responsibility in which the 'unpaid amateur' had always loomed large. As Clanchy states, 'the use of juries is a good example of how English law contained monarchical, feudal and communal elements and drew on customary procedures'. Yet, 'ultimately it was juries of the neighbourhood, and not royal judges or feudal lords who decided the fates of men and property by their verdicts'.[125] In both civil and communal cases the essential decisions were made by the verdicts of 'neighbours' and not by judges from Westminster. Superficially presenting the appearance of a centralized system, centripetal in relation to the King's court, in reality it was rooted in local opinion, although its undoubted coherence rested upon an obvious symbiosis in society of an inward-looking periphery and an outward-looking centre rather than on the incorporation of the former by the latter. It is important to draw attention to the contrast that existed between England in the later twelfth century with its common law, and much of Europe, where Roman law was sweeping all before it. There is no space here to consider this issue in detail beyond noting the implications of these very real differences between England and her neighbours on the Continent in the matter of centre–periphery relations. Within the Roman law areas resolution of disputes and the application to it of the law revolved around

170

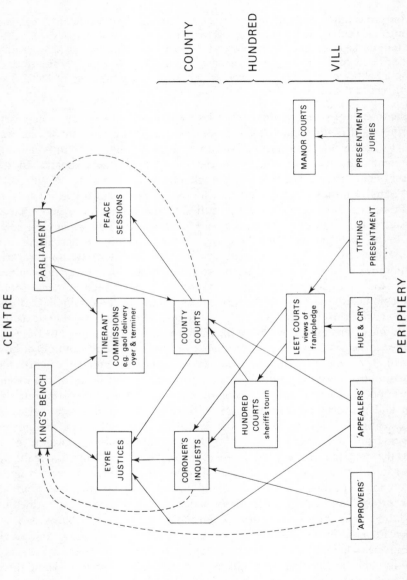

Figure 2

CENTRE

PERIPHERY

COUNTY

HUNDRED

VILL

PARLIAMENT

KING'S BENCH

PEACE SESSIONS

ITINERANT COMMISSIONS
e.g. gaol delivery
oyer & terminer

EYRE JUSTICES

COUNTY COURTS

CORONER'S INQUESTS

HUNDRED COURTS
sheriff's tourn

LEET COURTS
views of frankpledge

TITHING PRESENTMENT

HUE & CRY

'APPEALERS'

'APPROVERS'

MANOR COURTS

PRESENTMENT JURIES

the inquisitorial procedure according to which an official inquisitor or judge, who directed all the proceedings, often in secret, gathered the evidence and gave the judgement. Emphasis was placed upon written evidence and confessions often under torture. English kings however, made do with very few powerful justices who got through the business by peremptorily demanding simple answers from assembled juries: yes or no? Secret interrogation may well have been a more likely development in societies in which a 'participatory' tradition in the policing and trial of 'crime' was poorly developed or only weakly related to the instructions sent out from central government. Furthermore, the jury system of presentment and trial did require regular and frequent movement of relatively large numbers of people to attend court meetings at appointed moments in time. This would be difficult in a situation either of fragile political stability or of inward-looking communities. Of course, in raising these issues we are in danger of confusing causes with effects. The implications of the differences in trial procedures and the documents these yielded is nowhere more apparent than in the mundane but very extensive material generated by the English legal system in the medieval period – both the data at the level of the King's and manorial courts and the patchy but spectacular evidence produced by the inquisition. No English village could be studied in the same way as the now celebrated Montaillou.[126] Even when allowance is made for its geographically isolated position, the behaviour patterns revealed in the rich inquisitorial evidence show Montaillou to have been the archetypal 'unincorporated' community.

One further but important difference between the two systems concerns the personnel employed in their operation. The legal net with its remarkably 'tight mesh' could be spread for instance over England using just 5,000 unpaid J.P.s and fifteen appeal court judges at the end of the seventeenth century. In France, with an admittedly large population but a loosely woven system of law enforcement, there were 5,000 royal and 75,000 seigneurial judges along with a further 12,000 appeal court judges, all of whom were stipendiary:[127] such figures strikingly confirm the view of those who believe that unlike France 'England had a centralized government before she had a bureaucracy'.[128]

Some issues surrounding the 'law' and the 'community' in medieval England

Many of the issues I have considered above would be regarded by certain historians as irrelevant or of only marginal significance to the vast bulk of the populace, because the establishment of a common law by the Angevin monarchy provided a legal machinery only for freemen who held their land directly from the Crown. The judges of the royal courts would be seen as only interested in providing a forum for free tenants and would be, in Hilton's words, 'prepared to abandon customary tenants to the jurisdiction of the manorial courts'.[129] We have in this interpretation a monarchy apparently trying to extend royal justice and jurisdiction at the expense of the barons' private courts, but at the same time abandoning the customary villein tenants to their lords, whose private jurisdictions at the manorial level developed strongly. The paradox is therefore posed as a situation in which centralization of justice for a partial sector of the populace occurs at the same time as the 'unfree' are confined in their curial activities to localized courts in the private possession of their landlords. Hilton suggests that there is no problem, for it was in the interests of the King and indeed of his justices that this should be so, since they were all lords of manors, much of whose wealth was derived from direct cultivation of their demesnes in the early and middle thirteenth century.[130] In fact Hilton is inclined to see a definite conspiratorial relationship between the growth of a common law of villeinage in the later twelfth and early thirteenth centuries and the resumption of direct cultivation of their demesnes by the great estate owners.[131] The recent historian of villeinage and its treatment in the royal courts, P. R. Hyams, sees this as accidental but nevertheless highly detrimental to the interests of the villeins who were exposed to the arbitrary judgements of lords or their officials.[132] This interpretation would constitute a major plank in any argument founded upon presenting manorial villein populations as unincorporated nationally, whilst the central courts would be seen as agencies indirectly concerned with facilitating the removal of socially derived surpluses from the 'peasant' sector, in as much as landlords would be left free to raise rents and other charges on their tenants with no external constraints whatsoever.[133] To accept this portrayal of the situation in the thirteenth century would require some assessment, first of the share of the population represented by those of definitely unfree status and, secondly, of customary law and the tribunals in which it was for the most part operated.

Any attempt to estimate the unfree population would need to take into account both geographical variation in the incidence of villeinage and likely demographic differences between the villein and free population. Of the latter we know next to nothing and of the former our evidence is far from comprehensive. However two recent attempts to answer this question indicate that the unfree in the thirteenth century were a clear minority, and most likely no more than one third of the total population.[134]

There can be little doubt that there were attempts by lords to insist upon villein status for tenants who regarded themselves as free in the early thirteenth century, and there were equally strong moves on the part of such tenants to resist what they regarded as the removal of their free status. The evidence in the rolls of *curia regis* suggests that this friction was occasionally accompanied by violence.[135] Ironically, the reaction of landlords to the claims of their tenants for free status in the eyes of the King's justices brought about an increase in the corpus of manorial sources (ranging from custumals and surveys to manorial court records), as these tenants and their holdings were listed and their actions in customary tribunals recorded.[136] However, customary tenants derived some not inconsiderable benefits from this 'formalization of custom', as lords, for instance, subsequently found it less easy to increase obligations when defined by villagers or inquest juries under oath and perpetuated in writing than it had been in a world of oral law and custom.[137]

It would appear, too, that the manorial courts did not themselves remain hermetically sealed from developments in the legal procedure occurring in the Crown courts. In no area were they affected more than in their increasing use of juries of presentment and inquest, for which the King's courts provided the models. It would seem that presentment juries emerged first in village leet courts or views of frankpledge. With central government after 1215 becoming unconcerned with the management of minor infringements of the King's peace – in matters, for example, to do with the sale of diseased foods, the use of dishonest weights and measures, the maintenance of highways and water courses, and minor assaults – the 'bread and butter' of leet court business fell into the private hands of landlords, whose gains thereby in revenue were not inconsiderable.[138] Presentment juries extended subsequently into other areas of manorial affairs where plaints had been previously initiated either by individuals or manorial officers. By the late 1270s trial juries were also being used to investigate land disputes and came increasingly to employ the rolls of the court as a record they would consult for precedent or factual information in the making of their decisions.[139]

These developments were of great significance for relationships within the village, a view which accords well with that of those who suggest that the jury has always been a medium for the expression of the distribution of power in society and can be expected to act in the interests of the dominant people. It seems from the evidence from thirteenth- and fourteenth-century manorial courts that jurors came disproportionately from the upper echelons of the customary landholders and had at their disposal tools which they could use for their own advantage. However, in drawing attention to this capacity for social discrimination in the operation of the customary tribunals, we should not fail to note that developments in the legal instruments of those courts brought numerous benefits to tenants by providing means for recording economic transactions of indescribable variety. In addition these same tenants derived very considerable security in their tenure of customary land by inheritance and transmission through gift, lease or alienation. We can observe also a significant trend towards the standardization of terms and forms, many of which had originated in the higher courts, this suggesting a most notable homogenization of the landscape of 'customary law'.[140]

There is good reason to suppose that, in the specific demographic and economic conditions of the thirteenth century and the first third of the fourteenth, the 'jury-serving' section of the customary population advanced considerably at the expense not only of its less affluent neighbours but of some of its fellow villagers possessing freehold. Freeholders were not protected from inflationary forces, as the terms under which their land was held were less 'sticky' than those applying to customary land.[141] It remains a very open question whether in the context of these developments the elites or 'better sorts' among the villein population saw their livelihood so firmly bound up with the collective spirit of village resistance to overbearing lordship. One further point connected with these developments concerns the meaning to be attached to terms such as *tota curia* or *tota villata* so frequently encountered in manorial courts of this period. By the early fourteenth century, with juries effectively determining so much of what came before manorial courts and the decisions in personally initiated plaints, these 'collective' terms were no more than 'fictional relics' far detached from whatever meaning they may have possessed at an earlier date.[142]

Certain implications for the character of the villagers' relationships with royal agencies of law and order follow from the processes fostering internal differentiation of customary tenants in village society. A recent study by Barbara Hanawalt presents some highly suggestive patterns. In it she follows the fortunes of individuals (for the most part customary tenants of the Abbot of Ramsey) who have been identified by Raftis and his colleagues, through their participation in manorial courts, in the early fourteenth century gaol delivery records of Huntingdonshire – presents some highly suggestive patterns.[143] She notes that, while those villagers were guided by common law traditions already discussed and by the Statute of Winchester (1285) which stated that larceny, burglary, receiving, homicide, rape and arson were matters to be referred to the King's court, the Huntingdonshire village jurors displayed considerable latitude in their interpretation of such categories of 'crime'.[144]

Although her analysis has been undertaken using the highly problematic categorization of individuals appearing in manorial courts adopted by the 'Toronto School', she produces certain findings sufficiently unambiguous to suggest that they are not solely an artefact of her method. Although indictments, whether by individual plaint or through presentment jurors, showed a wide distribution across the village social and economic hierarchies, a noticeable socially specific pattern of eventual convictions was detected. It should be noted that there was considerable overlap in the personnel of both presenting and trial juries, suggesting a strong 'community' role for both policeman and judge in these matters. The conviction rate, at only 19 per cent, was low, like that identified by students of early modern English crime; among the prominent villagers (A-type) the rate of conviction was less than 5 per cent, but it was as high as 40 per cent for those from the lower levels of village society. The same xenophobic patterns that Ingram detected in early seventeenth-century Wiltshire were also observable, for when the accused were 'strangers' the conviction rate was 37.5 per cent. But, given the deliberately selective features of the system of indictment to which we have made such frequent reference in this discussion, the underlying driving force behind this system of communal justice was a prerogative in the hands of prominent villagers, who would use legal machinery deriving from the Crown in a selective fashion.[145] Such findings as these are also perfectly consistent with Britton's evidence concerning the sharp rise of convictions, particularly for so-called property offences, by lower-status villagers of Broughton during the period of economic difficulties brought on by recurrent harvest failures in the years 1310–19[146] or with Hanawalt's own analysis, covering the same years, of the growth in the incidence of property crimes in the gaol delivery records of whole counties.[147] Such variability suggests considerable flexibility in the social definition of 'crime'.

Of course in considering the appearance of villagers, whether free or villein, in the records of gaol delivery we have been observing a class of 'major' crimes rather than the humdrum melange of petty misdemeanours that constituted almost all the business of manorial, and especially of leet, courts and a lower but still sizeable proportion of the cases in such records, left by the fourteenth-century commissioners of peace, as have survived – in a rather sporadic fashion. In the latter part of the fourteenth century one major area of regulative activity in the hands of the J.P.s was the enforcement of the 1351 Statute of Labourers, which, along with the setting of definite day-work and piece-work wage rates for various occupations, made specific provisions for various conditions of employment and labour discipline. Servants, for instance, were to be sworn twice each year before the village constables among others. Many cases in the peace sessions deal with the failure of labourers to take oaths or to enter employment when ordered by constables. Indeed there is substantial evidence to indicate that petty constables bore the bulk of the labourers' resentments against what was certainly unpopular legislation.[148]

Constables chosen annually are regularly seen to come from the elite layers of village society and to bear an uncanny resemblance to that same village officer that students of the seventeenth century have portrayed as labouring under the burden of imposing legislated norms upon members of their own communities.[149] A recent study suggests, furthermore, that village constables in later fourteenth-century England were also likely to have come from the employer category of tenant farmers; and, when this is considered alongside the evidence suggesting that major gentry or aristocratic landlords figured very little among the employers named in indictments of labourers, it is possible to see the Statute of Labourers as more than just a body of legislation emanating from a Parliament stuffed with the landed interest.[150] When we add to this the significant numbers of village by-laws – most likely promulgated by the leading landholders in rural communities who also attempted to control labour migration and terms of employment – we find ample evidence to suggest the presence of outward-orientated village notables who might find in labour legislation originating at the centre, a tool they would see as, though enforced, nevertheless advantageous to them. Such enforcement would always, given the coercive powers at their disposal, present great difficulty.

We have reviewed evidence indicative of noteworthy flows of information, concepts and, most likely, personnel between courts which in theory were to do with both the freeholding and customary sectors of rural society. This suggests certain difficulties involved in any attempt to treat as 'closed' the contexts within which the rural inhabitants of medieval England came into contact with either common or customary law. For although the scope of medieval manorial jurisdiction over economic transactions and interpersonal litigations was certainly greater than that of Tudor and Stuart manor courts or leets, it does not necessarily follow – as Razi, for example, argues on the basis of his research into Halesowen – that as far as the individual was concerned 'the mediaeval village community was far more important than any local organization in later periods, because in no other period of English history were so many disputes concerning property and rights, as well as inter-personal conflicts, resolved locally by the villagers themselves through the mechanisms of the manorial courts'.[151] This 'closed' perspective arises quite simply from an almost total dependence upon evidence drawn from manorial courts. Indeed, the only evidential contexts within which Razi considers the Worcestershire manor are those in which landlord–tenant conflicts are likely to have loomed large. Moreover, in a recent consideration of these tensions he nowhere reflects on the implications of the fact that customary tenants used the apparatus of the common law as instruments for resolving their grievances.[152] Awareness of, and willingness of customary tenants to use, these wider common law institutions (as in the case of the tenants of Darnhall and Over in Cheshire, who knew what to do when the abbot of Vale Royal claimed them as villeins in 1336, or as in that of similar actions by inhabitants of Wawne in Holderness against the Abbey of Meaux in 1356), should not be regarded as aberrant behaviour or the work of desperate men; on the contrary, these cases indicate just how great a strain it would put upon interpretation to take a narrow definition of the 'political nation'.[153] As litigants men were prepared to use elements of the nation's administrative and legal machinery for securing their assumed rights. Nor were the courts, whether manorial or common law, isolated entities, for both information and people flowed between them.[154] Moreover, the participants in the local disturbances of the summer of 1381 exhibited considerable political awareness in the discrimination they exercised in selecting certain individuals as victims of their anger.[155]

I have noted, too, the implications that a socially differentiated village structure had for the selective utilization of the law in courts, whether considered at the level of the village, of the hundred or of the county. The options that this gave the village elites, who overwhelmingly staffed the law enforcement agencies, enabled them on some occasions to align themselves with the rules and values of the more distantly located elites and on others actually to protect those below them from such forces. Such flexibility of behavioural options would seem to indicate the existence neither of a medieval England of corporate village bodies nor of collectivities whose prime *raison d'être* was to resist the imposition of lordly pressures.

Conclusion

It would be all too easy to conclude from this discussion that an attempt has been made here to provide yet another account of English society in which nothing is assumed to have changed over the course of time. This unfortunate response is sometimes found in the work of certain early modernists who take the trouble to familiarize themselves with the writings on the period which precedes 'their own'.[156] Historical writing within an *immobiliste* tradition is as unsatisfactory as the writing of history in terms of the decline of the assumed characteristics of an older society. As Wrightson notes, this latter interpretative habit is easy to criticize, harder to escape – as his own writing unavoidably indicates.[157]

In the attempt to strike a balance in assessing the degree of change in the relations between community and State over the centuries, it becomes clear that we are dealing with changes in intensity and degree rather than with a major transformation in structure such as is implied by the 'incorporationist' perspective, whereby local communities are seen to have been absorbed into a wider political entity. In this gradual change of emphasis the relationship between the courts was modified as certain categories of their business moved from one to another and the residential locus and the political allegiances of their officials were adjusted. For example, the eyres became swamped by litigants who came to them with Appeals of Felony by oral complaint, thereby necessitating resort to special local commissions such as gaol delivery or the infamous oyer and terminer and trailbaston. Similarly, there was increasing use of J.P.s, men of the 'county' rather than itinerant representatives of the centre, in a widening range of activities both as judges and as enforcers of regulative legislation.

These developments clearly changed the character of centre–periphery linkages from that which obtained in the twelfth and thirteenth centuries. For example, conventional views suggest that the disturbances of later medieval England owe much to the potential for a growth in 'bastard' feudal relations as the county gentry aligned themselves with the various territorial magnates rather than with a weakened centre. For instance, Harding writes of this period as one in which the stream of judicial authority was reversed, 'flowing back to the localities and to the landlord, who found himself again keeping a "peace" – though this time it was in theory the king's . . .'.[158]

Indeed, it might be readily assumed that 'lordship' was everywhere predominant and 'community' subordinate – in contrast to the position in the seventeenth century. However, J. R. Maddicott has warned us that in the fourteenth century these contrasts are perhaps more apparent than real, just as Clive Holmes, in discussing early seventeenth-century England, has drawn our attention to the fact that 'county communities' and a 'national' political culture are not to be viewed as mutually exclusive. For in their 'participation in local administration, the gentry were continuously reminded that England was a centralized polity, governed by a common law . . .'.[159] Similarly, in discussing the fourteenth century Maddicott has remarked that we cannot assume that in the county's political business it was the magnates who alone mattered. For it was in the county's court that representatives in the national Parliament were elected. Moreover, the actual attendance of these representatives in Parliament was in theory guaranteed by the locality – that is by freeholders from the village in which their principals lived – and often the reeve, almost always a customary tenant, would act as a guarantor for a manorial lord.[160]

I have been, in the broadest possible sense, reviewing issues connected with the relationship between the State (defined in rather general terms) and the social structure. Relationships between groups which at some times have appeared polarized and at others overlapping, wholly or partially, have been stressed. I have, without wishing to specify these relationships too concretely in spatial terms, been concerned with issues to do with the forces in society promoting institutional coherence. The patterns of economic individualism that MacFarlane describes with reasonable accuracy for medieval English rural society have, if they are to be fully understood, to be assessed against a supporting back-cloth of collectivist institutions which have set limits to, and ground rules for, what was regarded as acceptable behaviour, and which have been responsible in a very general sense for the minimization of perceived personal risks and the restricted development of 'images of limited good'.[161] For in reality, because of the integration of its institutions, English rural society was neither in a state of Hobbesian 'warre' nor a geographical scattering of small, introspective corporate republics waiting to be integrated into a larger body politic by the outward-orientated 'middling sorts' at some point in the early seventeenth century. The absence of both these characteristics remains a feature of English rural society which must be taken into account in any attempt fully to understand England's highly distinctive historical experience. A major task awaiting students of society –

whether geographers, historians or sociologists – is to increase our under-standing of the long-term dialectic of economic individualism and political and philosophical collectivism that exists as a recurring theme in England both past and present.[162] To comprehend better, for instance, the nature of English serfdom, landlord–tenant relationships, the old Poor Law and its predecessors and successors, the position of women, the kinship system and its relationship to the demographic regime – these representing some among many issues – will require just such a commitment.[163]

Acknowledgement

I am particularly grateful to Dr Roger Schofield for his most helpful com-ments on an earlier draft of this essay. I, of course, retain responsibility for the views expressed in the final version.

All Souls College, Oxford

6

Some *terrae incognitae* in historical geography: an exploratory discussion[1]

ALAN R. H. BAKER AND DEREK GREGORY

ALAN BAKER: That debate should be a central concern of historical geographers is, I suppose, the premise on which this collection of essays is based. They were initially written as papers to be read at one of the Cambridge Occasional Discussions in Historical Geography and have, of course, been revised in the light of comments made at that time. Each is offered as a contribution to a debate. As I tried to show in my own essay, a willingness, even an eagerness, to be polemical, to engage in intradisciplinary and especially interdisciplinary discussion, has undoubtedly been one of the strengths of the *Annales* school of history for more than fifty years. In marked contrast, the reticence and relative isolation of historical geographers in France during that same period accounts for the discipline's weaker intellectual position and lower academic status. As far as historical geography in Britain is concerned, even as late as the end of the 1960s it was reasonable to argue that it relied almost entirely on enthusiasms and insights generated by its own practitioners, drawing little on concepts and methods developed in other fields. This is no longer the case, and British historical geography's enhanced reputation reflects, I think, its dual insistence both upon the scholarly interpretation of sources and upon an explicit concern with methodology, with what Clifford Darby called 'the problem of geographical description'.

As insiders, Ron Cooke and Brian Robson recorded in 1980 that historical geography in Britain had 'made immense strides' in the mid-1970s, and a number of outsiders have made the same point. In his review of history in Britain, Harold Parker praised 'the excellent articles and monographs in local and regional history produced by the British school of historical geographers'; an American, Gary Dunbar, has expressed the view that 'the new historical geography has been most successfully practiced in Great Britain'; a Frenchman, Paul Claval, has referred to 'the powerful school of British historical geography'; an Italian, Massimo Quaini, has observed within human geography in Britain 'the connections between geography and Marxist historiography which form the basis for a development of historical geography unparalleled in any other European country'; for a German audience, Anngret Simms has investigated the condition of British historical geography and concluded that during the last two decades it 'has become more and more one of the most productive fields of research within geography'; and a Russian, Vladimir Annenkov, has cast a critical but appreciative eye upon what he calls the 'new horizons of historical geography' in the English-speaking world. To some extent, the founding in 1973 of the Historical Geography Research Group of the Institute of British Geographers and the establishing in 1975 of the *Journal of Historical Geography* provide evidence to support such views: both measures have provided historical geographers in Britain with a more coherent sense of identity (the *Journal* is, of course, internationally significant but it is principally edited from Britain). Supporting roles have probably also been played by the Studies in Historical Geography edited by Brian Harley and myself since 1970 and by the Historical Geography Series edited by Robin Butlin since 1977. The effect of the Historical Geography Research Group (H.G.R.G.) has particularly been to promote discussion, not only among British historical geographers but also between us and our colleagues abroad, especially in the United States, Canada, France and Germany, where the Group has arranged symposia in cooperation with historical geographers from those countries.

Even so, the character and scale of discussion have as yet been relatively limited. For example, during the first seven years of its existence, the *Journal of Historical Geography* has staged debates on building cycles in Victorian cities; on the nineteenth-century *Gazette* corn returns; on the historical origins of the English wolds; on field systems; and on the geographical distribution of wealth in medieval England. The scope of such discussions could – and should – be considerably expanded.

DEREK GREGORY: Debates within the *Journal* have been limited in their range. On the other hand, the H.G.R.G. has had a markedly more catholic series of meetings. Although its original *raison d'être* was to compile a glossary of agrarian landscape terms, a remarkable achievement in itself, its seminars, symposia, conferences and publications have become much more wide-ranging: think, for example, of the debates over the transition from feudalism to capitalism and over the Industrial Revolution.

ALAN BAKER: I agree with that, and progress in historical geography has arguably been impressive during the last two decades or so; but there is no room for complacency. I concur whole-heartedly with Robin Butlin, who recently concluded that 'what is badly needed is debate, between geographers and their colleagues from other disciplines and between geographers and geographers, for the literature of British historical geography shows little evidence of passionate debate on critical issues'. What, for example, do you consider to be the main consequences for historical geography of the convergence between the other historical disciplines and a more formal social theory?

DEREK GREGORY: I would certainly identify that *rapprochement* as one of the most significant modern developments in the historical disciplines, and the contributions to this volume clearly reflect that, so it's a good example with which to begin. I think there are two main consequences. The first is the central concern with methodological issues, which you have already mentioned, and the second – which flows from it – is the search for non-functionalist forms of explanation.

In themselves, of course, methodological writings are scarcely novel: although neither Clifford Darby nor Carl Sauer (for example) regarded himself as a 'methodologist' and both of them affected disdain for methodological discussion, both published substantial essays about the 'nature' or 'spirit and purpose' of historical geography. But for the most part they were concerned to establish disciplinary boundaries, and in some measure to police them. This is far removed from our own views, I know. As Mark Billinge once suggested, 'it should no longer surprise the historical geographer that not all the fairies at the bottom of the garden are fellow geographers. Neither is there anything revolutionary or even new in the assertion that geography possesses a number of related and well-endowed neighbours, whose gardens have frequently appeared rather more ordered than our own.' Maybe not; but, to continue the analogy, much of classical historical geography was rather less concerned with opening up the broad vistas of Capability Brown and rather more worried about keeping the pigeons off its cabbage patch. In part this must have been a reflection of the small numbers working on Darby's allotment – and we shouldn't lose sight of that – but, whatever the reason, in the 1960s and early 1970s what I suppose we have to call a 'horticultural revolution' intruded on this familiar ground. And in the course of its rotations methodological writings came to be regarded – by their authors, if not always, by their readers! – as much more *central* to the sub-discipline.

But much of this was reactive and defensive. The rise of the so-called 'New Geography' was always more than a formalization of positivism (if it was that at all), and certainly much more than an endorsement of geography as spatial science, a science in which 'the only relations that matter are spatial ones', as Schaefer had put it. There were sustained criticisms of both these views, of course, perhaps most cogently by Cole Harris and other members of the Department of Geography at Toronto. But what seems to me most notable about the methodological writings of that period, taking historical geography as a whole, was their *acceptance* of the new protocols of geographical inquiry. Ron Johnston described historical geographers as 'relatively untouched' by the manoeuvres of the 'New Geography' – I'm never sure whether that was intended to be congratulation or condemnation – but they were surely no less touched than any other sort of geographer. Like the rest, they could be found crawling along the isotropic plane, scambling under the hexagonal netting and worming their way up the central-place hierarchies. While there were some who never made it out of boot-camp – soldiering on in the Royal Army Pay Corps, so to speak – it is simply wrong to suggest that historical geography somehow evaded the call-up. What was novel about its enlistment, however, and what I take to be the main reason for its defensive capitulation, was the way in which the 'New Geography' entailed a definite commitment to a functionalism which set its face against genetic ('historical') explanation. The origins of the dispute lay, of course, in geomorphology (which Darby had represented as one of the twin pillars of the subject, alongside historical geography). But although the distinctions were presumably clear enough in the natural sciences, and particularly to those whose interests lay not in denudation chronology, but in the analysis of short-term process–response systems, commentators like Clifford Smith insisted all along that in the human and social sciences the opposition was far more apparent than real. Even so, I still think it fair to say that even the supposedly 'dynamic' models in human geography – whether we're talking about the statistical models of (say) Markov processes or the substantive models of (say) diffusion theory – were moments in a definite functionalist movement which was unequivocally opposed to historical geography on any terms other than as a 'testing ground' for general propositions which rejected any suggestion of space–time specificity as a corrosive residue of the old 'idiographic' tradition. I regard the distinction between 'idiographic' and 'nomothetic' knowledges as thoroughly unhelpful, but, as I tried to argue in the *Dictionary of Human Geography*, the ease with which the terrain of historical geography could be redefined in this way was in large measure a result of the logical interdependencies between the classical preoccupation with the cartographic analysis of historical sources and the neo-classical predilection for the geometric disclosure of 'spatial structures'.

But more recently our methodological writings, for all their pretensions and confusions, have been characterized by a determined break with functionalism. Discussions of idealism and a phenomenologically informed humanism, of the limitations of structuralism and the construction of a realist social science, and of their conjunction in various models of structuration: all these, despite their differences, signal a profound departure from the deeply sedimented partitions between 'cross section' and 'vertical theme' or between 'synchronic' and 'diachronic'. Now none of this is simply the result of developments within historical geography: it is to David Harvey and Torsten Hägerstrand as much as to anyone that we have to look to understand the new sense of *historicity* now abroad within the discipline. But it may well be that today historical geography is poised to regain the central place it had within the wider subject when Darby wrote that classic essay 'On the relations of history and geography' exactly thirty years ago.

ALAN BAKER: The problem of the policing of boundaries was a very real one, and it was by no means confined to Britain. With hindsight, one can now see that one of the unfortunate consequences of the limited contact between geographers and those working in cognate disciplines was a failure to explore the relations between regional geography and total history, both of which were being propounded as holistic concepts. Both concepts grew in the fertile intellectual soil of France, but French historians have tended to be more successful than French geographers in practising what they preached. The *Annales* school adopted wholesale the nexus of geographical concepts developed within *la tradition vidalienne* and, unlike many – especially American – historians, *Annalistes* have moved far beyond a view of geography simply as setting, as the physical stage upon which historical dramas were enacted.

DEREK GREGORY: But even if historical geographers are no more than, as it were, scene-shifters and property masters, it seems to me astonishing how bare the set has been allowed to become. Apart from the contributions of people like Martin Parry, there has been remarkably little modern work on the relations between society and nature.

ALAN BAKER: Yes, but that can't be done very effectively *in vacuo*. The regional histories of the *Annales* school incorporate concepts borrowed from *all* the schools of geography (as identified by Peter Haggett in 1965): those of areal differentiation, landscape, ecology and location. French historians have had no reservations at all about the extent to which they may legitimately call upon geographical concepts in their own efforts to produce historical syntheses. By contrast, French geographers have been reluctant to call upon history in their own endeavours to write regional syntheses, doing so for the most part only in so far as the past could be charged with holding keys to the present. Such a self-denying ordinance impeded the development of historical geography in France and impoverished even the study there of contemporary human geography. Regional geography came in practice to be much less holistic than its logical counterpart, total history.

Even accepting the detachment of French human geographers from currents within history, their relative isolation (with a few notable exceptions) from the whole intellectual revolution that was to transform French social theory from the 1930s onwards – with the convergence of Marxism and existentialism – is none the less remarkable and regrettable; not least because the notion of holism is fundamental to these philosophies, which thereby become of direct significance to the synthetic purposes and practices of both total history and regional geography. There has, of course, been some dialogue between *Annalistes* and Marxist historians, and there is a developing discussion of Marxist concepts among human geographers, but there remains an opportunity for historical geographers to explore the relevance to their own work of Marx's concept of the totality of the historical process and of Sartre's conception of the totalization of history, with their dual emphasis upon synthesis and specificity. While closer acquaintance with these concepts might further our own understanding of places in the past, there exists also the possibility of a fruitful 'geographization' (to employ Peter Burke's apt but ugly term) of existential Marxist ideas about history.

DEREK GREGORY: The adjective there is highly necessary, though, because it's far from easy to provide a definitive assessment of the role of Marxism. The difficulty is partly a result of the different readings of Marx – which were already in contention in the 1890s. Today, one hundred years after Marx's death, perhaps all we can hope for is what Richard Johnson calls 'the best Marx', that is to say, one which recognizes the *complexity* of the terrain explored by Marx and which does not exempt his own writings from *criticism*. Certainly, claims to have divined 'what Marx really meant' have to be set alongside the extraordinary textual richness of the various Marxian 'traditions' (as Edward Thompson terms them), which, if nothing else, confirm that the easy distinction between an early 'humanist' Marx and a mature, 'scientific' Marx is both overdrawn and misleading. In any case, modern Marxism is not closed around the original writings of Marx (and Engels); and the second source of difficulty is exactly the widely discrepant range of evaluations made by modern commentators. Let me give just two examples. G. A. Cohen has provided a determined defence in *Karl Marx's Theory of History*, where he insists on the centrality of the dialectic between the forces and relations of production (and on the primacy of the forces themselves) in providing what he sees as a necessarily 'functional' explanation of historical change. Yet Tony Giddens' *Contemporary Critique of Historical Materialism* is predicated on exactly the opposite view: that 'only if historical materialism is regarded as embodying the more abstract elements of a theory of human praxis' and distanced from any conception of historical eventuation as 'the progressive augmentation of the forces of production' does it remain 'an indispensable contribution to social theory today' – which Giddens understands in avowedly non-functionalist terms. Of the two, I am closer to Giddens. I don't think it is quite as easy to dispense with the concept of a mode of production as he makes out (indeed, I think it a mistake), and I would also want to retain the sense in which Marx's concepts were clearly of several different *orders* (in ways which his own are not); but I'm quite sure that Giddens' discussion of the importance of a bounded conception of 'human agency' is absolutely vital for historical inquiry.

ALAN BAKER: That is why I stand by the importance of an *existential* Marxism. I have argued elsewhere that much historical geography has been based on a 'false consciousness' which personified *places* which were none the less described with little reference to the *people* who inhabited them, to the makers of the changing landscapes. One of the principal achievements of the *Annales* school, again, was its humanization of history, its insistence that all individuals and social groups – not merely the elites – have their historians. Nowhere is this more evident than in a remarkable section in Jacques Le Goff's book on *La Civilisation de l'Occident médiévale*, which he devotes to a consideration of heretics, lepers, Jews, sorcerers, sodomites, cripples, foreigners and outcasts. Advocacy of a total historical geography is intended not to undermine the substantial achievements of the landscape school of historical geography, but instead to build upon them by opening up new realms for inquiry by the humanization of historical geography.

DEREK GREGORY: I now have an image of Darby's Domesday maps adjusted not 'for serfs' but 'for heretics, lepers . . .' and the rest! This 'humanization' is clearly a very necessary task, and an extraordinarily difficult one: it's much easier to see the landscape as 'made' by the great figures of the past – the Vermuydens, the Reptons, the Cokes – than it is to probe into the great mass of people tucked away into the background. And we forget far too often that these included women and children as well as men. But how far do you think your 'humanized' historical geography really *is* compatible with Darby's vision of the subject?

ALAN BAKER: To a considerable degree, but in ways which both attend upon and extend beyond that vision. Perhaps I could make two points? First, history as humanization incorporates within it a notion of *progress*.

There are two criteria of progress which we can usefully employ: whether the power of people over nature is increased, and whether the power of people over other people is diminished. As historical geographers, therefore, I believe we should focus our attentions not only on the creation of cultural landscapes but also on the geography of social cooperation and domination. One challenge confronting us is to endeavour to assess progress not only in terms of material production, but also in terms of human emancipation. To date, most historical geographies have been cast in the mould of Whig histories of progress, practical demonstrations of modernization theories; it is, perhaps, now time to see how comfortably environmental destruction and pollution on the one hand and social control and surveillance on the other fit into that particular mould. There is sound, logical justification for extending the concern of historical geography well beyond the 'success stories' of changing landscapes.

Secondly, I know that it is believed by many geographers (and historians) that Darby's prime concern has been with cross-sectional reconstructions of past geographies, notably the Domesday Geography of England. In fact, he now refers to the 'Domesday Geography' as his 'albatross'; in practice, he has been an explorer, discovering sources and methodologies, himself undertaking, as well as encouraging others, to map out new territories of inquiry. So I think it quite erroneous to interpret what Anngret Simms has called 'the crusade against empirical positivism' as 'a strong reaction against H. C. Darby's method'; it would be more appropriate to view it as a logical extension of his own mission for the improvement of historical geography. But my argument is about more than 'humanization': it also involves an *holistic* conception of historical geography, which incorporates a number of implications for its practice, because of its inclusion not merely of the past but also of the present and the future, which it makes theoretically available and practically real. It provides logical justification for historical geographers to be concerned not only with the past *sensu stricto* but also with *la géographie humaine rétrospective et prospective*. This would require an attempt to make our discipline more comprehensive in terms of the period, places and problems studied. Most research by British and North American historical geographers during the last decade or so has been concerned with the nineteenth century, and as much as two-thirds of the current research effort deals with the eighteenth and nineteenth centuries. Some justification might be offered for this focus – in terms of the pivotal significance of the problems being studied during this period of industrial capitalism and in terms of the plethora of sources – but there is a logical necessity also to ensure that both earlier and later periods receive more and closer attention. There are, undoubtedly, ample precedents for historico-geographical research into medieval and early modern periods but relatively few for studies of the twentieth century: the inter-war years might be considered the real Dark Ages as far as historical geographers are concerned, but the First and Second World Wars themselves also deserve examination. Indeed, logically, an holistic approach implies that historical geographers should not be in any way deterred from bringing their studies through from the past to the present, because this approach rejects the artificiality of the distinction between the two.

Filling in the missing periods needs to be complemented by efforts to widen our horizons so that neglected places receive appropriate attention. There are, after all, areas within Britain and North America whose historical geography is hardly known, even though almost two out of every three British and North American historical geographers study their own countries (ignoring, for the moment, the proposition that the past itself is 'another country'). Perhaps the energies of more apprentices to our discipline should be applied on more distant shores, there to develop (both through their own personal researches and through cooperation with scholars overseas) understandings of the historical geographies of other lands which would be of both intrinsic and comparative interest. Studies of the historical geography of particular places could perhaps be integrated into historical geographies of interdependent development and of modes of production. Each of us is contributing, ultimately, to an historical geography of the world.

And this returns us to Marx again, because a specifically Marxist approach would surely see the writing of history as an integral part of the making of history. The purposes of historical geography are as much in need of exploration as are its practices. There is, it seems to me, little to commend the self-indulgence of a Richard Cobb, who confessed: 'I do not know what history is about, nor what social function it serves. I have never given the matter a thought . . . I do, however, find enormous enjoyment in research and in the writing of history. I am happy in it, and that is the main thing.' While the writing of history should undoubtedly be personally enjoyable for the *individual* author, it should surely also acknowledge his *social* responsibility both to other professional historians and to the public at large.

Of course, the abuse of history – for example, its conscription as an instrument of the State – has understandably led to the defence of history studied 'for its own sake', 'objectively'. But the need for a critical independence on the part of the historian does not require his constant confinement, either in solitary or in the limited company of his peers. Such isolation is, of course, very necessary at times, but not as a permanent condition. As an holistic and humanistic endeavour, history asks questions of the past – as Lucien Febvre put it, 'in terms of Humanity's needs today'. So, the historical geography which we write needs to make sense, to have meaning, for the present. It also needs to reach out to popular audiences as well as to a professional clientele: the vulgarization of scholarship constitutes a challenging task, an undervalued duty, part of a project whereby geographies of the past are restored to the people. The paths of exploration here lead, for example, to popular magazines and to broadcasting as well as to primary and secondary school textbooks and to adult education.

Once again, as more and more such paths are sketched, the challenge of historical geography becomes formidable, once again Darby's favourite aphorism becomes apposite: 'the harvest is great, the labourers are few'. Inevitably, an obvious danger of adopting such an holistic approach is that it lays its advocates and practitioners alike open to the charge of eclecticism and/or opportunism. It is crucial, therefore, while exploring intradisciplinary frontiers not to lose sight of the central concerns of geography.

DEREK GREGORY: One needs to be careful here, of course. I think it's fairly clear that most of the early encounters between modern geography and Marxism were little more than a defiant exegesis of the classical texts and a desperate demonstration that questions of geography were, as Quaini puts it in his *Geography and Marxism*, 'indelibly present' in them. Harvey's *Limits to Capital* is no exception, but it does at least sharpen the horns of a genuine dilemma. 'The historical geography of capitalism has been nothing short of remarkable', says Harvey, and its 'surface appearance of extraordinary historical–geographical change cries out for theoretical examination'. Yet 'it would be all too easy in the face of such diversity to succumb to that "spatial fetishism" that equalizes all phenomena *sub specie spatii* and treats the geometric properties of spatial patterns as fundamental. The opposite danger is to see spatial organization as a mere reflection of the processes of [capital] accumulation and class reproduction.' Examples of both are not difficult to find. If what I called earlier 'neo-classical' historical geography was seduced by the ordered world of spatial science, there is some justification in the complaint that some more recent excursions in historical geography have turned their backs on any serious examination of the salience of spatial structures to the production and reproduction of social practices. A recovery of these concerns does not entail a return to conventional spatial analysis; on the contrary. But I think a central task of historical geography is to clarify the ways in which human history *is instantiated in human geography*: to show how spatial structures are at once condition and consequence of social practice. Discussions of (let us say) the transition from feudalism to capitalism – a stock-in-trade of Marxist historiography – are likely to be much more incisive if the geography of the transformation is treated as something other than incidental to the outcome.

ALAN BAKER: I can agree with that because for me the core of our discipline – what distinguishes it from other academic disciplines – is the study of places. But the distinctiveness of geography needs to be retained, indeed sustained, even and especially when undertaking interdisciplinary excursions, otherwise it will all too easily be lost. Just as it was necessary for an earlier generation of historical geographers to reject the Hartshornian fallacy which defined geography and history as mutually exclusive studies in respectively chorology and chronology, so it is today necessary to reject the fallacy of equating geography with spatial organization. I can only reiterate my view that geography is no more the science of space than history is that of time: both space and time are as much the concern of other social scientists as they are of geographers and historians. Concepts of spatial organization and of temporal organization are essentially interdisciplinary rather than quintessentially geographical or historical. I have argued elsewhere that the analytical emphasis of much time-geography and space-geography seems to carry with it the danger of fragmenting time–space into an artificial plurality instead of synthesizing it into a genuine unity of period and place. That this tendency is considered as a danger follows logically from a view of geography as being centrally concerned with *place syntheses* rather than with *space–time analyses* (although the latter can and should contribute to the former).

We should be examining the social organization of space and time, not the spatial and temporal organization of society, because that puts the cart before the horse. We need more studies of the social control of time and space as scarce resources, as integral components of the process of social structuration and regional transformation. The last few years have seen a gradual renewal of interest in a new kind of regional geography with a strongly historical emphasis. My own contention that historical geography is properly concerned with periods and places rather than with times and spaces finds confirmation in the concept of *locale* recently elucidated by Tony Giddens, even though he prefers this term to that of *place*. Both probably owe much to the concept of the *pays* and its associated nexus of ideas developed by the French school of geography and adopted by the *Annales* school of history. Attachment to – and alienation from – place or locale play a significant role in the process of structuration.

DEREK GREGORY: I accept that, but isn't there a danger in this of becoming over-parochial? You spoke just now of the possibility of 'historical geographies of interdependent development'; but most of our studies seem to have been so bounded by the region, by what Harvey once identified as geography's characteristic 'resolution level', that we have rarely brought together the complexities of the local milieu with their wider national and international settings. Don't you think that decontextualized studies of this sort snap the connections *between* 'resolution levels' and all but dismember the *articulations* which were surely a primary concern of the *Annales* school?

ALAN BAKER: One answer might be to interpret the role of the region as that of mediating between the locality and the nation, in a way somewhat analogous to the group's mediation between the individual and society. The significance of place to specific social groups in the 'historic present' thereby becomes a critically important geographical concern. The transformation of geopieties is another avenue worth exploring. For example, the 'modernization' thesis of geographical change tends to presuppose a gradual extension of the economic and social organization of space, with local communities being absorbed into national structures, with attachment to a *pays* being replaced by that to a nation, as part of a process of cultural standardization. In reality, the process is likely to have been more complicated than that. It might have taken place very unevenly, in time and in space, so that regional differences might just as easily have been accentuated as reduced. 'Modernization' did not necessarily mean that all regions within a country 'developed' at the same rate and, moreover, the gap between the 'advanced' and the 'backward' regions within a country might well have been increased rather than diminished. More importantly, an attachment to 'regionalism' might in some circumstances have interposed itself as a potent political force between 'localism' and 'nationalism'. Furthermore, while it is possible to detect a process of regional transformation which involved the increasing *economic integration of space*, it might also be possible to detect a process of regional transformation which involved the increasing *spatial disintegration of society*: as the sense of place was transformed from a local to a national consciousness, so the *sense of community* might have ceded to a *sense of class* whose bonds might lie contiguously within a particular geographical region or hierarchically within a certain economic sector, in which case the sense of class would have dominated over any residual sense of place. Few historical geographers have yet explored the territory of regional consciousness and still fewer that of regionally based class consciousness.

DEREK GREGORY: Doreen Massey has argued that 'the social and economic structure of any given local area will be a complex result of that area's succession of roles within the series of wider, national and international, spatial divisions of labour'; and, although she would probably want to reject 'modernization' theories – and I think she would be right to do so – notions like yours do seem to be broadly comfortable with an emerging and really rather rich series of arguments about the 'territoriality' of class relations. But, at the same time, John Urry has emphasized that these 'localities' are also the complex result of 'a succession of roles within the temporally/spatially structured civil society and of the state, not merely of the "economic" division of labour'. This is surely important, because so much of neo-classical historical geography, especially in Britain, has been confined to a narrowly *economic* geography of the past. Matters have begun to change, of course: there are now much more substantial investigations of the intricacies of culture and the symbolic landscape (and here I have in mind the work of Denis Cosgrove in particular) and of the social texture of communities and their systems of intersubjective interaction – although there have been precious few attempts to take the *political* process seriously and chart the changing topographies of the State and the State apparatus in any detail. Even so, the point is surely that all these various studies will have to be convened within some plenary 'anatomy', as Urry calls it: that is to say, within some more inclusive – to use your term, *holistic* – sense of social formation.

The 'anatomy' of society is perhaps a less partisan phrase than 'social formation', but it has the more particular merit of suggesting the salience of both *structure* – of concepts of articulation and determination – and *spatiality*: what Edward Soja refers to as the 'materiality' of space. Of course, it is now something of a truism that conventional social theory failed to grasp the 'time–space constitution of social systems', and in some respects this can be traced back to those early arguments between Durkheim and Vidal de la Blache. But I think it is also the case that in seeking to remedy these deficiencies – through Giddens' theory of structuration, which you mentioned a moment ago – there has been a marked tendency to seize on the least 'geographical' of all geographies: Hägerstrand's time-geography. This has been preoccupied with the problematic of *time*; anyone who doubts that has only to look at the speed with which what started out as three-dimensional representations of intersubjective interaction, of Allen Pred's 'weaving dance in space and time', collapse into two-dimensional representations of simple vectors. It's not difficult to see how writings of this sort can be conjoined to theories of structuration which are so strongly influenced by Heidegger and Marx. Both these traditions have something to say about space, of course: about 'dwelling' and 'reach', for example, or about 'combined and uneven development' and 'the annihilation of space by time'. But that last phrase of Marx's is a peculiarly pregnant one. Traditions like these are indeed dominated by an almost overwhelming sense of *historicity*, and the basic *geography* of social life becomes a series of marginal notations to the text, dropped into the footnotes, so to speak, which have to be picked up and stitched together in ingenious reinterpretations. I don't mean this as a sort of special pleading for the geographer's straw man; rather, as a reminder of the importance of concepts of spatial structure *other* than those derived from spatial interaction (which is all Hägerstrand's 'paths and projects' are about) to the social sciences as a whole. I'm thinking particularly of questions of *location*. Time-geography characteristically treats the bases for spatial interaction as givens, and then shows how paths and projects in space and time are spun out within this framework: in other words, how geometry bounds 'human agency' through its translation into a series of structural 'constraints'. This is immensely important, of course, and I have found these representations extremely helpful in my own work, in clarifying the dynamics of the domestic system in the woollen industry: in showing how workshops, fulling mills and Cloth Halls were bound together by skeins of movement which were not incidental to the workings of the labour process. But neither were they detached from the restructuring and recomposition of the labour process and the emergence of the factory system, and in these transformations questions of *location* and *relocation* become intrusive. As I've said already, I'm not suggesting an uncritical return to spatial analysis, but it does seem to me that many of the traditional concerns if not the concepts of (say) location theory or diffusion theory, appropriately reworked and integrated into wider theorems of production and reproduction, ought to be of central importance to an understanding of what historical geography is about.

ALAN BAKER: Yes, those traditions are in danger of being overlooked and, as you say, they necessarily go beyond economic geography. Frameworks within which to conceptualize change have been devised within the traditions of historical and cultural geography established primarily by Darby and Sauer. The search for orderly descriptions of 'man's role in changing the face of the earth' resulted in the construction of some templates which have been employed for a wide range of periods and places. Darby's identification of some of the major 'vertical' themes of landscape change has been an inspiration for many, while his adoption of Broek's interdigitation of 'vertical' themes with 'horizontal' cross-sections to build a narrative staircase of landscape transformation has been followed by some. The ideas developed by Sauer about the diffusion of cultural forms through time and over space became a central concern of the 'Berkeley School' of cultural geography. Writings in both these traditions have been described as being informal and metaphorical, descriptive of pattern more than understanding of process. They undoubtedly promoted many 'good works' in historical geography, but their failure to get to grips with the processes of change has been seen by some as a serious shortcoming. Building upon these traditions, but also drawing upon ideas from contemporary human geography, Andrew Clark and – although his contribution is not always fully acknowledged – Clifford Smith explicated a concept of 'geographical change' which has come to be identified with the practice of historical (as opposed to cultural) geography in North America. Clark in particular was keen to encourage the study of a regional historical geography which focused upon processes and upon regions as 'continually changing entities'.

During the late 1960s there emerged a more rigorous attempt to formulate some basic concepts of geographical change, as part of the 'model-building' enterprise. At the outset, however, Harvey had offered both hope and hesitation. While he believed that the development of cultural forms over space was not a haphazard process and that principles of spatial evolution could be developed, he also warned that 'no simple monolithic principle holds the key to explanation, nor, even, do few principles combined offer an adequate explanation of the tremendous complexity of change in the real world'. The combination of caution and optimism is also found running through Harvey's dissection of temporal modes of explanation in geography. Similarly, John Langton's thoroughgoing critique of a systems approach to the study of change in human geography circumspectly balanced its merits against its limitations, concluding both that 'systems theory offers concepts about processes which are unrivalled in their analytical scope' and that 'the adoption of their approach to causal analysis involves many fundamental problems', particularly in connection with the concept of controlled feedback and with difficulties of calibrating such models with surviving historical sources. Nevertheless, Langton's own study of coal-mining in Lancashire in the seventeenth and eighteenth centuries, *Geographical Change and Industrial Revolution*, stands as the most sustained endeavour by an historical geographer to employ such an approach to the analysis of geographical change. Whatever one thinks about systems theory in general or Löschian economics in particular, Langton's monograph demonstrates the value of explicitly adopting a theoretical and interdisciplinary approach to what is fundamentally recognized as an empirical analysis in historical geography.

There is paradoxically even a good *theoretical* case for claiming that there exists no useful alternative to *empirical* analysis in the study of non-equilibrium situations. But the recognition of historical specificity need not exclude – indeed, must be reconciled with – the acknowledgement of historical structures: the personality of a place may be viewed as the outcome of *événements, conjonctures* and *structures* which involve both contingencies and causalities. If this is so, then we ought not to seek for, or expect to be able to sustain, either a *single* concept of geographical change, of regional transformation, or an *infinity* of concepts. It is the middle ground between these two poles that still awaits thorough exploration.

University of Cambridge

Notes

Notes to Chapter I

1 Just as this essay was basically inspired by Clifford Darby's concern with the method of historical geography, so its title owes much to one of his classic papers: H. C. Darby, 'On the relations of history and geography', *Transactions and Papers of the Institute of British Geographers*, 19 (1953), 1–11. A summary of an earlier version of this present essay has been published: A. R. H. Baker, 'On the relations of historical geography and the *Annales* school of history', *Proceedings of the 24th International Geographical Congress, Section 9; Historical Geography* (Tokyo, 1982), 318–22.

2 A general essay such as this one must assume on the part of its readers some acquaintance with the background literature. Furthermore, the field which it covers is extensive. These notes and references, therefore, are not exhaustive. Instead, they cite principal works and provide support for those statements most likely to be contested. Furthermore, although this essay explores the relations of history and geography principally in France it does so mainly with an English-speaking audience in mind, so that it is an exercise not only in interpretation, but also, though less importantly, in translation: for this reason, publications referred to are predominantly those readily available in English.

3 L. Febvre, *La terre et l'évolution humaine; introduction géographique à l'histoire* (Paris, 1922); C. O. Sauer, 'The morphology of landscape', *University of California Publications in Geography*, 2 (1925), 19–54; M. Bloch, *Les caractères originaux de l'histoire rurale française* (Oslo and Paris, 1931); H. C. Darby, *An historical geography of England before A.D. 1800* (Cambridge, 1936).

4 A. Buttimer, 'Charism and context: the challenge of *la géographie humaine*' in D. Ley and M. S. Samuels (eds), *Humanistic geography: prospects and problems* (London, 1978), pp. 58–76.

5 The innovatory roles of Febvre and Bloch will be considered later in this essay; for those of Sauer and Darby, see: M. Williams, '"The apple of my eye": Carl Sauer and historical geography', *Journal of Historical Geography*, 9

195

(1983), 1–28; P. J. Perry, 'H. C. Darby and historical geography: a survey and review', *Geographische Zeitschrift*, 57 (1969), 161–78.

6 H. C. Darby, 'Some reflections on historical geography', *Historical Geography*, 9 (1979), 9–13.

7 An extensive and convenient – although not consistently convincing – critique of the *Annales* school of history is T. Stoianovich, *French historical method: the Annales paradigm* (Ithaca, N.Y., 1976).

8 A. R. H. Baker (ed.), *Progress in historical geography* (Newton Abbot, 1972); H. C. Prince, 'Historical geography in 1980' in E. H. Brown (ed.), *Geography yesterday and tomorrow* (Oxford, 1980), pp. 229–41.

9 X. De Planhol, 'Historical geography in France' in Baker (ed.), *Progress*, pp. 29–44.

10 H. S. Hughes, *The obstructed path: French social thought in the years of desperation* (New York, 1968), pp. 19–64; P. Burke (ed.), *Economy and society in early modern Europe: essays from 'Annales'* (London, 1972), pp. 1–10; P. Burke (ed.), *A new kind of history: from the writings of Febvre* (London, 1973), pp. ix–xvi; T. N. Clark, *Prophets and patrons: the French university and the emergence of the social sciences* (Cambridge, Mass., 1973); G. Iggers, *New directions in European historiography* (Middleton, Conn., 1975), pp. 43–79; W. R. Keylor, *Academy and community: the foundation of the French historical profession* (London, 1975); Stoianovich, *French historical method*, pp. 25–61.

11 Keylor, *Academy and community*, p. 211; M. Siegel, 'Henri Berr's *Revue de synthèse historique*', *History and Theory*, 9 (1970), 322–34.

12 L. Febvre, *Philippe II et la Franche Comté: étude d'histoire politique, religieuse et sociale* (Paris, 1912); L. Febvre, *La terre et l'évolution humaine*.

13 G. Huppert, 'The *Annales* school before the *Annales*', *Review*, 1 (1978), 215–19.

14 T. S. Kuhn, *The structure of scientific revolutions* (Chicago, 1972). A summary critique of the paradigm concept is D. R. Stoddart, 'The paradigm concept and the history of geography' in D. R. Stoddart (ed.), *Geography, ideology and social concern* (Oxford, 1981), pp. 70–80.

15 Iggers, *New directions*, pp. 43–5.

16 M. Bloch and L. Febvre, 'A nos lecteurs', *Annales d'histoire économique et sociale*, 1 (1929), 1–2; Burke, *Economy and society*, p. 4.

17 Burke, *A new kind of history*, p. xv.

18 L. Gallois, *Régions naturelles et noms de pays* (Paris, 1908).

19 Stoianovich, *French historical method*, pp. 76–88.

20 Febvre, *La terre*; Bloch, *Les caractères originaux de l'histoire rurale française*.

21 L. Febvre, review of *Cinquantième anniversaire du Laboratoire de Géographie, Université de Rennes* (Rennes, 1952), *Annales: économies, sociétés, civilisations* (1953), 372–7, on p. 374.

22 A. Buttimer, *Society and milieu in the French geographic tradition* (Chicago, 1971), p. 84; P. Claval, *Les mythes fondateurs des sciences sociales* (Paris, 1980), p. 160.

23 *Annales d'histoire économique et sociale*, 1 (1929), 606–11.

24 R. Mandrou, 'Géographie humaine et histoire sociale', *Annales: économies sociétés, civilisations*, 12 (1957), 619–26.

25 L. Febvre, 'Histoire et géographie: Sisyphe et les géographes', *Annales: économies, sociétés, civilisations*, 5 (1950), 87–90.

26 F. Braudel, *La Méditerranée et le monde mediterranéen à l'époque de Philippe II* (Paris, 1949); F. Braudel, 'En guise de conclusion', *Review*, 1 (1978), 243–53. A selection of his essays, translated into English, is: F. Braudel, *On history* (London, 1980).

27 R. M. Andrews, 'Some implications of the *Annales* school and its methods for a revision of historical writing about the United States', *Review*, 1 (1978), 165–80; M. Aymard, 'The *Annales* and French historiography (1929–72)', *Journal of European Economic History*, 1 (1972), 491–511; B. Bailyn, 'Braudel's geohistory – a reconsideration', *Journal of Economic History*, 11 (1951), 277–82; G. Dunbar, 'Geosophy, geohistory and historical geography: a study in terminology', *Historical Geography*, 10, no. 2 (1980), 1–8; J. Glenisson, 'France' in G. Iggers and H. T. Parker (eds), *International handbook of historical studies* (Westport, Conn., 1979), pp. 175–92; C. Higounet, 'La géohistoire' in C. Samaran (ed.), *L'histoire et ses méthodes* (Brussels, 1961), pp. 68–91; Huppert, 'The *Annales* school before the *Annales*', p. 218; S. Kinser, 'Annaliste paradigm? The geohistorical structuralism of Fernand Braudel', *American Historical Review*, 86 (1981), 63–105; M. M. Knight, 'The geohistory of Fernand Braudel', *Journal of Economic History*, 10 (1950), 212–16; I. Woloch, 'French economic and social history', *Journal of Interdisciplinary History*, 4 (1974), 43–57.

28 M. Harsgor, 'Total history: the *Annales* school', *Journal of Contemporary History*, 13 (1978), 1–13; Huppert, 'The *Annales* school before the *Annales*', p. 222.

29 F. Braudel, 'L'histoire et les sciences sociales: la longue durée', *Annales: économies, sociétés, civilisations*, 4 (1958), 725–53. This essay is translated and reprinted in Burke (ed.), *Economy and society*, pp. 11–42 and also in Braudel, *On history*, pp. 25–54.

30 G. McLennan, *Marxism and the methodologies of history* (London, 1981), pp. 129–44; R. C. Rhodes, 'Emile Durkheim and the historical thought of Marc Bloch', *Theory and Society*, 5 (1978), 45–73; C. Tilly, 'Anthropology, history and the *Annales*', *Review*, 1 (1978), 207–13; A. Burguière, 'The new *Annales*: a redefinition of the late 1960s', *Review*, 1 (1978), 195–205.

31 The comparative method imbues much work of the *Annales* school. For specific discussions of the method, see: M. Bloch, 'A contribution towards a comparative history of European societies' in *Land and work in medieval Europe: selected papers by Marc Bloch* (London, 1967), pp. 44–81; this essay was first published in 1928 in *Revue de synthèse historique*; J. A. Raftis, 'Marc Bloch's comparative method and the rural history of mediaeval England', *Mediaeval Studies*, 26 (1962), 349–68; W. H. Sewell, 'Marc Bloch and the logic of comparative history', *History and Theory*, 6 (1967), 208–18.

32 Samples – not necessarily selected as being representative – of the work of the *Annales* have been translated into English. See, for example: M. Bloch, *Feudal society*, 2 vols (London, 1961 and 1962); *idem, French rural history: an essay on its basic characteristics* (London, 1966); *idem, Land and work*; *idem, The Ile-de-France: the country around Paris* (London, 1971); F. Braudel,

The Mediterranean and the Mediterranean world in the age of Philip II, 2 vols (London, 1972 and 1973); *idem, Capitalism and material life* 1400–1800 (London, 1973); *idem, On history*; *idem, Civilisation and capitalism 15th–18th century*, 2 vols (London, 1900 and 1982); G. Duby, *Rural economy and country life in the medieval West* (London, 1968); E. Le Roy Ladurie, *Times of feast, times of famine: a history of climate since the year* 1000 (London, 1972); *idem, The peasants of Languedoc* (London, 1974); *idem, The territory of the historian* (Hassocks, 1979); *idem, Montaillou: Cathars and Catholics in a French village* 1294–1324 (Harmondsworth, 1980). Selected articles from the *Annales* are being published in English translation in a series edited by R. Forster and O. Ranum: 1 *Biology of man in society* (London, 1975); 2 *Family and society* (London, 1976); 3 *Rural society in France* (London, 1977); 4 *Deviants and the abandoned in French society* (London, 1978).

33 D. Fenlon, 'Encore une question: Lucien Febvre, the Reformation and the school of *Annales*', *Historical Studies*, 9 (1974), 65–81; J. Revel, 'The *Annales*: continuities and discontinuities', *Review*, 1 (1978), 9–18; I. Wallerstein, '*Annales* as resistance', *Review*, 1 (1978), 5–7.

34 See, for example; P. Veyne, *Comment on écrit l'histoire* (Paris, 1971); E. Le Roy Ladurie, *Le térritoire de l'historien*; P. Chaunu, *Histoire, science sociale* (Paris, 1974); J. Le Goff and P. Nova, *Faire de l'histoire*, 3 vols (Paris, 1974); M. de Certeau, *L'écriture de l'histoire* (Paris, 1975).

35 A recent example is: P. Vilar, *Une histoire en construction: approche marxiste et problématiques conjoncturelles* (Paris, 1982).

36 R. Cobb, 'Nous des *Annales*' in *A second identity: essays on France and French history* (London, 1969), pp. 76–83; O. Hufton, book review in *Economic History Review*, 35 (1982), 140–5. An ambivalent attitude towards the *Annales* school is also well expressed in B. Bailyn, 'Braudel's geohistory – a reconsideration', *Journal of Economic History*, 11 (1951), 277–82 and 'Review article', *Journal of Economic History*, 37 (1977), 1028–34.

37 Andrews, 'Some implications of the *Annales* school', p. 166; M. Aymard, 'The geo-history faces with the human sciences: the case of *Etudes Rurales*', *Journal of European Economic History*, 3 (1974), 493–504; R. Forster, 'Achievements of the *Annales* school', *Journal of Economic History*, 38 (1978), 58–76; Stoianovich, *French historical method*, pp. 232–9; F. R. Willis, 'The contribution of the *Annales* school to agrarian history: a review essay', *Agricultural History*, 52 (1978), 538–48.

38 D. C. North, 'Comment', *Journal of Economic History*, 38 (1978), 77–80; D. H. Pinkney, 'The dilemma of the American historian of modern France reconsidered', *French Historical Studies*, 9 (1975–6), 170–81.

39 Kinser, '*Annaliste* paradigm?', pp. 103–5.

40 P. Goubert, *Beauvais et le Beauvaisis de 1600 à 1730: contribution à l'histoire sociale de la France du XVIIe siècle* (Paris, 1960); E. Le Roy Ladurie, *Les Paysans de Languedoc* (Paris, 1965).

41 Iggers, *New directions*, pp. 43–5.

42 N. Birnbaum, 'The *Annales* school and social theory', *Review*, 1 (1978), 225–35; McLennan, *Marxism*, p. 132.

43 Iggers, *New directions*, pp. 71–3.
44 Braudel, 'L'histoire et les sciences sociales', pp. 725–53.
45 J. S. Cohen, 'The achievements of economic history: the Marxist school', *Journal of Economic History*, 38 (1978), 29–57; E. J. Hobsbawm, 'Comments', *Review*, 1 (1978), 157–62; Iggers, *New directions*, pp. 123–74; 'Marxism and modern social history'; McLennan, *Marxism*; Stoianovich, *French historical method*, pp. 111–18.
46 Birnbaum, 'The *Annales* school and social theory', pp. 233–4.
47 McLennan, *Marxism*, pp. 129, 136 and 141.
48 G. Iggers, 'Introduction: the transformation of historical studies in historical perspective' in G. Iggers and H. T. Parker (eds), *International handbook of historical studies* (Westport, Conn., 1979), pp. 1–13.
49 A. Sheridan, *Michel Foucault: the will to truth* (London, 1980), pp. 91–2 and 128–9; J. Weeks, 'Foucault for historians', *History Workshop Journal*, 14 (1982), 106–19.
50 P. Burke, 'Reflections on the historical revolution in France: the *Annales* school and British social history', *Review*, 1 (1978), 147–56. See also remarks upon this paper by Hobsbawm, pp. 157–62.
51 G. S. Jones, 'History: the poverty of empiricism' in R. Blackburn (ed.), *Ideology and social science: readings in critical social theory* (Glasgow, 1972), pp. 96–115; H. C. Prince, 'Fernand Braudel and total history', *Journal of Historical Geography*, 1 (1975), 103–6.
52 T. W. Freeman, 'Vidal de la Blache: a regional and human geographer' in *The geographer's craft* (Manchester, 1967), pp. 44–71; R. E. Dickinson, 'Vidal de la Blache (1845–1918)', in *The makers of modern geography* (London, 1969), pp. 208–12.
53 Burke, *Economy and society*, p. 4.
54 De Planhol, 'Historical geography in France', p. 29.
55 R. Harrison Church, 'The French school of geography' in G. Taylor (ed.), *Geography in the twentieth century* (London, 1951), pp. 70–91; De Planhol, 'Historical geography in France', p. 31.
56 L. Mirot, *Manuel de géographie historique de la France* (Paris, 1929); Darby (ed.), *An historical geography of England before A.D. 1800*.
57 H. C. Darby (ed.), *A new historical geography of England* (Cambridge, 1973); R. A. Dodgshon and R. A. Butlin (eds.), *An historical geography of England and Wales* (London, 1978); M. Dunford and D. Perrons, *The arena of capital* (London, 1983).
58 Buttimer, *Society and milieu*, p. 80.
59 *Ibid.*, pp. 43–58 and 73–85; P. Claval, 'De Vidal de la Blache au structuralisme' in P. Claval and J.-P. Nardy (eds), 'Pour le cinquantenaire de la mort de Paul Vidal de la Blache: études de l'histoire de la géographie', *Cahiers de Géographie de Besançon*, 16 (1968), 111–25.
60 P. Vidal de la Blache, *Tableau de la géographie de la France*, vol. 1 of E. Lavisse (ed.), *Histoire de France* (Paris, 1903). The concept is appraised in G. Dunbar, 'Geographical personality' in H. J. Walker and W. G. Haag (eds), *Man and cultural heritage: papers in honor of Fred B. Kniffen* (Baton Rouge, La, 1974), pp. 25–33.

61 A. Demangeon, *La Picardie et les régions voisines* (Paris, 1905), p. 456.
62 A. Meynier, 'Cinquante ans de géographie française' in *Cinquantième Anniversaire du Laboratoire de Géographie (1902–52) de l'Université de Rennes* (Rennes, 1952), pp. 47–65.
63 A. Demangeon, *Les sources de la géographie de la France aux Archives Nationales* (Paris, 1905).
64 Buttimer, *Society and milieu*, p. 84; Claval, *Les mythes fondateurs*, pp. 161–2.
65 Sister Mary Annette, 'The changing French region', *Professional Geographer*, 17 (1965), 1–5; *idem*, 'French geography in the sixties', *Professional Geographer*, 20 (1968), 92–7; Claval, 'De Vidal de la Blache au structuralisme', pp. 118–20.
66 Aymard, 'The *Annales* and French historiography', pp. 114–15; Glenisson in Iggers and Parker, *International handbook*, p. 177; V. Berdoulay, 'The Vidal–Durkheim debate' in D. Ley and M. S. Samuels (eds), *Humanistic geography: prospects and problems* (London, 1978), pp. 77–90.
67 P. Claval, 'Contemporary human geography in France', *Progress in Geography*, 7 (1974), 253–92.
68 De Planhol, 'Historical geography in France', pp. 40–4; J. L. M. Gulley, 'The practice of historical geography: a study of the writings of Professor Roger Dion', *Tijdschrift voor Economische en Sociale Geografie*, 52 (1961), 169–83.
69 R. Dion, 'La géographie humaine rétrospective', *Cahiers Internationaux de Sociologie*, 6 (1949), 3–27; Darby, 'On the relations of history and geography', p. 6.
70 R. Dion, 'La géographie historique' in G. Chabot, R. Clozier and J. Beaujeu-Garnier (eds), *La géographie française au milieu du XXe siècle* (Paris, 1957), 183–6.
71 Dion retired from the Collège de France in 1968. A summary of his lecture course there during his final year indicates the considerable degree to which he had abandoned the ideas which he had propounded twenty years earlier: R. Dion, 'Géographie historique de la France', *L'Annuaire du Collège de France*, 68 (1968–9), 503–18.
72 Buttimer, *Society and milieu*, p. 97; P. Claval, 'La pensée géographique: introduction à son histoire', *Publications de la Sorbonne. Série N. S. Recherches* 2 (1972), 34–5.
73 For example: L. Champier, 'La recherche française en matière d'histoire et de géographie agraire depuis un quart de siècle', *Revue de Géographie de Lyon*, 31 (1956), 319–27; A. Meynier, *Les paysages agraires* (Paris, 1958); E. Juillard, A. Meynier, X. De Planhol and G. Sautter (eds), 'Structures agraires et paysages ruraux', *Annales de l'Est*, 17 (1957), 1–188; E. Juillard, Géographie rurale française: travaux récents et tendances nouvelles', *Etudes Rurales*, 13 (1964), 47–70.
74 M. Sorre, 'Le rôle de l'explication historique en géographie humaine' in *Mélanges géographiques offerts à Philippe Arbos* (Clermont-Ferrand, 1953), pp. 19–22. This has been published in English as 'The role of historical explanation in human geography' in P. L. Wagner and M. W. Mikesell (eds), *Readings in cultural geography* (Chicago, 1962), pp. 44–7.
75 E. Juillard, 'Aux frontières de l'histoire et de la géographie', *Revue historique*,

215 (1956), 267–73; H. C. Darby, 'Historical geography' in H. P. R. Finberg (ed.), *Approaches to history* (London, 1962), pp. 127–56.
76 De Planhol, 'Historical geography in France', pp. 29–44.
77 Higounet, 'La géohistoire', pp. 71–82.
78 A. R. H. Baker, 'On the historical geography of France', *Journal of Historical Geography*, 6 (1980), 69–76. See also: H. D. Clout, 'The practice of historical geography in France', in H. D. Clout (ed.), *Themes in the historical geography of France* (London, 1977), pp. 1–19.
79 M. Mollat and P. Pinchemel, 'Rencontres de la géographie et de l'histoire' in Comité National Français de Géographie, *Recherches géographiques en France* (Paris, 1972), pp. 13–18.
80 J.-C. Boyer, 'Formes traditionnelles et formes nouvelles de la géographie historique: leur place dans la recherche en géographie', *Comité des Travaux Historiques et Scientifiques: Bulletin de la Section de Géographie*, 82 (1978), 55–63.
81 H. Clout, review in *Journal of Historical Geography*, 9 (1983), 72–3.
82 J. P. Ferrier, J. B. Racine and C. Raffestin, 'Vers un paradigme critique: matériaux pour un project géographique', *L'Espace Géographique*, 8 (1978), 291–7.
83 For three related reviews of the debate, see: A. R. H. Baker, 'Historical geography', *Progress in Human Geography*, 1 (1977), 465–74; *idem*, 'Historical geography: understanding and experiencing the past', *Progress in Human Geography*, 2 (1978), 495–504; *idem*, 'Historical geography: a new beginning?', *Progress in Human Geography*, 3 (1979), 560–70. See also V. V. Annenkov, 'New horizons of historical geography', *Historicka Geografia*, 20 (1982), 261–96.
84 Darby, 'Historical geography' in Finberg, *Approaches to history*, pp. 127–56.
85 P. Claval, 'Géographie historique', *Annales de Géographie*, 90 (1981), 669–71; Darby, 'On the relations of history and geography'; H. C. Darby, 'An historical geography of England: twenty years after', *Geographical Journal*, 126 (1960), 147–59; *idem*, 'Historical geography' in Finberg, *Approaches to history*, pp. 127–56; *idem*, 'The problem of geographical description', *Transactions and Papers of the Institute of British Geographers*, 30 (1962), 1–14.
86 Darby, 'Some reflections on historical geography', p. 10.
87 Darby, *An historical geography*.
88 Darby, 'On the relations of history and geography'.
89 H. C. Darby, *The theory and practice of geography* (London, 1947), pp. 19–20; *idem*, 'On the relations of history and geography', p. 6.
90 H. C. Darby, 'The changing English landscape', *Geographical Journal*, 117 (1951), 377–94.
91 Darby, 'On the relations of history and geography', p. 11.
92 Darby, 'An historical geography of England: twenty years after', p. 149.
93 Darby, *A new historical geography*.
94 Darby, 'An historical geography of England: twenty years after', p. 155.
95 D. Whittlesey, 'The horizon of geography', *Annals of the Association of American Geographers*, 35 (1945), 1–36.
96 Darby, 'The problem of geographical description', p. 8.

97 Darby, 'Historical geography', pp. 127–56.
98 Darby, 'The problem of geographical description', pp. 7–8.
99 A. R. H. Baker and M. Billinge (eds), *Period and place: research methods in historical geography* (Cambridge, 1982).
100 Baker, 'Historical geography: a new beginning?', p. 560.
101 D. Gregory, 'Historical geography' in D. Gregory, P. Haggett, D. M. Smith and D. R. Stoddart (eds), *The dictionary of human geography* (Oxford, 1981), pp. 146–50.
102 L. W. Hepple, 'Epistemology, model-building and geography', *Geographical Articles*, 10 (1967), 42–8; R. C. Harris, 'Theory and synthesis in historical geography', *Canadian Geographer*, 15 (1971), 157–72; A. H. Clark, 'Historical geography in North America' in Baker (ed.), *Progress in historical geography*, pp. 129–43.
103 A. H. Clark, 'The whole is greater than the sum of its parts: a humanistic element in human geography' in D. R. Deskins, G. Kish, J. D. Nystuen and G. Olsson (eds), *Geographic humanism, analysis and social action* (Ann Arbor, Mich., 1977); R. C. Harris, 'The historical mind and the practice of geography', pp. 123–37.
104 D. Gregory, 'The discourse of the past: phenomenology, structuralism and historical geography', *Journal of Historical Geography*, 4 (1978), 161–73.
105 D. Gregory, 'Social change and spatial structures' in T. Carlstein, D. Parkes and N. Thrift (eds), *Making sense of time* (London, 1978), pp. 38–55.
106 D. Gregory, *Ideology, science and human geography* (London, 1978), p. 172.
107 D. Gregory, 'Human agency and human geography', *Transactions of the Institute of British Geographers*, 6 (1981), 1–18.
108 D. Gregory, 'Action and structure in historical geography' in Baker and Billinge (eds), *Period and place*, pp. 244–50. For a recent discussion among historians about the writing of history, see: L. Stone, 'The revival of narrative: reflections on a new old history', *Past and Present*, 85 (1979), 3–24; E. J. Hobsbawm, 'The revival of narrative: some comments', *Past and Present*, 86 (1980), 3–8; P. Abrams, 'History, sociology and historical sociology', *Past and Present*, 87 (1980), 3–16. Perceptive reflections upon the writing of history are also to be found in T. Zeldin, 'Social history and total history', *Journal of Social History*, 10 (1976), 237–45.
109 M. Billinge, 'In search of negativism, phenomenology and historical geography', *Journal of Historical Geography*, 3 (1977), 55–67.
110 M. Billinge, 'Reconstructing societies in the past: the collective biography of local communities' in Baker and Billinge (eds), *Period and place*, pp. 19–32.
111 A. Giddens, *New rules of sociological method* (London, 1976); idem, *Central problems in social theory: action, structure and contradiction in social analysis* (London, 1979); idem, *A contemporary critique of historical materialism, Vol 1: Power, property and the state* (London, 1981).
112 A. R. H. Baker, 'On ideology and historical geography' in Baker and Billinge (eds), *Period and place*, pp. 233–43.
113 J. P. Sartre, *Critique de la raison dialectique* (Paris, 1960), translated as *Critique of dialectical reason* (London, 1976).
114 Useful critiques of Sartre's existential Marxism are to be found in two works

by M. Poster: *Existential Marxism in post-war France* (Princeton, N.J., 1975) and *Sartre's Marxism* (London, 1978).

115 R. Thabault's *Mon village 1848–1914: l'ascension d'un peuple* (Paris, 1945), translated as *Education and change in a village community: Mazières-en-Gâtine 1848–1914* (London, 1971).

116 E. B. Ackerman, *Village on the Seine: tradition and change in Bonnières, 1815–1914* (London, 1978).

117 T. Judt, 'The development of socialism in France: the example of the Var', *Historical Journal*, 18 (1975), 55–83; idem, *Socialism in Provence 1871–1914* (Cambridge, 1979).

118 T. Zeldin, *France 1848–1941, Vol. 1: Ambition, love and politics* (Oxford, 1973), pp. 130–97.

119 A. R. H. Baker, 'Ideological change and settlement continuity in the French countryside: the development of agricultural syndicalism in Loir-et-Cher during the late-nineteenth century', *Journal of Historical Geography*, 6 (1980), 163–77.

120 G. Wright, *Rural revolution in France: the peasantry in the twentieth century* (London, 1964).

121 A. Soboul, 'The French rural community in the eighteenth and nineteenth centuries', *Past and Present*, 10 (1956), 78–95; P. Gratton, *Les luttes des classes dans les campagnes* (Paris, 1971); M. Agulhon, *La République au village* (Paris, 1979), trans. as *The Republic in the village* (Cambridge, 1982).

122 M. Agulhon and M. Bodiguel, *Les associations au village* (Le Paradou, 1981).

123 E. Weber, *Peasants into Frenchmen: the modernisation of rural France 1870–1914* (London, 1977).

124 W. H. Sewell, *Work and revolution in France: the language of labor from the Old Regime to 1848* (Cambridge, 1980).

125 E. Shorter and C. Tilly, *Strikes in France 1830–1968* (Cambridge, 1974).

126 Y. Lequin, *La formation de la classe ouvrière régionale: les ouvriers de la région lyonnaise (1848–1914)* (Lyons, 1977).

127 H. D. Clout, *The land of France* (London, 1983).

Notes to Chapter 2

1 M. Billinge, 'Reconstructing societies in the past: the collective biography of local communities' in Alan R. H. Baker and M. Billinge (eds), *Period and place: research methods in historical geography* (Cambridge, 1982), pp. 19–32.

2 See for example, D. Gregory, 'Human agency and human geography', *Transactions of the Institute of British Geographers*, 6 (1981), 1–18; M. Billinge, 'Reconstructing societies in the past' in Baker and Billinge (eds), *Period and place*, pp. 19–21.

3 R. Gray, 'Bourgeois hegemony in Victorian Britain' in The Communist University of London (ed.) *Class, hegemony and party* (London, 1977), pp. 73–93; R. Williams, *Marxism and literature* (Oxford, 1977).

4 E. P. Thompson, 'The peculiarities of the English' in R. Miliband and J. Saville (eds), *The Socialist Register* (London, 1965), p. 357; Gray, 'Bourgeois hegemony' p. 75; N. Poulantzas, 'Marxist political theory in Great Britain',

New Left Review, 43 (1967). This common formulation by the three authors locates hegemony in the bourgeoisie and therefore necessarily views the landed interests' position as that of a fraction of capital. Debatable as this is for the mid-nineteenth century it appears to have absolutely no validity for the eighteenth century when the bourgeoisie can hardly be considered to have achieved even counter-hegemonic status. The location of hegemony was one of those issues fruitfully debated by Perry Anderson and E. P. Thompson in the mid-1960s. See also P. Anderson, 'Origins of the present crisis', *New Left Review*, 23 (1964).

5 M. J. Wiener, *English culture and the decline of the industrial spirit 1850–1880* (Cambridge, 1981).

6 For a full discussion of Weber's differentiation between class and status – the former tied to the means of production and the ability of social groups to develop particular life-styles, the latter tied to normative concepts of social rank and social esteem – see J. Scott, *The upper classes* (London, 1982).

7 This division of the bourgeoisie into 'grande bourgeoisie' and ordinary bourgeoisie is crucial, though it tends to be blurred in most accounts of nineteenth-century social development. However radically active it was at the beginning of the century, the grande bourgeoisie was to align itself with the landed interest and thereby bolster its flagging fortunes by mid-century. The ordinary bourgeoisie maintained its opposition to landed hegemony and ultimately inherited it itself.

8 The argument presented is a much condensed version of the author's Ph.D. thesis, 'Late Georgian and early Victorian Manchester: a cultural geography', University of Cambridge, 1982. This truncated version cannot hope to engage all the issues tackled in the larger work, nor can its treatment of a number of complex issues do more than caricature the argument. A fuller version is to appear in due course as *A cultural geography of industrialisation*.

9 Williams, *Marxism and literature*, pp. 108–14.

10 *Ibid.*, p. 111.

11 A. Gramsci, *A modern prince and other writings* (London, 1957); *idem*, *Prison notebooks* (London, 1970).

12 Williams, *Marxism and literature*, p. 112.

13 J. Foster, *Class struggle and the Industrial Revolution* (London, 1968). Foster's concept is considerably less subtle than Gramsci's hegemony, though it is indisputably better known to geographers, who have begun to adopt it just as historians and sociologists have begun to reject it. For Foster false consciousness is that system of values deliberately formulated by the bourgeoisie and imposed upon the working class in place of its own natural consciousness, in order to subdue its revolutionary tendencies and break down an emerging solidarity into smaller and more manageable interest groups. It is the implied knowledgeability, together with the implicitly mechanical character of the model, that has aroused the greatest objection. Hegemony avoids both these features.

14 This is in contradistinction to the current use of ideology within geography. Following the popularity and wide critical acclaim accorded to Derek Gregory's *Ideology, science and human geography* (London, 1978) ideology is frequently taken to mean 'unexamined discourse' – i.e. a science which does not critically

evaluate its own preconceptions. See also A. R. H. Baker, 'On ideology and historical geography' in Baker and Billinge (eds), *Period and place*, pp. 233–43. The definition of ideology adopted here – somewhat broader in scope – follows that outlined in Williams, *Marxism and literature*, pp. 55–74.

15 Williams, *Marxism and literature*, p. 59.

16 Gramsci, *Prison notebooks*, pp. 205–23.

17 *Ibid.*, pp. 223–7. This appears to be, in terms of social history in the nineteenth century, a fruitful and commonplace conception. Much recent work from E. P. Thompson's *Making of the English working class* (Harmondsworth, 1970) through Foster, *Class struggle*, to Raphael Samuel's 'The workshop of the world', *History Workshop*, 3 (1977), 6–72, has assumed (not perhaps incorrectly) that the fundamental task of social history is to chart the 'coming to itself' of the working class – its emancipation from ruling hegemonic ideas, and the attempt of dominant groups to subvert its natural historic mission through instrumental control. Other themes are also important.

18 Williams, *Marxism and literature*, p. 110.

19 *Ibid.*, p. 110.

20 See James F. Becker, *An outline of Marxist political economy* (Cambridge, 1978); Louis Althusser and Etienne Balibar, *Reading 'Capital'* (London, 1970) and Louis Althusser, *For Marx* (London, 1977). Culture always appears to fit uncomfortably within historical materialist analyses.

21 Thompson, 'The peculiarities of the English', p. 356.

22 Williams, *Marxism and literature*, pp. 112–13.

23 Gramsci, *Prison notebooks*, p. 223.

24 See for example Thompson, *The making of the English working class*; Gray, 'Bourgeois hegemony', pp. 79–81.

25 Thompson would of course insist that the working class was made long before this, and he is almost certainly right. Even the most reactionary of historians would accept that it was made by 1850, though Foster is busily unmaking it at about this time.

26 Poulantzas, 'Marxist political theory'; Gray, 'Bourgeois hegemony', pp. 74–5.

27 Gray, 'Bourgeois hegemony', p. 76.

28 *Ibid.*, pp. 73–9.

29 See Billinge, *Late Georgian and early Victorian Manchester*, pp. 49–95 and 446–511, and, from a different perspective, Scott, *Upper classes*, pp. 11–13.

30 For the actual agencies through which this was effected, see Billinge, 'Late Georgian and early Victorian Manchester', pp. 139–51 and, for a general outline, E. P. Thompson, *Whigs and hunters: origins of the Black Act* (London, 1975); H. T. Dickinson, *Liberty and property in eighteenth century Britain* (London, 1977), pp. 10–31.

31 J. Brewer, *Party ideology and popular politics at the accession of George III* (Cambridge, 1976) discusses this formation in an earlier phase, whilst E. Halévy, *England in 1815* (London, 1924), provides a detailed analysis for the ensuing period. Despite certain shifts of emphasis (the eclipse of principled Whigism and the growth of a new Toryism) and party allegiance, the two pictures are remarkably congruent, emphasizing that the emergence of bourgeois hegemony was a mid-nineteenth-century phenomenon.

32 The distinction between aristocracy and nobility is an important though difficult one. For a discussion of the hierarchies within landed society, see F. M. L. Thompson, *English landed society in the nineteenth century* (London, 1963); Scott, *Upper classes.*

33 The details of this assertion are explored below. The concept of counter-hegemony and precisely how it emerges is a difficult issue both theoretically and empirically. It is discussed in greater depth in Gramsci, *Prison notebooks*, pp. 198–220 (for the theory) and Billinge, *Late Georgian and early Victorian Manchester*, pp. 103–428 (for the empirical detail).

34 B. Disraeli, *Coningsby, or The new generation* (London, 1844), quoted in P. Bloomfield, *Disraeli* (London, 1961), p. 25. For a fuller discussion of the significance of the fictional works of this most symbolic and charismatic figure see M. Masefield, *Peacocks and primroses: a survey of Disraeli's novels* (London, 1953). For a splendid study of Mrs Gaskell and other provincial novelists (in particular the origins of their distinctive voice), see W. A. Craik, *Mrs Gaskell and the English provincial novel* (London, 1975).

35 C. Dickens, *Hard Times* (London, 1854). Gradgrind is a superb creation and nothing captures his spirit better than the image of him 'sitting in the room with the deadly statistical clock, proving something no doubt – probably in the main that the Good Samaritan was a Bad Economist' (p. 73). There are of course numerous commentaries and as many sociological analyses of the Dickensian life-world; amongst which the considerable achievement of *Hard Times* has figured prominently. The novel is perhaps unequalled in its portrayal of the roots and consequences of utilitarianism in the industrial towns. Probably the most brilliant and didactic study of the novel's place in the evolving context of urban perception is to be found in R. Williams, *The country and the city* (London, 1973).

36 If there was agreement over the existence of such polarization, there was, amongst novelists in particular, no real consensus over the desirability of one succeeding the other. Corrupt as the landed interest was it generated some sympathy and respect, some confidence and some colour – an honest robustness many appear to have found preferable to the prospect of bourgeois rule, which, it is suggested, might have been fairer and more efficient but at some expense: dullness, priggishness, insensitivity and a *laissez-faire* attitude towards the suffering of individuals.

37 W. Bagehot, *The English constitution* (London, 1928).

38 Thompson, 'The peculiarities of the English'; *idem*, *The making of the English working class.*

39 Scott, *Upper classes*, pp. 7–13.

40 See, for example, M. Weber, *Interpretation of social reality*, ed. R. Eldridge (London, 1972).

41 E. P. Thompson, *William Morris: romantic to revolutionary*, 2nd edn (London, 1977), p. 8.

42 *Ibid.*, pp. 8–9.

43 See, for example, the account in Dickinson, *Liberty and property.*

44 A number of interesting descriptions, together with a comprehensive analysis of contemporary trends, appear in J. B. Owen, *The eighteenth century: 1714–*

1815 (London, 1974), especially in the sections on society and culture in the two half-centuries (pp. 123–69 and 295–338). G. Mingay, *English landed society in the eighteenth century* (London, 1963) also gives insight into the aristocratic life-style, though in general he is inclined to play down the playboy image of the gentry, arguing that they took their national responsibilities far too seriously to indulge in the frivolous or unproductive with quite the regularity ascribed by others. In this he appears to have accepted the Spring line (see below) and remains unrepentant, maintaining a very similar tale in a later book – see G. Mingay, *The gentry* (London, 1977). The gentry are not of course identical in economic, social or cultural make-up to the aristocracy, though they do constitute a complementary element in the same basic power bloc. Mingay's rehabilitation is not altogether convincing and the more licensed portrait depicted here, though unsubtle, may be closer to the truth – see D. Cannadine, 'Aristocratic indebtedness in the nineteenth century', *Economic History Review*, 30 (1977), 624–50.

45 For a thorough and stimulating account of both the Elgin expedition and its impact on English art and English art patronage see W. Gaunt, *Victorian Olympus* (London, 1952) especially pp. 9–19. Also useful are the accounts by T. Ashcroft, *English art and English society* (London, 1959); F. D. Klingender, *Art and the Industrial Revolution* (London, 1947) and, in a broader tradition, D. Pilcher, *The Regency style 1800–1830* (London, 1947). An unusual and interesting perspective on changing English tastes and their financial implications can be found in G. R. Reitlinger, *The economics of taste: the rise and fall of picture prices 1760–1960* (London, 1961).

46 This is exhaustively discussed in L. Namier, *The structure of politics at the accession of George III*, 2nd edn (London, 1957), an interpretation challenged more recently by Brewer, *Party ideology*, especially part II.

47 For a brief though informative discussion of latitudinarianism, see R. Porter, *English society in the eighteenth century* (Harmondsworth, 1982). More exhaustive treatments can be found in: N. Sykes, *Church and State in the eighteenth century* (Cambridge, 1934); S. C. Carpenter, *Eighteenth century Church and people* (London, 1959). Also useful are: R. N. Stromberg, *Religious liberalism in eighteenth century England* (London, 1954); G. R. Cragg, *Reason and authority in the eighteenth century* (Cambridge, 1964). Briefly, latitudinarianism preached religious moderation, was 'anti-enthusiasm' and preferred to regard itself as a general feature of life rather than as an apodictic code. One contemporary christened it 'Christianity without tears', and two texts became central to its teaching: 'Be not righteous overmuch' and 'His commandments are not grievous'. It was precisely this attitude that was challenged, first by Wesley and subsequently by the Tractarians of the Oxford Movement.

48 This is, of course, the argument pursued in R. H. Tawney, *Religion and the rise of capitalism* (Harmondsworth, 1967). There is not space here to enter into the complexities of the issue, though the thesis has been subjected to intense scrutiny. See for example O. Chadwick, *The secularization of the European mind in the nineteenth century* (Cambridge, 1976), pp. 1–9.

49 See Sykes, *Church and State*, for the constitutional basis and background. For the role of religion more generally, see A. D. Gilbert, *Religion and society in*

industrial England; church, chapel and social change 1740–1914 (London, 1976), pp. 51–124. This quasi-quantitative account charts the changes in religious persuasion of the period in the wider context of the political tensions evident in the transition from proto-industrialized to industrialized society. It is an important theme also taken up in W. R. Ward, *Religion and society in England 1710–1850* (London, 1972) and in O. Chadwick, *The Victorian Church*, 2 vols (London, 1971). Some idea of the total exclusion suffered by Nonconformists, particularly in respect of institutional training and office, is offered in H. McLachlan, *English education under the Test Acts* (London, 1931) and in M. R. Watts, *The Dissenters* (Oxford, 1978).

50 For a discussion of the role of the local clergy see J. Hurt, *Education in evolution* (London, 1972), pp. 39–67; Gray, 'Bourgeois hegemony', pp. 82–4. The theme is more fully explored in Billinge, *Late Georgian and early Victorian Manchester*, pp. 87–92.

51 See Chadwick, *Secularization of the European mind*, pp. 1–47. This fascinating study addresses a number of important and unusual themes in the emergence of a modern, more secular, mentality – from liberalism to science, from Marxism to Darwinism.

52 Evangelism seems to have emerged partly as a reaction to the laxities of latitudinarianism and partly as a challenge to Nonconformity, the spectacular successes of which were beginning to threaten the stability of Anglicanism. Whether this was a strictly theological issue (the capturing of souls) or a political issue (the constitutional position of the Church) is another matter. Tractarianism and the Oxford Movement emerged again in response both to latitudinarian shortcomings and to the belief that the Church should assert its independence of Parliamentary controls: that the relations between Church and State had become one-sided and inimical to the spiritual interests and needs of the country.

53 Gray, 'Bourgeois hegemony', p. 82.

54 These two necessarily went hand in hand, albeit on different time-scales. I will argue later that it was the economic decline of the landed interest that set in train a whole series of reactions, which culminated in the loss of political power and control. Since political control was amongst the most precious of aristocratic possessions, the struggle to retain it was as long as it was intense. The mechanisms of its loss – other than the purely economic – are discussed below.

55 E. Hobsbawm, *The age of capital* (London, 1975), p. 248.

56 The details of the Rothschild and Brookes families are taken from several sources including L. H. Grindon, *Manchester banks and bankers* (Manchester, 1877). A great deal of similarly useful information can be found in V. A. C. Gatrell, 'The commercial middle class in Manchester', unpublished Ph.D. dissertation, University of Cambridge, 1972. For a more general account, see C. Moraze, *The triumph of the middle classes* (London, 1966).

57 See Billinge, *Late Georgian and early Victorian Manchester*, pp. 118–31.

58 See N. Gash, *Politics in the age of Peel* (London, 1953). Gash's account can be instructively compared with accounts of the politics of the earlier age of George III. See also J. F. C. Harrison, *The early Victorians 1832–51* (London, 1971).

59 See Thompson, *Making of the English working class*, pp. 515–628.

60 See T. Tholfsen, *Working-class radicalism in mid-Victorian Britain* (London, 1976); Foster, *Class struggle*, pp. 125–202. For specific protest movements see, for example, E. Hobsbawm and G. Rudé, *Captain Swing* (London, 1969) and, for Luddism, D. Gregory, *Regional transformation and industrial revolution* (London, 1982).

61 Gray, 'Bourgeois hegemony', pp. 77–83.

62 Thompson, *The Socialist Register*, p. 326.

63 See note 47 above.

64 This will be discussed in more detail below. Some indication of the scale of such sales can be found in D. Cannadine, 'Aristocratic indebtedness in the nineteenth century', especially pp. 630–1.

65 See for example C. P. Darcy, *The encouragement of the fine arts in Lancashire 1760–1860* (Manchester, 1975), pp. 20–41 and 63–79.

66 F. M. L. Thompson, *English landed society in the nineteenth century*, pp. 76–108. See also Mingay, *English landed society in the eighteenth century*; C. Wood, *Victorian panorama* (London, 1976) and, for a slightly earlier period, Halévy, *England in 1815*, pp. 486–524.

67 The scientific involvement of the bourgeoisie has been extensively documented, as has its instrumental role in the foundation and promulgation of the scientific society movement. Specific references will be given later where appropriate, and it is clearly impractical to list here all those volumes which would be of use to readers interested in this aspect of the late eighteenth century. A very full bibliography appears in Billinge, *Late Georgian and early Victorian Manchester*. Perhaps the most useful general indication of the wealth of material, and an obvious starting point for bibliographic research is the work by A. E. Musson and E. Robinson, *Science and technology in the Industrial Revolution* (Manchester, 1969), together with A. E. Musson (ed.), *Science, technology and economic growth in the eighteenth century* (London, 1972) and J. B. Morrell, 'Individualism and the structure of British science in 1830', *Historical Studies of the Physical Sciences*, 3 (1971), 184–201. Two journals have become particularly associated with attempts to chart the scientific involvement of the middle class, one English (*Business History*) and one American (*Science Studies*).

This, curiously, is one of the few issues on which Marxist and non-Marxist orthodoxies agree. Typical formulations are those of Halévy, *England in 1815*, pp. 524–5 ('It is in Nonconformist England excluded from the national Universities, in industrial England with its new centres of population and civilization, that we must seek the institutions which gave birth to the utilitarian and scientific culture of the new age'); S. F. Mason, *A history of the sciences: main currents of scientific thought* (London, 1953) ('The men of the industrial revolution with their scientific education . . . and technical interest forwarded institutions to promote . . . the sciences in their own locales'), and from the Marxist perspective J. D. Bernal, *The social functions of science* (London, 1939) ('It was in Leeds, Manchester, Birmingham, Glasgow and Philadelphia, rather than Oxford, Cambridge and London, that the science of the Industrial Revolution took root'). See also J. D. Bernal, *Science in history*, 3rd edn, vol. 2 (Harmondsworth, 1965).

68 Disraeli, *Coningsby*, p. 148.
69 See for example Musson and Robinson, *Science and technology*; D. S. L. Cardwell, *The organisation of science in England* (London, 1957); *idem* (ed.), *John Dalton and the progress of science* (Manchester, 1968); *idem, Artisan to graduate* (Manchester, 1974); R. H. Kargon, *Science in Victorian Manchester* (Manchester, 1977); A. Thackray, 'Science and technology in the Industrial Revolution', *History of Science*, 9 (1970); and, on a more discursive note, M. Neve, 'The Mancunian model; *Times Literary Supplement*, 21 July 1978. It could truly be said that the study of science and industry in Manchester has itself become a science and an industry.
70 B. Love, *Manchester as it is, or notices . . . of the metropolis of manufacturers* (Manchester, 1839). Another useful source is *Everett's panorama of Manchester* (Manchester, 1834).
71 Details of the city's institutions can also be found in *Bradshaw's Manchester Journal*, 1 (1841); *Slater's Manchester and Salford Directory* (Manchester, various dates); *Piggot's Manchester Directory* (Manchester, 1785); *Raffald's Manchester Directory* (Manchester, 1772 and 1781), etc.; and, for the later period, *The Yearbook of Scientific and Learned Societies of Great Britain and Northern Ireland*, 1 (1884). For an individual and highly entertaining view of the cultural life of the city later in the nineteenth century, see M. Kennedy (ed.), *The autobiography of Charles Hallé* (London, 1972).
72 There is, of course, considerable room for definitional haggling, and a great deal of fruitless discussion has concerned the logical and practical differences between scientist, natural philosopher and technologist. This argument has been summarized and brilliantly dismissed for the red herring it is by Rupert Hall: see A. R. Hall, 'What did the Industrial Revolution in Britain owe to science?' in N. McKendrick (ed.), *Historical perspectives: studies in English thought and society in honour of J. H. Plumb* (London, 1974), pp. 129–51. The Manchester 'school' which has been most obviously responsible for establishing the positive equation between science and technology has produced a number of very remarkable studies, the usual framework being one in which contemporary science either can or cannot be specifically linked to a given piece of technology. The empiricist argument on the other hand seeks to establish more generally that processes of industrial manufacture were operative long before their efficacy could be rationalized and explained scientifically. Alternatively the role of science has been reduced to that of making 'strategic' improvements to well-established craft techniques. Certain inventions have been singled out for particular appraisal – most notably the steam engine and chlorine bleaching, two areas where science ought to have had much to contribute. For differing interpretations of each (as well as a detailed review of the rift between the two positions) see Hall, 'What did the Industrial Revolution in Britain owe to science?'; Musson and Robinson, *Science and Technology*; P. Mathias, 'Who unbound Prometheus?' in Musson (ed.), *Science, technology and economic growth*.
73 This statement will be discussed at length later. It is worth noting at this juncture, however, that contemporary opinion did not idealize science as either a profession or a disconnected activity. Indeed it was at this time that

science became part of the cultural equipment of the *generally* literate. The divorce of science from the grasp of the averagely intelligent was a much slower process in Britain than in the rest of Europe, and though this may explain the relative backwardness of some British science in comparison to French and German achievements, it should also be noted that the demise of such 'amateurism' was accompanied in Britain by a constant and vocal expression of regret.

74 T. S. Ashton, *The Industrial Revolution* (London, 1948); Mathias, 'Who unbound Prometheus?'; Bernal, *Science in history*; R. E. Schofield, *The Lunar Society of Birmingham* (Oxford, 1963); *idem*, 'The industrial orientation of the Lunar Society of Birmingham', *Isis*, 48 (1957), 408–15.

75 There has always been a strong element of dissent from this positive formulation of science and technology, both from the point of view of empirically evidenced non-interactions and, more subtly, in the refutation of the position of scientific societies as simple research and development institutions. A few outstandingly well-argued examples of the former are: D. Landes, *The unbound Prometheus* (Cambridge, 1969); E. Ashby, *Technology and the academics* (London, 1958); Hall, 'What did the Industrial Revolution in Britain owe to science?'; A. P. Usher, *A history of mechanical invention* (Boston, 1954); C. C. Gillespie, 'The natural history of industry', *Isis*, 48 (1957), 398–407. Somewhat more equivocal are the accounts by D. S. L. Cardwell, *Technology, science and history* (London, 1972) and, by one of the founding fathers of the debate, R. K. Merton, 'Science, technology and society in seventeenth century England', *Osiris*, 4 (1938), 360–632.

76 Hall, 'What did the Industrial Revolution in Britain owe to science?', p. 129.

77 *Ibid.*, p. 151.

78 Ashby, *Technology*, pp. 50–1.

79 It is difficult to keep track of the many studies now appearing as scientific societies once again become the vogue in research in science history. Most of these studies concentrate on provincial institutions, since many of the metropolitan foundations (notably the Royal Society) were next to moribund at this time. A complete list of societies is available in the yearbook (*op. cit.*; see n. 71 above), and, for an earlier period, in A. Hume, *The learned societies and printing clubs of Great Britain* (London, 1854). A general overview of the research potential of societies can be found in R. E. Schofield, 'Histories of scientific societies: needs and opportunities for research', *History of Science*, 2 (1963), 70–83: M. Ornstein, *The role of scientific societies in the seventeenth century* (Chicago, 1928); D. McKie, 'Scientific societies to the end of the eighteenth century' in A. Ferguson (ed.), *Natural philosophy through the 18th century* (London, 1948), 133–43. Also useful is Cardwell, *Organisation of science*. For a bibliography of specific studies, see Billinge, *Late Georgian and early Victorian Manchester*.

80 Manchester institutions have been as exhaustively treated as Manchester scientists. See Cardwell (ed.), *Artisan to graduate* for studies of the two Mechanics' Institutes, the Royal Manchester Institution, the Municipal School of Technology, the Manchester College of Science and Technology and the University of Manchester Institute of Science and Technology; Kargon, *op. cit.*

for the Natural History Society, Geology Society and others; and, for the Statistical Society, T. S. Ashton, *Economic and social investigations in Manchester 1833–1933* (London, 1934).

81 Kargon, *Science in Victorian Manchester*, p. 33.

82 F. Nicholson, 'The Literary and Philosophical Society 1781–1851', *Memoirs of the Manchester Literary and Philosophical Society*, 68 (1924), 119–20.

83 *Ibid.*, p. 127.

84 Members' names can be identified from the *Complete List of Members and Officers of the Manchester Literary and Philosophical Society* (Manchester, 1896). Their occupations, religious affiliations, social backgrounds, etc., have been identified from contemporary directories, obituaries and local histories. Family papers, church records and other, miscellaneous sources have provided additional information. The complete study of over 600 members of the Society confirms the sketchy outline presented here and can be found in Billinge, *Late Georgian and early Victorian Manchester.* Where necessary, I shall indicate general sources here, but particular biographical events will not be closely referenced in what is an exploratory essay, not a definitive account.

85 See B. Abel-Smith, *The hospitals 1800–1948* (London, 1949); M. J. Peterson, *The medical profession in mid-Victorian London* (Berkeley, Calif., 1978).

86 E. M. Brockbank, *Sketches of the honorary medical staff of the Manchester Royal Infirmary* (Manchester, 1904).

87 *Ibid.*

88 T. Turner, *An address to the inhabitants of Lancashire* . . . (London, 1825); F. W. Jordan, *The life of Joseph Jordan, surgeon* (Manchester, 1904), pp. 52–3.

89 Brockbank, *Sketches*; and *Complete List of Members.*

90 Kargon, *Science in Victorian Manchester*, p. 7. This is also very clear from the official account of the Society's foundation, which appears as a Preface to Volume 1 of the *Memoirs.*

91 See Sir T. Baker, *Memorials of a Dissenting chapel . . . being a sketch of the rise of nonconformity in Manchester* (London, 1884); this volume, usefully contains a full list (with some bibliographic details) of the Cross Street trustees. See also E. L. H. Thomas, *Illustrations of the Cross Street chapel* (Manchester, 1917). For a broader contextual account of the position of Cross Street, its clientele and Unitarianism generally, see: H. McLachlan, *The Unitarian movement in the religious life of England* (London, 1934); R. V. Holt, *The Unitarian contribution to social progress in England* (London, 1952).

92 Rev. R. Harrison, *A sermon preached at the Dissenting chapel in Cross Street Manchester . . . by Ralph Harrison, together with a discourse . . . at the public commencement of Manchester Academy by Thomas Barnes* (Warrington, 1786). It is worth remembering that, as a sect, Unitarianism underwent a slow and complex evolution in the half-century after 1760. It was of course legally proscribed until 1813, but despite divisions of opinion within the Unitarian ranks, it was never in danger of schism, unlike the less exclusive and more factional Methodists. In this sense Joseph Priestley (see below) was characteristic of all parties loyal to the central Unitarian belief.

93 A. Raistrick, *Quakers in science and industry* (Newton Abbot, 1968); Holt, *The Unitarian contribution.*

94 Baker, *Memorials of a Dissenting chapel*, p. 70.

95 See, for example S. Shapin, 'The Potteries Philosophical Society', *Science Studies*, 2 (1972); *idem*, 'Property, patronage and the politics of science: the founding of the Royal Society of Edinburgh', *British Journal for the History of Science*, 7 (1974); A. D. Orange, 'The British Association for the Advancement of Science: the provincial background', *Science Studies*, 1 (1971); *idem*, 'The origins of the British Association for the Advancement of Science', *British Journal for the History of Science*, 6 (1972); *idem*, *Philosophers and provincials: the Yorkshire Philosophical Society 1822–44* (Leeds, 1973); M. Berman, 'The early years of the Royal Institution 1799–1810', *Science Studies*, 2 (1972); *idem*, *Social change and scientific organisation: the Royal Institution 1799–1844* (London, 1978).

96 The achievement of office in most of the 'ancient' professions required aristocratic patronage and usually a seal of approval such as that granted by public school or university (an exception was significantly the medical profession – ancient in one sense, it did not have the social kudos of the other professions, being related still to the blood-letting, barber tradition. Thus, important as the profession was, it had no status – hence the medical thrust of the Literary and Philosophical Society's founders). In the case of the other professions, natural aversion to the 'Old Corruption', together with social or legal exclusion from many of the establishments which fed the professions, made the law, Civil Service, education, etc., a closed shop to the ascendant middle class. Science on the other hand was a bourgeois preserve and combined in practice as well as in theory the principles of merit and self-help. Success, respect and reward through effort was its motto, and it was a theme taken up with a good deal of, albeit Hobsonian, vigour.

97 See, for example, A. Aspinall, *Politics and the press* (London, 1949). Such a view of the genteel professions was also widely promulgated in the institutes – even in fact in the Mechanics' Institutes and the Society for the Diffusion of Useful Knowledge: for further details, see E. Storella, '"Oh what a world of profit and delight": the Society for the Diffusion of Useful Knowledge', unpublished Ph.D. dissertation, Brandeis University, 1969. For Mechanics' Institutes and the inculcation of the working classes into bourgeois professional prejudice, see M. Tylecote, *The Mechanics' Institutes of Lancashire and Yorkshire before 1957* (Manchester, 1957). *Blackwood's Magazine* carries such sentiments as a recurring theme.

98 Such associations would, of course, fit nicely into Foster's idea of conscious ideological imposition.

99 'Within safe social limits' was something of a key-note. As I have already suggested, the role of the humble came to occupy a central position in scientific interpretations of the self-help movement identified with the name of Samuel Smiles. The judicious balancing act consisted of upholding unequivocally Smiles' doctrinaire propositions (the very justification for non-intervention in the economic systems which oppressed the working class) yet at the same time controlling the political and social ambitions of those not only 'helping themselves' but demanding their just rewards for so doing. In a religous age one might suppose that this left a good deal of scope for divine intervention,

but in the early nineteenth century it was the middle class rather than God who decided whether or not to 'help those who helped themselves'. It was a dangerous message, since the bourgeoisie palpably did not reward the most ambitious artisans – only those who strove to improve themselves without losing their sense of deference or position. Self-help, like Newtonian science, was a double-edged weapon which required delicate handling. Such skills were only acquired after a good deal of trial and – unfortunately – error.

100 T. Henry, 'On the advantages of literature and philosophy in general and especially on the consistency of literary and philosophical with commercial pursuits', *Memoirs of the Manchester Literary and Philosophical Society*, 1 (1785), 14.

101 Sir B. Heywood, *Addresses delivered at the Manchester Mechanics' Institution* (London, 1843), p. 17.

102 Dickens, *Hard Times*. From the very first page of the novel the small children (known only by their number) are referred to as 'pitchers' since they are nothing more than empty vessels waiting to be filled with facts. For an excellent discussion of education at this time, as well as of the spirit and method of the Lancaster and Bell system, see Hurt, *Education in evolution*, chapter 1; and, more generally, J. Lawson and H. Silver, *A social history of education* (London, 1973).

103 J. Priestley, *Experiments and observations on different kinds of air* (London, 1774), p. xiv. Joseph Priestley was forever the Establishment's scourge, so much so that in 1791 he was physically attacked by Church and King rioters. Throughout his life he was branded a radical and an atheist, despite his strong Unitarian persuasions. As scientist, philosopher, lecturer and later Non-conformist minister he was a symbol of bourgeois activism and a convenient target for Anglican/Tory retaliation. At no stage in his remarkable career did he compromise his beliefs, but it was his reply to Burke's *Reflections on the French Revolution*, following closely on the heels of yet another theological polemic – *History of early opinions concerning Jesus Christ* (1786) – that finally precipitated the crisis in 1791, when a large mob broke into his home and laboratory in Birmingham. His books, manuscripts and scientific apparatus were destroyed in a violent act of aristocratically sponsored exorcism. The Manchester Literary and Philosophical Society proposed not only its condolences but a subscription to replace his damaged belongings.

104 See M. J. Cullen, *The statistical movement in early Victorian Britain* (London, 1975).

105 See A. Redford, *The history of local government in Manchester* (London, 1939); S. D. Simon, *A century of city government: Manchester 1838–1938* (London, 1938). This pattern of rapid colonization by Literary and Philosophical Society alumni is mirrored in national politics as well. By the end of the nineteenth century some twenty-one members of the Society had become M.P.s. The dates of their election to Parliament chart the changing status of the Manchester elite and the success of its social overtures outside the city. Having been without an M.P. before 1832, the Society was continuously represented for the rest of the nineteenth century, and after 1859 there were only four years in which the Society had fewer than three members simultaneously in the House.

106 See Billinge, *Late Georgian and early Victorian Manchester*. The only Mancunian family known to have made the complete transition within a generation was that of the Unitarian banker John Jones: his son-in-law built up the family fortune to an estimated £5,000,000, becoming 'one of the wealthiest subjects in the world' and the first Lord Overstone. See D. P. O'Brien, *The correspondence of Lord Overstone* (Cambridge, 1971); F. M. L. Thompson, *English landed society*, p. 39.

107 Billinge, *Late Georgian and early Victorian Manchester*, pp. 490–511.

108 Attributed to Peel in the *Everyman dictionary of quotations & proverbs* (London, 1951).

109 F. M. L. Thompson, *English landed society*, p. 63.

110 Details of the Greg family are assembled from several sources including: F. Collier, 'Samuel Greg and Styal Mill', *Memoirs of the Manchester Literary and Philosophical Society*, 85 (1943); the obituary of R. H. Greg in the *Manchester Guardian*, 23 Feb. 1875. Details of the Heywoods can be found in T. Heywood, *A memoir of Sir Benjamin Heywood* (Manchester, 1888) and in Baker, *Memorials of a Dissenting chapel*, pp. 108, 115, 123.

111 Stone, L. *The crisis of the aristocracy 1558–1641* (Oxford, 1965).

112 See Cannadine, 'Aristocratic indebtedness', p. 626.

113 See D. A. Spring, 'English land owners and nineteenth century industrialism', together with J. T. Ward, 'Landowners and mining' and R. W. Sturgess, 'Landownership, mining and urban development in nineteenth century Staffordshire', all in J. T. Ward and R. G. Wilson (eds), *Land and industry: the landed estate and the Industrial Revolution* (Newton Abbot, 1971).

114 T. J. Raybould, 'The development and organisation of Lord Dudley's mineral estates 1774-1845', *Economic History Review*, 21 (1968); Cannadine, 'Aristocratic indebtedness'.

115 Spring has published extensively on this theme. Some of his major statements are: 'The English landed estate in the age of coal and iron 1830-80', *Journal of Economic History*, 11 (1951); 'The Earls of Durham and the great northern coalfield 1830-80', *Canadian Historical Review*, 33 (1952); 'English land ownership in the nineteenth century: a critical note', *Economic History Review*, 9 (1957); *The English landed estate in the nineteenth century: its administration* (Baltimore, Md, 1963).

116 Sturgess, 'Landownership, mining and urban development'.

117 Quoted in Cannadine, 'Aristocratic indebtedness', p. 640. See also M. Girouard, *The Victorian country house* (Oxford, 1971), pp. 125–30; J. Mordaunt Crook, 'Patron extraordinary: John Third Marquis of Bute (1847–1900)' in *Victorian South Wales: architecture, industry and society*, Victorian Society: Seventh Conference Report (London, 1969), pp. 5–22.

118 Mordaunt Crook, *Victorian South Wales*, p. 17.

119 The Thompsonian view, like Spring's, has been reiterated several times, notably in F. M. L. Thompson, 'The end of the great estate', *Economic History Review*, 8 (1955); *idem*, 'English great estates in the nineteenth century (1790–1914)' in *Contributions to the First International Conference of Economic History* (Paris, 1960); and, of course, Thompson, *English landed society*.

120 See G. C. Brauer, *The education of a gentleman: theories of gentlemanly education in England 1660–1775* (New York, 1959); Stone, *Crisis of the aristocracy*, pp. 303–17.

121 See Cardwell, *The organisation of science*, pp. 45–50.

122 See Musson and Robinson, *Science and technology*. Chapter 5 ('Training captains of industry') details the development of the education of Matthew Robinson Boulton Jr (1770–1842) and James Watt Jr (1769–1848). It is clear that neither took their European tours quite as seriously as their fathers might have wished.

123 See Cardwell, *Organisation of science*, pp. 20–1. Musson and Robinson supply an alternative explanation for the decline of dissenting academies: see their *Science and technology*, p. 85.

124 See F. Musgrove, 'Middle class education and employment in the nineteenth century', *Economic History Review*, 12 (1959); H. J. Perkin, 'Middle class education and employment in the nineteenth century: a critical note', *Economic History Review*, 14 (1961).

125 Letter to Rev. Mr Deane, 2 November 1780, quoted in Musson and Robinson, *Science and technology*, p. 203.

126 See Darcy, *Encouragement of the fine arts* and for an interesting if idiosyncratic side-light G. E. Fussell, *James Ward R.A.: animal painter 1769–1859 and his England* (London, 1974), chapter 3.

127 Many prominent members of the middle class turned to the court painters during the early nineteenth century in this way. No longer satisfied with the work of lesser artists, they employed the best and, perhaps not coincidentally, the manner of their portrayal changed. Never keen to emphasize a commercial connection, they quickly learned the value of a rusticated setting and an equestrian pose – the bread and butter of the court painters. Even artists like Joseph Wright of Derby, who had made the romanticized industrial scene an acceptable genre, found, when it came to portraits, a fashionable demand for a less authentic style: see B. Nicolson, *Joseph Wright of Derby: painter of light*, 2 vols (London, 1958).

128 See W. Weber, *Music and the middle class* (London, 1975).

129 *Ibid.*, pp. 53–84.

130 G. Best, *Mid-Victorian Britain* (London, 1971), pp. 218–78; W. L. Burn, *The age of equipoise: a study of the mid-Victorian generation* (London, 1968). Also interesting, though a little more diffuse, is R. D. Altick, *Victorian people and ideas* (London, 1973), pp. 1–33 and 269–91, together with W. F. Houghton, *The Victorian frame of mind* (New Haven, Conn., 1957).

131 See E. P. Thompson, *William Morris*; W. Gaunt, *The Pre-Raphaelite tragedy* (London, 1942); Wood, *Victorian panorama*.

132 See, for example, J. Betjeman and J. Gay, *London's historic railway stations* (London, 1972).

133 For a general account of the Gothic Revival in Britain, see K. Clark, *The Gothic Revival: a study in the history of taste* (London, 1950).

134 Kennedy (ed.), *The autobiography of Charles Hallé*.

135 *Prospectus of the Royal Manchester Institution:* 'Proposal of 1823' in Packet B4, Archives of the RMI, Manchester Central Reference Library.

136 See for example D. Gadd, *Georgian summer: Bath in the eighteenth century* (London, 1971); R. Lennard, *Englishmen at rest and play* (London, 1931); P. J. N. Havins, *The spas of England* (London, 1976); J. Lowerson and J. Myerscough, *Time to spare in Victorian England* (London, 1977), pp. 23–46.

Notes to Chapter 3

1 E. Gaskell, *Mary Barton: a tale of Manchester life* (London, 1848), Preface.

2 The phrase is that of Eric Hobsbawm, who provides a summary survey of the continental European revolutions in his *The age of capital 1848–1875* (London, 1975).

3 T. Nairn, 'The English working class', *New Left Review*, 24 (1964), 43.

4 P. Anderson, 'Origins of the present crisis', *New Left Review*, 23 (1964), 196.

5 G. Stedman Jones, 'Society and politics at the beginning of the world economy', *Cambridge Journal of Economics*, 1 (1977), 77–92.

6 For illuminating introductions to these themes, see J. Urry, 'Duality of structure: some critical issues', *Theory, culture and society*, 1 (1982), 100–6; B Hindess, 'Power, interests and the outcomes of struggles', *Sociology*, 16 (1982), 498–511.

7 The following paragraphs derive from J. Foster, *Class struggle and the Industrial Revolution* (London, 1974) and his response to Musson's critique: J. Foster, 'Some comments on "Class struggle and the labour aristocracy, 1830–1860"', *Social History*, 3 (1976), 357–66.

8 Foster, 'Comments', p. 363; G. Stedman Jones, 'Class struggle and the Industrial Revolution', *New Left Review*, 90 (1975), 37.

9 Foster, *Class struggle*, p. 3.

10 N. Poulantzas, *State, power, socialism* (London, 1978); J. Urry, 'Social relations, space and time' in D. Gregory and J. Urry (eds), *Social relations and spatial structures* (London, forthcoming).

11 P. Anderson, *Arguments within English Marxism* (London, 1980), pp. 31–2. Anderson also identifies a third thesis, the implication of 'closure': the claim that the English working class was in some sense 'made' by the early 1830s. This intersects with the first two theses; it is considered in both sections of the essay which follow because it entails a discussion not simply of class formations in the 1830s and early 1840s but also of 'hegemony' in the late 1840s and 1850s; as Anderson asks, 'if the same class could be made by the 30s, unmade after the 40s, and remade during the 80s, how ultimately satisfactory is the whole vocabulary of making itself?'. Anderson, *Arguments*, pp. 46–7. The following paragraphs derive from E. P. Thompson, *The making of the English working class* (Harmondsworth, 1968); *idem*, 'Patrician society, plebeian culture', *Journal of Social History*, 7 (1974), 382–405; *idem*, 'Eighteenth-century English society: class struggle without class?', *Social History*, 3 (1978), 133–65; *idem*, *The poverty of theory and other essays* (London, 1978).

12 N. Thrift, 'On the determination of social action in space and time', *Society and Space*, 1 (1983), 28.

13 P. Abrams, *Historical sociology* (Shepton Mallet, 1982), p. xiv; *idem*, 'History, sociology, historical sociology', *Past and Present*, 87 (1980), 3–16.

14 D. Gregory, 'Human agency and human geography', *Transactions of the Institute of British Geographers*, 6 (1981), 1–18.
15 Anderson, *Arguments*, p. 39.
16 R. Johnson, 'Edward Thompson, Eugene Genovese and socialist–humanist history', *History Workshop Journal*, 6 (1978), 79–100.
17 There is no space here to review the continuing debate, but my own views concur with those of G. McLennan, 'Richard Johnson and his critics: towards a constructive debate', *History, Workshop Journal* 8 (1979), 157–66 and A. Warde, 'E. P. Thompson and poor theory', *British Journal of Sociology*, 33 (1982), 224–37.
18 Anderson, *Arguments*, pp. 22, 33–4 and 39. I have made some attempt to bind these objective coordinates into the course of class struggle between the 1790s and the 1830s in my *Regional transformation and Industrial Revolution: a geography of the Yorkshire woollen industry* (London, 1982). The struggles of the early period, and in particular the campaigns of the Luddites, are largely ignored in the discussions which follow, but it is of course essential to locate any more complete historical geography in such a context: all I can offer here *are* 'sketches'.
19 In his review of Foster, Thompson identified 'a critical area of any Marxist analysis' as 'the weighting of the relations between "social being" and "social consciousness"'. 'What Foster does', he continued, 'is to place a very firm, indeed "hard" re-emphasis upon "social being" . . . I welcome this re-emphasis; and it is done with a force and a precision which does indeed make many previous studies (and I do not exclude my own) of social being appear impressionistic' (E. P. Thompson, 'Testing class struggle', *Times Higher Education Supplement*, 8 March 1974).
20 J. Saville, 'Class struggle and the Industrial Revolution' in R. Miliband and J. Saville (eds), *The Socialist Register* (London, 1974), pp. 226–40.
21 A. Cutler, B. Hindess, P. Hirst and A. Husain, *Marx's 'Capital' and capitalism today*, Vol. 1 (London, 1977), p. 164.
22 E. O. Wright, *Class, crisis and the state* (London, 1978).
23 D. Harvey, 'The urban process under capitalism: a framework for analysis', *International Journal of Urban and Regional Research*, 2 (1978), 112–13; see also his 'third-cut' at crisis theory in *idem, The limits to capital* (Oxford, 1982).
24 Saville, 'Class struggle', p. 231.
25 J. O'Connor, 'The meaning of crisis', *International Journal of Urban and Regional Research*, 5 (1981), 331.
26 Saville, 'Class struggle', p. 231.
27 O'Connor, 'Meaning of crisis', p. 318.
28 Saville, 'Class struggle', p. 233.
29 Wright, *Class, crisis and the state*.
30 These paragraphs are derived from Foster, *Class struggle*.
31 R. J. Morris, *Class and class consciousness in the Industrial Revolution 1780–1850* (London, 1979), p. 42.
32 F. Crouzet, 'Toward an export economy: British exports during the Industrial Revolution', *Explorations in Economic History*, 17 (1980), 48–93; K. Barr, 'Long waves and the cotton-spinning enterprise, 1789–1849' in T. K. Hopkins

and I. Wallerstein (eds), *Processes of the world-system* (Beverly Hills, Calif., 1980), pp. 84–100; F. Engels, *The condition of the working class in England* (London, 1969), p. 117 – this was first published in German in 1845 and in English in 1892.

33 L. Faucher, *Manchester in 1844; its present condition and future prospects* (London, 1844), p. 16. I am indebted to Humphrey Southall for the transformed data on which Figure 1 is based. Maps like these can only be indicative, of course, and much finer quantitative analysis is needed before firm conclusions can be drawn; and these will always be limited by the deficiencies of the data. Hepple's preliminary findings, however, indicate that the county bankruptcy series reported in the *London Gazette* follows the business cycle reference series very closely, and his inter-county cross-spectral analysis suggests 'considerable leads and lags' within the space economy, with Lancashire and the East Midlands – both centres of the cotton industry – as leading areas and London and the south as lagging areas. See L. Hepple, 'Spectral techniques and the study of interregional economic cycles' in R. F. Peel, M. Chisholm and P. Haggett (eds), *Processes in physical and human geography: Bristol essays* (London, 1975), pp. 392–408.

34 Faucher, *Manchester*, p. 140: for modern analyses of cotton exports, see Crouzet, 'Export economy'; D. Farnie, *The English cotton industry and the world market 1815–1896* (Oxford, 1979).

35 S. D. Chapman, *The cotton industry in the Industrial Revolution* (London, 1972), p. 45.

36 Farnie, *English cotton industry*, p. 130; see also R. Smith, 'Manchester as a centre for the manufacturing and merchanting of cotton goods, 1820–1830', *University of Birmingham Historical Journal*, 4 (1953), 47–65.

37 Engels, *Condition*, p. 115.

38 British Parliamentary Papers (1842), XXII.

39 S. D. Chapman, 'Financial restraints on the growth of firms in the cotton industry 1790–1850', *Economic History Review*, 32 (1979), 50–69.

40 Faucher, *Manchester*, pp. 15–16; cf. Engels, *Condition*, p. 76.

41 H. B. Rogers, 'The Lancashire cotton industry in 1840', *Transactions and Papers of the Institute of British Geographers*, 28 (1960), 135–53.

42 V. A. C. Gatrell, 'Labour, power and the size of firms in Lancashire cotton in the second quarter of the nineteenth century', *Economic History Review*, 30 (1977), 95–139. The figures are:

	Full time/full capacity	Short time/short capacity	Short time/short capacity	Stopped
Fine spinning	73%	4%	19%	5%
Coarse spinning	60%	6%	19%	15%
Combined mills	55%	12%	25%	8%
Power weaving	58%	2%	25%	15%
Total	59%	7%	21%	12%

43 Figure 3 is derived from Horner's report in PP (1842), XXII. It suffers from all the usual disadvantages of 'snap-shots'. Horner reckoned that 13 per cent

of the work-force were unemployed: if all the mills had been working at full capacity a further 25,000 jobs would have become available. But figures like these understate the severity of the depression; although some 87 per cent of mills were working, Horner cautioned that 'it would be a great error to infer that this is a proof that they were making a profit'. The fixed charges on capital which they incurred whether their machinery was running or not were so onerous that they were for the most part minimizing their losses: see G. N. Von Tunzelmann, *Steam power and British industrialization to 1860* (Oxford, 1979), pp. 212–17. By early spring 1842, and in direct consequence, Horner was reporting that 'a reduction of wages appears to be becoming general', of the order of 10 or 12 per cent.

44 Rodgers, 'Lancashire cotton industry', pp. 350–2.

45 Gatrell, 'Labour, power'; cf. Chapman, 'Financial restraints'.

46 R. A. Sykes, 'Some aspects of working-class consciousness in Oldham 1830–1842', *Historical Journal*, 23 (1980), 168–9.

47 D. Gadian, 'Class consciousness in Oldham and other north-west industrial towns 1830–1850', *Historical Journal*, 21 (1978), 161–72; see also C. Calhoun, *The question of class struggle: social foundations of popular radicalism during the Industrial Revolution* (Oxford, 1982), pp. 198–201.

48 Stedman Jones, 'Class struggle'.

49 A. J. Taylor, 'Concentration and specialization in the Lancashire cotton industry 1825–1850', *Economic History Review*, 1 (1949), 114–22. The diffusion of the 'self-actor' in the 1830s was restricted to coarser counts of yarn (nos 16s – 40s) and did not dominate counts up to no 60s for another thirty years, so that Taylor's claim is plausible.

50 Sykes, 'Some aspects', p. 170.

51 See Von Tunzelmann, *Steam power*, pp. 212–17; R. A. Sykes, 'Early Chartism and trade unionism in south-east Lancashire' in J. Epstein and D. Thompson (eds), *The Chartist experience: studies in working class radicalism and culture 1830–1860* (London, 1982), pp. 181–2.

52 Sykes, 'Early Chartism', p. 165.

53 *Replies of Sir Charles Shaw to Lord Ashley* (London, 1843), p. 9; cf. Lees' claim that 'a town's place in the English urban hierarchy influenced the way in which political information spread to it and through it' (L. Lees, 'The study of social conflict in English industrial towns', *Urban History Yearbook* (Leicester, 1980), p. 38). There is considerable scope for a study of information diffusion during the early Industrial Revolution, and it is more than puzzling that ten years after Pred's suggestive analyses for the United States no comparable work has appeared on this side of the Atlantic: A. Pred, *Urban growth and the circulation of information: the United States system of cities 1790–1840* (Cambridge, Mass., 1973).

54 Cf. Gash's claim that 'Hungry bellies filled the ranks of the Chartists; the return of economic prosperity after 1843 thinned them' (N. Gash, *Aristocracy and people* (London, 1979), p. 210). See also G. Kitson Clark, 'Hunger and politics in 1842', *Journal of Modern History*, 25 (1953), 55–74.

55 F. C. Mather, 'The General Strike of 1842' in J. Stevenson and R. Quinault (eds), *Popular protest and public order* (London, 1974), pp. 115–40; M. Jenkins,

The General Strike of 1842 (London, 1980). See also A. G. Rose, 'The Plug Riots of 1842 in Lancashire and Cheshire', *Transactions of the Lancashire and Cheshire Antiquarian Society*, 67 (1957), 75–112.

56 Jenkins, *General Strike*, p. 159.
57 Sykes, 'Early Chartism', pp. 174–5.
58 Sykes, 'Early Chartism', p. 172.
59 G. Stedman Jones, 'The language of Chartism' in Epstein and Thompson (ed.), *Chartist experience*, p. 48.
60 The *Northern Star* was first published in Leeds on 18 November 1837; by the end of 1838 its circulation exceeded that of any other provincial paper, and in 1839 it sold over 50,000 copies a week and 'already rivalled the circulation of the largest London paper, *The Times*'; even after the failure of the first National Petition its circulation was still 30,000 and in the depths of the depression it remained above 12,000. See E. Haraszti, *Chartism* (Budapest, 1978), pp. 52–3; J. Epstein, 'Fergus O'Connor and the *Northern Star*', *International Review of Social History*, 21 (1976), pp. 51–97. Other indications of the changing geography of Chartism are provided in D. Jones, *Chartism and the Chartists* (London, 1975), 9–10.
61 A. Briggs, 'The local background of Chartism' in A. Briggs (ed.), *Chartist studies* (London, 1959), pp. 1–28.
62 P. Richards, 'State formation and class struggle 1832–48' in P. Corrigan (ed.), *Capitalism, state formation and Marxist theory* (London, 1980), pp. 49–78; Gregory, *Regional transformation*, pp. 256–7.
63 Sykes, 'Some aspects', pp. 173 and 179.
64 Faucher, *Manchester*, p. 138.
65 Stedman Jones, 'Class struggle'.
66 P. Deane and W. A. Cole, *British economic growth 1688–1959* (Cambridge, 1967), p. 191; Von Tunzelmann, *Steam power*, pp. 234–6; Saville, 'Class struggle', p. 232. The diffusion of the self-actor was partially interconnected with that of the power-loom because it produced a more uniform yarn.
67 W. Lazonick, 'Industrial relations and technical change: the case of the self-acting mule', *Cambridge Journal of Economics*, 3 (1979), 231.
68 Thompson, *Making of the English working class*.
69 Foster, *Class struggle*.
70 Richards, 'State formation'.
71 Stedman Jones, 'Class struggle', p. 66.
72 R. Gray, 'Bourgeois hegemony in Victorian Britain' in J. Bloomfield (ed.), *Class, hegemony and party* (London, 1977), p. 73.
73 W. Cooke Taylor, *Notes of a tour in the manufacturing districts of Lancashire* (London, 1842).
74 E. P. Thompson, 'The peculiarities of the English', reprinted in Thompson, *Poverty*, p. 70; Anderson, *Arguments*, p. 48.
75 Lazonick, 'Industrial relations', pp. 231–2; *idem*, 'The subjection of labour to capital: the rise of the capitalist system', *Review of Radical Political Economy*, 10 (1978), 8.
76 R. Price, 'The labour process and labour history, *Social History*, 8 (1983), 57–8.

77 M. Anderson, *Family structure in nineteenth-century Lancashire* (Cambridge, 1977) has an unduly instrumentalist conception of the working-class family, which flows (in part) from his over-simplified version of exchange theory; see also *idem*, 'Sociological history and the working-class family: Smelser revisited', *Social History*, 3 (1976), 317–34. The interpretation here is derived from J. Humphries, 'Class struggle and the persistence of the working class family', *Cambridge Journal of Economics*, 1 (1977), 241–58; *idem*, 'The working-class family, women's liberation and class struggle: the case of nineteenth-century British history', *Review of Radical Political Economy*, 9 (1977), 25–41; G. Stedman Jones, 'Working-class culture and working-class politics in London, 1870–1900: notes on the remaking of a working class', *Journal of Social History*, 7 (1974), 460–508; Foster, *Class struggle*, p. 138.

78 Lazonick, 'Industrial relations'; M. Holbrook-Jones, *Supremacy and subordination of labour: the hierarchy of work in the early labour movement* (London, 1982), pp. 154–85.

79 Von Tunzelmann, *Steam power*, pp. 210–15 and 226–40; Farnie, *English cotton industry*, pp. 89–90 and 198–9.

80 K. Burgess, *The challenge of labour* (London, 1980), p. 14.

81 Thompson, 'Peculiarities', p. 71.

82 T. J. Nossiter, *Influence, opinion and political idioms in reformed England* (Brighton, 1975); P. Joyce, 'The factory politics of Lancashire in the later nineteenth century', *Historical Journal*, 18 (1975), 525–33; *idem*, *Work, society and politics: the culture of the factory in later Victorian England* (Brighton, 1980).

83 Gash, *Aristocracy*, p. 165.

84 The unequal size of constituencies, their uneven geographical distribution and the complexity of voting behaviour in multi-member constituencies are only some of the most obvious.

85 Nossiter, *Influence*, p. 184: see also his Table 34 and Appendix A.

86 N. Gash, *Reaction and reconstruction in English politics 1832–1852* (Oxford, 1965), pp. 134–6. The Conservative share of the poll is derived from Nossiter, *Influence*, p. 182, but Fraser argues that his method consistently overestimates Conservative support (D. Fraser, *Urban politics in Victorian England* (Leicester, 1976), pp. 226–7). In any event, these results confirm Nossiter's view that 'the local basis of politics was already breaking down by 1841' and that an incipient regionalism was forming which, so Nossiter argues, was to become decisive by the late 1860s and to dominate the electoral geography of the country until the 1880s (Nossiter, *Influence*, p. 191).

87 W. Aydelotte, 'Voting patterns in the British House of Commons in the 1840s', *Comparative Studies in Society and History*, 5 (1963), 134–63; see also *idem*, 'Parties and issues in early Victorian England', *Journal of British Studies*, 5 (1966), 95–114.

88 Richards, 'State formation', p. 76.

89 Stedman Jones, 'Language of Chartism', p. 51.

90 Foster, *Class struggle*, pp. 186–7.

91 R. Gray, 'Politics, ideology and class struggle under early industrial capitalism: a critique of John Foster', *Marxism Today*, 21 (1977), 369; cf. O'Connor, 'Meaning of crisis', p. 318.

92 G. McLennan, *Marxism and the methodologies of history* (London, 1981), p. 217.

93 R. Bhaskar, *The possibility of naturalism* (Brighton, 1979). This is to make a claim for a realist approach to the analysis of social relations and spatial structures: see D. Gregory, 'Solid geometry: notes on the recovery of spatial structure' in P. Gould and G. Olsson (eds), *A search for common ground* (London, 1982), pp. 187–219; *idem, Social theory and spatial structure* (London, forthcoming); J. Urry, 'Social relations'.

94 Anderson, *Arguments*, p. 55; G. A. Cohen, *Karl Marx's theory of history: a defence* (Oxford, 1979).

95 G. A. Cohen, 'Forces and relations of production' in B. Matthews (ed.), *Marx: a hundred years on* (London, 1983), pp. 111–34.

96 Foster, *Class struggle*; *idem*, 'Comments'.

97 J. Foster, 'How imperial London preserved its slums', *International Journal of Urban and Regional Research*, 3 (1979), 110–11.

98 Foster, *Class struggle*.

99 D. Harvey, 'Class structure in a capitalist society and the theory of residential differentiation' in Peel, Chisholm and Haggett (eds), *Processes*, pp. 354–69; see also I. Katznelson, 'Community, capitalist development and the emergence of class', *Politics and Society*, 9 (1979), 203–37.

100 These paragraphs are derived from Foster, *Class struggle* and *idem*, 'Comments'; see also E. Yeo, 'Culture and constraint in working-class movements, 1830–1850' in E. Yeo and S. Yeo (eds), *Popular culture and class conflict: explorations in the history of labour and leisure* (Brighton, 1981), pp. 155–86. I shall not be concerned to discuss the concept of a 'labour aristocracy' in any detail here, but an important set of exchanges is H. F. Moorhouse, 'The Marxist theory of the labour aristocracy', *Social History*, 3 (1978), 61–82; A. Reid, 'Politics and economics in the formation of the British working class: a response to H. F. Moorhouse', *Social History*, 3 (1978), 347–61; H. F. Moorhouse, 'History, sociology and the quiescence of the British working class: a reply to Reid', *Social History*, 4 (1979), 481–90; A. Reid, 'Response', *Social History*, 4 (1979), 491–3. Useful summaries of the wider literature include J. Field, 'British historians and the concept of the labor aristocracy', *Radical History Review*, 19 (1978–9), 61–85; G. McLennan, '"The labour aristocracy" and "incorporation": notes on some terms in the history of the working class', *Social History*, 6 (1981), 71–81; *idem, Methodologies*, pp. 206–32; R. Gray, *The aristocracy of labour in nineteenth-century Britain, c. 1850–1914* (London, 1981).

101 Burgess, *Challenge*, p. 23.

102 Stedman Jones, 'Class struggle', pp. 46–8.

103 See, for example, A. Schmidt, *History and structure: an essay on Hegelian-Marxist and structuralist theories of history* (Cambridge, Mass., 1981).

104 R. Conquest, *Lenin* (London, 1972), pp. 39–40 provides a convenient summary of a complex issue.

105 McLennan, *Methodologies*, p. 217.

106 Thompson, 'Eighteenth-century English society', p. 148.

107 A. Giddens, *A contemporary critique of historical materialism, vol. 1: Power, property and the State* (London, 1981), p. 66.

108 G. Stedman Jones, 'Class expression versus social control? A critique of recent trends in the social history of "leisure"', *History Workshop Journal*, 4 (1977), 162–70.

109 Giddens, *Contemporary critique*, pp. 66 and 90.

110 Calhoun, *Question of class struggle*, pp. 149–50 and 174.

111 Thompson, *Making*.

112 Calhoun, *Question of class struggle*, pp. 166 and 172.

113 Calhoun, *Question of class struggle*, pp. 23–32.

114 Giddens, *Contemporary critique*.

115 K. Wrightson, 'Aspects of social differentiation in rural England, c. 1580–1660', *Journal of Peasant Studies*, 5 (1977), 35, 40–1. The particular argument I wish to make is not affected by the cogent criticisms of R. Smith, '"Modernization" and the corporate medieval village community in England: some sceptical reflections' in this volume.

116 Thompson, 'Eighteenth-century English society', p. 150.

117 E. P. Thompson, *Whigs and hunters* (London, 1975), p. 265.

118 N. Thrift, 'Flies and germs: a geography of knowledge' in Gregory and Urry (eds), *Social relations* (forthcoming).

119 R. Porter, *English society in the eighteenth century* (Harmondsworth, 1982), pp. 118–19.

120 J. Brewer, *Party ideology and popular politics at the accession of George III* (Cambridge, 1976), pp. 268–9.

121 See Brewer, *Party ideology*; A. Goodwin, *The Friends of Liberty* (London, 1979).

122 Thompson, 'Eighteenth-century English society', p. 154.

123 The best is J. Urry, *The anatomy of capitalist societies: the economy, civil society and the state* (London, 1981).

124 Thompson, 'Eighteenth-century English society', p. 124.

125 Anderson, 'Origins', pp. 204–5; Thompson, 'Peculiarities', p. 56.

126 Gray, 'Bourgeois hegemony', p. 88; see also *idem*, 'Politics, ideology and class struggle'; G. Crossick, *An artisan elite in Victorian society* (London, 1978); F. Hearn, *Domination, legitimation and resistance: the incorporation of the nineteenth-century English working class* (Westport, Conn., 1978).

127 Joyce, *Work, society and politics*, p. xvi.

128 T. Tholfsen, *Working-class radicalism in mid-Victorian Britain* (London, 1976), p. 243.

129 Anderson, 'Origins', pp. 204–5; Nairn, 'English working class'.

130 Joyce, *Work, society and politics*, pp. 92–4, 146, 168 and 172. Indeed, Joyce suggests that the second half of the nineteenth century saw 'the consolidation of a sense of community in the factory towns' (p. 110). Few authors have investigated the wider ramifications of this, but see J. D. Marshall, 'Colonisation as a factor in the planting of towns in north-west England' in H. J. Dyos (ed.), *The study of urban history* (London, 1968), pp. 215–30; R. J. Dennis, 'Distance and social interaction in a Victorian city', *Journal of Historical Geography*, 3 (1977), 237–50; D. Ward, 'Environs and neighbours in the "Two Nations": residential differentiation in mid-nineteenth-century Leeds', *Journal of Historical Geography*, 6 (1980), 133–62. Ward in particular emphasizes the

lack of residential differentiation between the 'labour aristocracy' and the rest of the working class, which offers some comparative confirmation of Joyce's claim.

131 H. Dutton, J. E. King, 'The limits of paternalism: the cotton tyrants of North Lancashire 1836–54', *Social History*, 7 (1982), 63.
132 Joyce, *Work, society and politics*, pp. 56–7 and 145.
133 K. Wrightson, *English society 1580–1680* (London, 1982), p. 64.
134 See for example Thompson, 'Peculiarities', pp. 72–4.
135 Stedman Jones, 'Class expression', p. 168. Indeed, many usages of 'hegemony' seem to ascribe what J. S. Duncan has called a 'superorganic' status to the cultural realm, and in doing so fail to explore its fragmentations and foliations: that is to say, its basic *geography*. See J. S. Duncan, 'The superorganic in American cultural geography', *Annals of the Association of American Geographers*, 70 (1980), 181–98.
136 Gray, 'Bourgeois hegemony', p. 84; Joyce, *Work, society and politics*, p. 92.
137 Gray, 'Bourgeois hegemony', p. 81. This was of course true at both the national level – witness the 'policy break' between 1838 and 1842 – and the local level: see J. Seed, 'Unitarianism, political economy and the antinomies of liberal culture in Manchester, 1830–1850', *Social History*, 7 (1982), 1–26; M. Billinge, 'Hegemony, class and power in late Georgian and early Victorian England: towards a cultural geography' in this volume. It is, however, of the first importance to avoid an excessive formalism and to clarify the *content* of these differential ideologies. In this sense, the claims of political economy seem to me more impressive than those of 'science', however this is conceived, since they entailed the articulation and contestation of clearly defined class interests. See D. Gregory, *Regional transformation*, pp. 221–3, 228–9, 239–42; M. Berg, *The Machinery Question and the making of political economy 1815–1848* (Cambridge, 1980); for an incisive critique of Berg, see G. Claeys and P. Kerr, 'Mechanical political economy', *Cambridge Journal of Economics*, 5 (1981), 251–72.
138 Dutton and King, 'Limits to paternalism', p. 62; see also *idem, Ten per cent and no surrender: the Preston strike of 1853–1854* (Cambridge, 1981).
139 A. E. Musson, 'Technological change and manpower', *History*, 67 (1982), 246.
140 Burgess, *Challenge*, p. 19.
141 Joyce, *Work, society and politics*, p. 93.
142 *Ibid.*, p. 124.
143 Reid, 'Politics and economics', p. 360.
144 Paradoxically Harvey does exactly this in *Limits to capital*, especially pp. 114–19.
145 Lazonick, 'Industrial relations', p. 231.
146 N. Poulantzas, 'Marxist political theory in Britain', *New Left Review*, 43 (1967), 60–1; see also the superb commentary in G. Eley, 'Re-thinking the political: social history and political culture in 18th and 19th century Britain', *Archiv für Sozialgeschichte*, 21 (1981), 427–57.
147 Gray, 'Politics, ideology and class struggle', p. 401.

Notes to Chapter 4

1 G. E. Mingay, 'The agricultural revolution in English history: a reconsideration', *Agricultural History*, 26 (1963), 123 tries to maintain the credibility of the phrase.

2 See also D. Woodward, 'Agricultural revolution in England 1500–1900: a survey', *Local Historian*, 9 (1971), 323–33.

3 Recent summaries are given in A. R. H. Baker, 'Historical geography', *Progress in Human Geography*, 1 (1977), 465–7; *idem*, 'Understanding and experiencing the past', *Progress in Human Geography*, 2 (1978), 495–504; *idem*, 'Historical geography: a new beginning?', *Progress in Human Geography*, 3 (1979), 560–70; R. A. Butlin, 'Developments in historical geography in Britain in the 1970s' in A. R. H. Baker and M. Billinge (eds), *Period and place: research methods in historical geography* (Cambridge, 1982), pp. 10–16.

4 A. Young, *General view of the agriculture of the county of Norfolk* (London, 1804), p. 31; W. F. Karkeek, 'On the farming of Cornwall', *Journal of the Royal Agricultural Society of England*, 6 (1846), 403; K. Marx, *Capital*, 3 vols (London, 1954), Vol. I, p. 697.

5 R. L. Prothero, 'The pioneers and prospects of English agriculture', *Quarterly Review*, 159 (1885), 323–59; *idem, Pioneers and progress in English farming* (London, 1888); Lord Ernle, *English farming past and present* (London, 1912); G. E. Fussell, 'Introduction, Part one: English farming before 1815' in Ernle, *English farming past and present*, 6th edn (London, 1963), pp. xxi–lxxv; O. R. McGregor, 'Introduction, Part two: English farming after 1815' in *ibid.*, pp. lxxix–cxlv. Ernle's book was more successful than W. H. R. Curtler, *A short history of English agriculture* (Oxford, 1909) or N. S. B. Gras, *A history of agriculture* (New York, 1925) and is more academic than books like C. S. Orwin, *A history of English farming* (London, 1949) and R. Whitlock, *A short history of farming in Britain* (London, 1965).

6 Ernle, *English farming past and present*, p. 149.

7 *Ibid.*, p. 174.

8 *Ibid.*, p. 156.

9 Curtler, *Short history of English agriculture*, pp. 162–3; P. Mantoux, *The Industrial Revolution in the eighteenth century* (London, 1928), pp. 156–61; Gras, *History of agriculture*, pp. 208–32.

10 Ernle, *English farming past and present*, pp. 190–5.

11 E. Kerridge, 'The agricultural revolution reconsidered', *Agricultural History*, 43 (1969), 463–76; T. B. Franklin, *A history of agriculture* (London, 1948), p. 124; P. S. Fry, *A short history of British life* (London, 1976), pp. 160–1.

12 H. W. Saunders, 'Estate management at Raynham in the years 1661–86 and 1706', *Norfolk Archaeology*, 19 (1915), 39–66; J. H. Plumb, 'Sir Robert Walpole and Norfolk husbandry', *Economic History Review*, 5 (1952), 86–9.

13 T. H. Marshall, 'Jethro Tull and the new husbandry', *Economic History Review*, 2 (1929), 41–60; G. E. Fussell, *Jethro Tull: his influence on mechanized agriculture* (Reading, 1973).

14 G. E. Fussell, 'The size of English cattle in the eighteenth century', *Agricultural History*, 3 (1929), 160–81.

15 N. Kent, *General view of the agriculture of the county of Norfolk* (London, 1796), p. 40; *idem*, 'On Norfolk turnips and fallowing', *Annals of Agriculture*, 22 (1794), 24; A. Young, 'Minutes in rural economy, taken at Rainham, the seat of Lord Viscount Townshend, in January 1785', *Annals of Agriculture*, 5 (1786), 120–9.

16 R. A. C. Parker, 'Coke of Norfolk and the agrarian revolution', *Economic History Review*, 8 (1955), 156–66; *idem, Coke of Norfolk: a financial and agricultural study, 1707–1842* (Oxford, 1975), pp. 157, 199.

17 In addition to references cited, see J. A. Walton, 'Agriculture 1730–1900' in R. A. Dodgshon and R. A. Butlin (eds), *An historical geography of England and Wales* (London, 1978), pp. 240–2.

18 J. Thirsk, 'The content and sources of English agrarian history after 1500', *Agricultural History Review*, 3 (1955), 79.

19 For example by E. L. Jones, 'Editor's introduction' in E. L. Jones (ed.), *Agriculture and economic growth in England 1650–1815* (London, 1967), pp. 1–48; M. Bloch, *French rural history* (London, 1966), pp. 197–8.

20 E. Kerridge, 'Turnip husbandry in High Suffolk', *Economic History Review*, 8 (1955), 390–2; *idem*, 'Agriculture 1500–1793' in *The Victorian histories of the counties of England. A history of Wiltshire, Volume 4* (London, 1959), pp. 43–64; *idem, The agricultural revolution* (London, 1967), pp. 13, 328.

21 J. Thirsk (ed.), *The agrarian history of England and Wales, Volume IV; 1500–1640* (Cambridge, 1967).

22 J. Thirsk, review, *History*, 55 (1970), 259.

23 Kerridge, *Agricultural revolution*, pp. 181–2; see also J. Broad, 'Alternate husbandry and permanent pasture in the Midlands, 1650–1800', *Agricultural History Review*, 28 (1980), 78–9.

24 J. D. Chambers and G. E. Mingay, *The agricultural revolution 1750–1880* (London, 1966); Mingay, 'Agricultural revolution: a reconsideration'.

25 Chambers and Mingay, *Agricultural revolution*, p. 54.

26 F. M. L. Thompson, 'The second agricultural revolution, 1815–1880', *Economic History Review*, 21 (1968), 62–77.

27 H. C. Darby, 'The draining of the English clay-lands', *Geographische Zeitschrift*, 52 (1964), 190–201; R. W. Sturgess, 'The agricultural revolution on the English clays', *Agricultural History Review*, 14 (1966), 104–21; A. D. M. Phillips, 'Underdraining and the English clay-lands, 1850–80: a review', *Agricultural History Review*, 17 (1969), 44–55.

28 For example, D. B. Grigg, *The agricultural revolution in south Lincolnshire* (Cambridge, 1966); T. W. Beastall, *The agricultural revolution in Lincolnshire* (Lincoln, 1978); N. Riches, *The agricultural revolution in Norfolk* (Chapel Hill, N.C., 1937).

29 Space precludes a list of these – there are over fifty of them. See M. Overton, 'Probate inventories and the reconstruction of agricultural landscapes' in M. Reed (ed.), *Discovering past landscapes* (London, 1983); M. Overton, *A guide to probate inventories*, Historical Geography Research Group Publication (Norwich, forthcoming).

30 See note 36 below.

31 L. A. Clarkson, *The pre-industrial economy in England 1500–1750* (London,

1971), pp. 57–8; D. C. Coleman, *The economy of England* 1450–1750 (Oxford, 1977), pp. 111–24; B. A. Holderness, *Pre-industrial England* (London, 1976), p. 74; I. Wallerstein, *The modern world-system, Vol. II* (London, 1980), p. 263.

32 E. L. Jones, *Agriculture and the Industrial Revolution* (Oxford, 1974), pp. 4–5.

33 Mingay, 'Agricultural revolution in English history', p. 123; G. E. Fussell, review of Mingay, *Agricultural revolution: changes in agriculture, Economic History Review*, 30 (1977), 713; B. H. Slicher van Bath, 'Eighteenth century agriculture on the continent of Europe: evolution or revolution?', *Agricultural History*, 43 (1969), 169; Woodward, 'Agricultural revolution: a survey', p. 330; Kerridge, 'Agricultural revolution reconsidered', p. 473. Compare these with E. D. Ross and R. L. Tontz, 'The term "agricultural revolution" as used by agricultural historians', *Agricultural History*, 22 (1948), 32–8.

34 Gras, *History of agriculture*, pp. 220–2.

35 Kerridge, *The Farmers of old England* (London, 1973), pp. 136 and 135.

36 E. L. Jones, 'Agriculture and economic growth in England, 1660–1750: agricultural change', *Journal of Economic History*, 25 (1965), 1–18, reprinted in Jones, *Agriculture and economic growth in England*, pp. 152–71, in Jones, *Agriculture and the Industrial Revolution*, pp. 67–84 and in W. E. Minchinton (ed.), *Essays in agrarian history*, 2 vols (Newton Abbot, 1968), Vol. I, pp. 205–19; *idem*, 'Eighteenth-century changes in Hampshire chalkland farming', *Agricultural History Review*, 8 (1960), 9–20, reprinted in Jones, *Agriculture and the industrial revolution*, pp. 22–40; *idem*, 'Editor's introduction' in *Agriculture and economic growth in England 1650–1815*, reprinted in Jones, *Agriculture and the Industrial Revolution*, pp. 85–127. All subsequent references to Jones' work follow the page numbering in his *Agriculture and the Industrial Revolution*. John's contributions include: A. H. John, 'The course of agricultural change, 1660–1760' in L. S. Pressnell (ed.), *Studies in the Industrial Revolution* (London, 1960), pp. 125–55, reprinted in Minchinton, *Essays in agrarian history*, Vol. I, pp. 223–53; 'Agricultural productivity and economic growth in England, 1700–1760', *Journal of Economic History*, 25 (1965), 19–34, reprinted in Jones, *Agriculture and economic growth in England*, pp. 172–93; 'Aspects of economic growth in the first half of the eighteenth century', *Economica*, 28 (1961), 176–90, reprinted in W. E. Minchinton (ed.), *The growth of English overseas trade in the sixteenth and seventeenth centuries* (London, 1969), pp. 165–83, and in E. M. Carus-Wilson, *Essays in economic history*, 3 vols (London, 1954, 1962), vol. 2, pp. 360–73.

37 Jones, *Agriculture and the Industrial Revolution*, p. 72; John, 'Course of agricultural change', pp. 124–7.

38 Jones, *Agriculture and the Industrial Revolution*, pp. 72, 78 and 27.

39 *Ibid.*, pp. 77–8; John, 'Course of agricultural change', p. 132.

40 Jones, *Agriculture and the Industrial Revolution*, pp. 74–6, 90–1; John, 'Course of agricultural change', pp. 132–3, *idem*, 'Aspects of economic growth', p. 167.

41 Jones, *Agriculture and the Industrial Revolution*, pp. 73–4.

42 John, 'Course of agricultural change', p. 141, n. 1.

43 W. Marshall, *The rural economy of Norfolk*, 2 vols (London, 1787), vol. 1, pp. 262–3.

44 W. Blith, *The improver improved or the survey of husbandry surveyed* (London, 1652), pp. 184–5; W. A. Ellis, *The modern husbandman or the practice of farming as it is now carried out by the most accurate farmers in several counties of England*, 8 vols (London, 1744–5), vol. 1 (February), p. 32.

45 E. J. Russell, 'Rothamsted and its experimental station', *Agricultural History*, 16 (1942), 161–83; Rothamsted Experimental Station, *Details of the classical and long-term experiments up to 1967* (Harpenden, 1970); A. D. Hall, *The book of the Rothamsted experiments* (London, 1919). An exception is G. P. H. Chorley, 'The agricultural revolution in northern Europe, 1750–1880; nitrogen, legumes and crop productivity', *Economic History Review*, 34 (1981), 71–93.

46 The table is derived from J. B. Lawes and J. H. Gilbert, 'Rotation of crops', *Journal of the Royal Agricultural Society of England*, 5 (1894), 584–646.

47 For the assumptions made in calculating output from a wheat, barley, fallow rotation, see M. Overton, 'Agricultural change in Norfolk and Suffolk, 1580–1740', unpublished Ph.D. thesis, University of Cambridge, 1981, pp. 284–5.

48 R. Morgan, 'The root crop in English agriculture, 1650–1870', unpublished Ph.D. thesis, University of Reading, 1978, p. 444; Kerridge, *Agricultural revolution*, pp. 272–5; R. Trow-Smith, *A history of British livestock husbandry up to 1700* (London, 1957), pp. 256–7; Chambers and Mingay, *Agricultural revolution*, p. 35.

49 V. H. T. Skipp, *Crisis and development: an ecological case study of the Forest of Arden, 1570–1674* (Cambridge, 1978), pp. 43, 45; Kerridge, *Agricultural revolution*, p. 24; R. B. Outhwaite, 'Rural England, 1500–1750', *Histoire Sociale – Social History*, 2 (1968), 85–97.

50 Anon., 'The state of husbandry in Norfolk', *Gentleman's Magazine*, 22 (1752), 502.

51 C. Clay, 'The price of freehold land in the later seventeenth and eighteenth centuries', *Economic History Review*, 27 (1974), 173–89.

52 Coleman, *Economy of England*, pp. 101–5.

53 Ernle, *English farming*, p. 166; Chambers and Mingay, *Agricultural revolution*, pp. 80–1.

54 Morgan, *The root crop in English agriculture*, pp. 7–60.

55 N. Whitley, 'On the climate of the British islands in its effects on cultivation', *Journal of the Royal Agricultural Society of England*, 11 (1850), 42.

56 Overton, 'Agricultural change', pp. 129–90.

57 Examples include: E. A. Cox and B. R. Dittmer, 'The tithe files of the mid-nineteenth century', *Agricultural History Review*, 13 (1965), 1–16; O. Ashmore, 'Inventories as a source of local history II – Farmers', *Amateur Historian*, 4 (1959), 186–95.

58 For example, M. Overton, 'English probate inventories and the measurement of agricultural change', *A. A. G. Bijdragen*, 23 (1980), 205–15.

59 Kerridge, 'Agricultural revolution reconsidered', p. 465.

60 Kerridge, *Agricultural revolution*, p. 116.

61 P. Deane and W. A. Cole, *British economic growth, 1688–1959*, 2nd edn (Cambridge, 1967), p. 67; G. E. Fussell, 'Population and wheat production in the eighteenth century', *History Teachers' Miscellany*, 7 (1929), 65–8, 84–8, 120–7 and 108–11.

62 Ellis, *Modern husbandman*, vol. 1 (January), p. 71.
63 W. O. Aydelotte, 'Quantification in history', *American Historical Review*, 71 (1966), 803–25.
64 G. E. Mingay, *The agricultural revolution: changes in English agriculture 1650–1850* (London, 1977), p. 5.
65 Kerridge, *Agricultural revolution*, p. 328.
66 R. E. Beringer, *Historical analysis: contemporary approaches to Clio's craft* (New York, 1978), pp. 193–201. See also; W. O. Aydelotte, *Quantification in history* (London, 1971); C. Erikson, 'Quantitative history', *American Historical Review*, 80 (1975), 351–65; C. H. Lee, *The quantitative approach to economic history* (London, 1977); A. R. H. Baker, 'Rethinking historical geography' in A. R. H. Baker (ed.), *Progress in historical geography* (Newton Abbot, 1972), pp. 17–20; H. N. Scheiber, 'Poetry, prosaism, and analysis in American agricultural history', *Journal of Economic History*, 36 (1976), 919–27.
67 For example, W. G. Hoskins, 'The Leicestershire farmer in the sixteenth century' in W. G. Hoskins (ed.), *Essays in Leicestershire history* (Liverpool, 1950), pp. 123–83. The tradition lives on: see M. F. Pickles, 'Agrarian society and wealth in mid-Wharfedale, 1664–1743', *Yorkshire Archaeological Journal*, 53 (1981), 63–78. The resistance of English agricultural historians contrasts with work on Western Europe. For example: J. C. Toutain, *Le produit de l'agriculture français de 1700 à 1958: II – La croissance*, in Cahiers de L'Institut de Science Economique Appliquée (Paris, 1961); W. H. Newell, 'The agricultural revolution in nineteenth-century France', *Journal of Economic History*, 33 (1973), 697–730; M. Morineau, *Les faux-semblants d'un démarrage économique: agriculture et démographie en France au XVIIIe siècle* (Paris, 1972); G. W. Grantham, 'The diffusion of the new husbandry in northern France', *Journal of Economic History*, 38 (1978), 311–37; P. K. O'Brien, D. Heath and C. Keyder, 'Agricultural efficiency in Britain and France, 1815–1914', *Journal of European Economic History*, 6 (1977), 339–91; H. van der Wee and E. van Canwenberghe (eds), *Productivity of land and agricultural innovation in the Low Countries (1250–1800)* (Louvain, 1978).
68 Overton, 'Agricultural change'; *idem*, 'Probate inventories and measurement', p. 213.
69 Kerridge, 'Turnip husbandry', pp. 390–2; *idem*, *Agricultural revolution*, pp. 270–7.
70 Overton, 'Agricultural change', pp. 171–4.
71 M. Overton, 'Computer analysis of an inconsistent data source: the case of probate inventories', *Journal of Historical Geography*, 3 (1977), 326.
72 E. M. Rogers and F. F. Shoemaker, *Communication of innovations*, 2nd edn (London, 1971), p. 182.
73 J. A. Yelling, 'The combination and rotation of crops in east Worcestershire, 1540–1640', *Agricultural History Review*, 17 (1969), 24–43, reprinted in A. R. H. Baker, J. D. Hamshere and J. Langton (eds), *Geographical interpretations of historical sources* (Newton Abbot, 1970), pp. 117–37; *idem*, 'Probate inventories and the geography of livestock farming', *Transactions of the Institute of British Geographers*, 51 (1970), 111–26; *idem*, 'Changes in crop production in east Worcestershire, 1540–1867', *Agricultural History Review*, 21 (1973),

18–34; J. A. Walton, *A study in the diffusion of agricultural machinery in the nineteenth century*, Oxford University School of Geography Research Papers, No. 5 (Oxford, 1973).

74 Overton, 'Agricultural change', pp. 171–4.

75 *Ibid.*, p. 275.

76 *Ibid.*, p. 280.

77 Overton, 'Crop yields', pp. 370–3.

78 *Ibid.*

79 Overton, 'Probate inventories and the measurement of agricultural change', p. 212.

80 Overton, 'Agricultural change', p. 271.

81 A. H. John, 'English agricultural improvement and grain exports, 1660–1765' in D. C. Coleman and A. H. John (eds), *Trade, government and economy in pre-industrial England* (London, 1976), pp. 47–51; Overton, *Agricultural change*, pp. 257–9.

82 Overton, 'Agricultural change', pp. 267–9.

83 H. H. Lamb, *Climate present past and future, Volume 2: Climatic history and the future* (London, 1977), pp. 440–73.

84 Overton, 'Agricultural change', pp. 254–6.

85 See Overton, 'Agricultural change'; *idem, The agricultural revolution in England: the transformation of the rural economy, 1500–1830* (Cambridge, forthcoming).

86 D. Gregory, *Ideology, science and human geography* (London, 1978), pp. 25–48.

87 G. G. S. Murphy, 'The "new" history', *Explorations in Entrepreneurial History*, 2 (1965), 132–46, reprinted in R. L. Andreano (ed.), *The new economic history: recent papers on methodology* (London, 1970), pp. 1–16; G. N. Von Tunzelmann, 'The new economic history: an econometric appraisal', *Explorations in Entrepreneurial History*, 5 (1968), pp. 175–200.

88 See, for example, I. Hacking, *The logic of statistical inference* (Cambridge, 1965).

89 They have discussed *what* should be studied rather than *how* it should be studied. For example, Thirsk, 'Content and sources'; R. Lennard, 'Agrarian history: some vistas and pitfalls', *Agricultural History Review*, 12 (1964), 83–98. E. L. Jones, 'Afterword', in W. N. Parker and E. L. Jones (eds), *European peasants and their markets* (London, 1975), pp. 327–60.

90 Chambers and Mingay, *Agricultural revolution*, pp. 3–4; Kerridge, *Agricultural revolution*, p. 332; G. E. Mingay, 'Dr. Kerridge's "agricultural revolution"; a comment', *Agricultural History Review*, 43 (1969), 497; R. B. Outhwaite, 'Rural England, 1500–1750', *Histoire Sociale – Social History*, 2 (1968), 85–97.

91 D. B. Grigg, *The agricultural revolution in south Lincolnshire* (Cambridge, 1966), pp. 190–1.

92 Overton, 'Crop yields', p. 371.

93 M. J. R. Healy and E. L. Jones, 'Wheat yields in England, 1815–1859', *Journal of the Royal Statistical Society*, 125 (1962), 574–9, reprinted in Jones, *Agriculture and the Industrial Revolution*, pp. 184–90.

94 For a recent review, see, G. R. McLennan, *Marxism and the methodologies of history* (London, 1981), pp. 66–111.

95 G. R. Elton, *The practice of history* (London, 1967), pp. 62 and 65.

96 E. H. Carr, *What is history?* (London, 1961), p. 11.

97 G. Stedman Jones, 'The pathology of English history', *New Left Review*, 46 (1967), 42, reprinted as 'History: the poverty of empiricism' in R. Blackburn (ed.), *Ideology in social science* (London, 1972), pp. 96–115.

98 'Editorial', *History Workshop Journal*, 6 (1978), 4; see also F. Redlich, 'Potentialities and pitfalls in economic history', *Explorations in Entrepreneurial History*, 6 (1968), 93–108, reprinted in Andreano, *The new economic history*, p. 87.

99 See pp. 119–23 above.

100 B. H. Slicher van Bath, *The agrarian history of Western Europe 1500–1850* (London, 1963), p. 17.

101 Skipp, *Crisis and development*, p. 78.

102 R. G. Wilkinson, *Poverty and progress: an ecological model of economic development* (London, 1973); D. B. Grigg, 'Population pressure and agricultural change', *Progress in Geography*, 8 (1976), pp. 133–76; *idem*, *Population growth and agrarian change* (Cambridge, 1980); *idem*, *The dynamics of agricultural change* (London, 1982).

103 E. A. Wrigley and R. S. Schofield, *The population history of England 1541–1871* (London, 1981), pp. 454–84.

104 A great variety of approaches call themselves, or have been called, 'ecological'. In addition to those cited see W. S. Cooter, 'Ecological dimensions of medieval agrarian systems', *Agricultural History*, 52 (1978), 458–77; J. D. Post, 'Famine, mortality, and epidemic disease in the process of modernisation', *Economic History Review*, 29 (1976), 14–37; Grigg, *Dynamics of agricultural change*, pp. 19–80.

105 Wrigley and Schofield, *Population histo, y*, p. 404.

106 Skipp, *Crisis and development*, p. 52, runs into this problem.

107 D. Harvey, 'Population, resources and the ideology of science', *Annals of the Association of American Geographers*, 66 (1976), 256–77.

108 P. O'Brien, 'Agriculture and the industrial revolution', *Economic History Review*, 30 (1977), 166–81.

109 Butlin, *Transformation of rural England*, p. 14.

110 N. F. R. Crafts, 'The eighteenth century: a survey' in R. C. Floud and D. N. McCloskey (eds), *The economic history of Britain since 1700*, 2 vols (Cambridge, 1981), vol. 1, pp. 1–16.

111 N. F. R. Crafts, 'Enclosure and labour supply revisited', *Explorations in Economic History*, 15 (1978), 172–83.

112 N. F. R. Crafts, 'Income elasticities of demand and the release of labour by agriculture during the British Industrial Revolution', *Journal of European Economic History*, 9 (1980), 153–68.

113 See p. 132–3 above.

114 For an introduction to Marxian theory which criticizes the neo-classical approach, see R. E. Rowthorn, 'Neo-classicism, neo-Ricardianism and Marxism', *New Left Review*, 86 (1974), 63–87; for an introduction which criticizes the 'Malthusian' view, see R. Brenner, 'Agrarian class structure and economic development in pre-industrial Europe', *Past and Present*, 70

(1976), 30–74. Some of the best introductions to Marxism include: M. R. Howard and J. E. King, *The political economy of Marx* (London, 1975); A. Brewer, *Marxist theories of imperialism* (London, 1980), pp. 27–60; W. H. Shaw, *Marx's theory of history* (London, 1978); G. A. Cohen, *Marx's theory of history: a defence* (Oxford, 1978).

115 Howard and King, *Political economy of Marx*, pp. 1–21; M. Hollis and E. J. Nell, *Rational economic man: a philosophical critique of neoclassical economics* (London, 1975), pp. 212–3; R. Keat and J. Urry, *Social theory as science* (London, 1975), pp. 96–118; E. J. Nell, 'Economics: the revival of political economy' in Blackburn (ed.), *Ideology and social science*, pp. 77–8.

116 Some interpretations of Marxism lead to the conclusion that the theory is ahistorical. For a counter-attack, see E. P. Thompson, *The poverty of theory and other essays* (London, 1978), pp. 193–397.

117 W. Lazonick, 'Karl Marx and enclosures in England', *Review of Radical Political Economy*, 6 (1974), 1–59.

118 K. Collins, 'Marx on the English agricultural revolution: theory and evidence', *History and Theory*, 6 (1967), 351–81; K. R. Popper, *Conjectures and refutations*, 4th edn (London, 1972), pp. 33–65.

119 J. Saville, 'Primitive accumulation and early industrialization in Britain', *The Socialist Register* (London, 1969), pp. 251–2.

120 K. Tribe, *Genealogies of capitalism* (London, 1981), pp. 35–100; idem, 'Capitalism and industrialization', *Intervention*, 5 (1975), 23–37.

121 I. Carter, *Farm life in northeast Scotland 1800–1914* (Edinburgh, 1979).

122 K. Tribe, *Land, labour and economic discourse* (London, 1978), pp. 53–79.

123 E. P. Thompson, 'The moral economy of the English crowd in the eighteenth century', *Past and Present*, 50 (1971), 76–136.

124 The 'transition debate' is reviewed by Tribe, *Genealogies of capitalism*, pp. 1–34. See R. H. Hilton (ed.), *The transition from feudalism to capitalism* (London, 1976).

125 Marx, *Capital*, vol. 1, pp. 677–81; idem, *Pre-capitalist economic formations*, trans. J. Cohen, ed. E. J. Hobsbawm (London, 1964), p. 67; idem, *Grundrisse*, trans. M. Nicolaus (London, 1973), pp. 497–514.

126 K. Tribe, 'Ground rent and the formation of classical political economy: a theoretical history', unpublished Ph.D. thesis, University of Cambridge, 1976, p. 61.

127 M. Dobb, *Studies in the development of capitalism*, revised edn (London, 1963), p. 226.

128 These are summarized in G. E. Mingay, *Enclosure and the small farmer in the age of the Industrial Revolution* (London, 1968); and M. Turner, *English Parliamentary enclosure* (Folkestone, 1980).

129 Mingay, *Small farmer*, p. 10; idem, 'The size of farms in the eighteenth century', *Economic History Review*, 14 (1962), 469–88; J. V. Beckett, 'The decline of the small landowner in eighteenth- and nineteenth-century England: some regional considerations', *Agricultural History Review*, 30 (1982), 97–111.

130 C. B. Macpherson, 'Capitalism and the changing concept of property', in E. Kamenka and R. S. Neale (eds), *Feudalism, capitalism and beyond* (London, 1975), pp. 105–24.

131 D. C. North and R. P. Thomas, *The rise of the Western world: a new economic history* (Cambridge, 1973); Kerridge, *Farmers of old England*, p. 135.
132 R. G. Collingwood, *An essay on metaphysics* (Oxford, 1940), pp. 34–48.
133 J. Robinson, *Economic philosophy* (London, 1962).
134 Harvey, 'Population, resources and ideology', p. 256.
135 H. Katouzian, *Ideology and method in economics* (London, 1980), p. 140.
136 McGregor, 'Introduction to Ernle', p. lxxxi; Mingay, *Agricultural revolution: changes in agriculture*, p. 2.
137 Kerridge, 'Agricultural revolution reconsidered', p. 472; E. Kerridge, *Agrarian problems in the sixteenth century and after* (London, 1969), pp. 9, 15.
138 Mingay, 'Agricultural revolution in English history', p. 125.
139 Keat and Urry, *Social theory as science*, p. 177; A. Giddens, *Central problems in social theory* (London, 1979), pp. 165–97.
140 W. H. Walsh, 'The limits of scientific history', *Historical Studies*, 3 (1961), 52; reprinted in W. H. Dray, *Philosophical analysis and history* (New York, 1966), pp. 66–74; see also D. M. Potter, 'Explicit data and implicit assumptions in historical study' in L. Gottschalk (ed.), *Generalization in the writing of history* (Chicago, 1963), p. 183.
141 Jones, *Agriculture and the Industrial Revolution*, p. 16.
142 Katouzian, *Ideology and method*, pp. 148–9.
143 Lazonick, 'Karl Marx and enclosures'.
144 Collins, 'Marx on the English agricultural revolution'.
145 Kerridge, 'Agricultural revolution reconsidered'.

Notes to Chapter 5

1 A comment in fact about the character of society in towns made by C. Phythian-Adams in *The fabric of the traditional community*, prepared by C. Phythian-Adams, K. Wilson and P. Clark (Milton Keynes, 1977), p. 38; but for comparable views presented in terms of the rural parish, see C. Phythian-Adams, *Local history and folklore: a new framework* (London, 1975), pp. 17–21.
2 C. Hill, *Society and Puritanism in pre-Revolutionary England* (London, 1964), p. 483.
3 *Ibid.*, p. 484.
4 J. Thirsk, 'The family', *Past and Present*, 27 (1964), 122, referring to Robert Mandrou, *Introduction à la France moderne* (Paris, 1961).
5 Most conveniently summarized in L. Stone, 'The rise of the nuclear family in early modern England' in C. E. Rosenberg (ed.), *The family in history* (Philadelphia, 1975), pp. 13–58.
6 K. Thomas, *Religion and the decline of magic: studies in popular beliefs in sixteenth and seventeenth century England* (London, 1971), p. 560.
7 *Ibid.*, p. 561.
8 *Ibid.*, pp. 547–60; A. Macfarlane, *Witchcraft in Tudor and Stuart England; a regional and comparative study* (London, 1970), pp. 192–206.
9 Macfarlane subsequently rejected his earlier interpretations in his 'Introduction' to *The origins of English individualism* (Oxford, 1978), pp. 1–6. Apart from the dependence of these arguments explaining the rise of witchcraft accusations

upon individualist processes undermining a sense of community, they were also noticeably couched in terms of structural functionalism – perhaps understandably, given its predominance in much of the anthropological literature with which Macfarlane and Thomas were familiar. For a critique of this aspect of their work, see C. Larner, *Enemies of God: the witch-hunt in Scotland* (London, 1981), pp. 20–3.

10 Hill, *Society and Puritanism*, p. 486.

11 K. Wrightson, 'Aspects of social differentiation in rural England, c. 1580–1660', *The Journal of Peasant Studies*, 5 (1978), 33–47.

12 R. H. Hilton, *The English peasantry in the later Middle Ages* (Oxford, 1975), pp. 51–5 and 91.

13 E. P. Thompson, 'Patrician society, plebeian culture', *Journal of Social History*, 7 (1974), 384, 389 and 393.

14 Wrightson, 'Aspects of social differentiation', p. 34.

15 R. Redfield, *Peasant society and culture* (Chicago, 1956), pp. 41–2. A concept applied to what is seen as a European-wide 'post-Breughelian' reform of popular culture by P. Burke, *Popular culture in early modern Europe* (London, 1978), pp. 207–45. For its supposed appearance in the form of increased middling and upper-class concern with the alehouse in seventeenth-century England, see P. Clark, 'The alehouse and the alternative society' in D. Pennington and K. Thomas (eds), *Puritans and revolutionaries: essays in seventeenth century history presented to Christopher Hill* (Oxford, 1978), pp. 47–72.

16 K. Wrightson, *English society 1580–1680* (London, 1982), pp. 222–3.

17 K. Wrightson and D. Levine, *Poverty and piety in an English village: Terling, 1525–1700* (London, 1979).

18 It has received a very warm welcome from Christopher Hill, who sees it as showing how demography controlled by historical imagination can contribute to a deeper understanding of changes in society and ideology. See his review in *Social History*, 6 (1981), 119–21. Hill is particularly intrigued by the 'revolutionary' potential of this emerging new social group in county government: see 'Parliament and people in seventeenth century England', *Past and Present* 92 (1981), 119; *idem*, 'A rejoinder', *Past and Present*, 98 (1983), 156–7.

19 See A. Everitt, 'The marketing of agricultural produce' in J. Thirsk (ed.), *The agrarian history of England and Wales, Volume IV: 1500–1640* (Cambridge, 1967), pp. 577–86; J. Chartres, 'The marketing of agricultural produce' in J. Thirsk (ed.), *The agrarian history of England and Wales, Volume V* (Cambridge, forthcoming); A. Kussmaul, 'Time and space, hoofs and grain: the seasonality of marriage in England', *Journal of Interdisciplinary History* (forthcoming); M. Spufford, *Contrasting communities: English villages in the sixteenth and seventeenth centuries* (Cambridge, 1974), pp. 138–9.

20 See B. W. Quintrell, 'The making of Charles I's Book of Orders', *English Historical Review*, 95 (1980), 553–72; P. A. Slack, 'Books of Orders: the making of English social policy, 1577–1631', *Transactions of the Royal Historical Society*, 30 (1980), 18–19; T. G. Barnes, *Somerset 1625–1642* (Oxford, 1961), chapter 6.

21 For a general but precise account, see G. R. Elton, *The Tudor constitution*, 2nd edn (Cambridge, 1982).

22 See the discussion in M. E. James, *Family, lineage and civil society; change and continuity in the Tudor north* (Oxford, 1974); R. B. Smith, *Land and politics in the England of Henry VIII* (Oxford, 1970); J. H. Gleeson, *The Justice of the Peace in England* (Oxford, 1969); A. Hassell Smith, *County and court: government and politics in Norfolk, 1558–1603* (Oxford, 1974); P. Clark, *English provincial society: religion, politics and society in Kent 1500–1640* (Hassocks, 1977).

23 P. Laslett, 'The gentry of Kent in 1640', *Cambridge Historical Journal*, 9 (1948), 158–61; A. Everitt, *The community of Kent and the Great Rebellion* (Leicester, 1966).

24 J. Samaha, *Law and order in historical perspective: the case of Elizabethan Essex* (New York and London, 1974); K. Wrightson, 'Two concepts of order: justice, constables and jurymen in seventeenth century England' in J. Brewer and J. Styles (eds), *An ungovernable people: the English and their law in the seventeenth and eighteenth centuries* (London, 1980), pp. 21–46; J. A. Sharp, 'Enforcing the law in the seventeenth century English village' in V. A. C. Gatrell, B. Lenman and G. Parker (eds), *Crime and the law: the social history of crime in Western Europe since 1500* (London, 1980), pp. 97–119.

25 For their likely participation in the electoral process, see D. Hirst, *The representatives of the people? Voters and voting in England under the early Stuarts* (Cambridge, 1974).

26 K. Wrightson, *English society*, pp. 206–20.

27 D. Cressy, *Literacy and the social order: reading and writing in Tudor and Stuart England* (Cambridge, 1980), pp. 118–74; Wrightson, *English society*, pp. 191–9.

28 An especially valuable discussion is J. S. Migdal, *Peasants, politics and revolution: pressures towards political and social change in the Third World* (Princeton, N.J., 1974).

29 J. R. Gusfield, 'Tradition and modernity: misplaced polarities in the study of change', *American Journal of Sociology*, 72 (1967), 351–62; C. S. Whittaker, 'A dysrhythmic process of political change', *World Politics*, 19 (1967), 198–201.

30 See Barrington Moore, Jr, *Social origins of dictatorship and democracy: lord and peasant in the making of the modern world* (Boston, Mass., 1966), pp. 453–83.

31 R. I. Rhodes, 'The disguised conservatism in evolutionary development theory', *Science and Society*, 32 (1968), 388; and of course E. R. Wolf, *Peasant wars of the twentieth century* (New York, 1969).

32 E. R. Wolf, *Peasants* (Englewood Cliffs, N.J., 1966), p. 11.

33 J. D. Powell, 'Peasant society and clientelist politics', *American Political Science Review*, 64 (1970), 413.

34 See Migdal, *Peasants, politics and revolution*, chapter 3.

35 F. G. Bailey, *Caste and the economic frontier: a village in highland Orissa* (Manchester, 1957), p. 255.

36 Behaviour superbly analysed in J. C. Scott, *The moral economy of the peasant: rebellion and subsistence in southeast Asia* (London, 1976).

37 Classically described in E. C. Banfield, *The moral basis of a backward society* (New York, 1958); and G. M. Foster, 'Peasant society and the image of limited good', *American Anthropologist*, 67 (1965), 293–315.

38 E. R. Wolf, 'An analysis of ritual co-parenthood (compadrazgo)' in J. M. Potter, M. N. Diaz and G. M. Foster (eds), *Peasant society: a reader* (Boston, Mass., 1966), pp. 174–99.

39 For an excellent synopsis of this literature, see Migdal, *Peasants, politics and revolution*, pp. 60–84.

40 Scott, *The moral economy*, pp. 91–113.

41 B. Hutchinson, 'The patron–dependent relationship in Brazil: a preliminary examination', *Sociologia Ruralis*, 6 (1966), 16–17.

42 S. Forman and J. F. Reigelhaupt, 'Market place and marketing system: towards a theory of peasant economic integration', *Comparative Studies in Society and History*, 12 (1970), 202.

43 Scott, *The moral economy*, pp. 56–90.

44 G. W. Skinner, 'Chinese peasants and the closed community: an open and shut case', *Comparative Studies in Society and History*, 13 (1971), 271.

45 E. R. Wolf, 'Aspects of group relations in a complex society: Mexico', *American Anthropologist*, 58 (1956), 1065.

46 Based on Migdal, *Peasants, politics and revolution*, p. 155.

47 E. Stokes, *The peasant and the Raj: studies in agrarian society and peasant rebellion in colonial India* (Cambridge, 1978), p. 19.

48 C. Dewey, 'Image of the village community: a study in Anglo-Indian ideology', *Modern Asian Studies*, 6 (1972), 295.

49 J. W. Burrows, 'The village community and the uses of history in late nineteenth-century England', in N. McKendrick (ed.), *Historical perspectives: studies in English thought and society in honour of J. H. Plumb* (London, 1974), p. 261.

50 Dewey, 'Images of the village community', p. 295.

51 *Ibid.*, p. 296.

52 E. A. Freeman, *The growth of the English constitution from the earliest times*, 3rd edn (London, 1876), pp. 1–2.

53 W. Stubbs, *The constitutional history of England*, 3rd edn (Oxford, 1883), p. 91.

54 J. R. Green, *The making of England*, 4th edn (London, 1904), p. 54.

55 Sir G. L. Gomme, *The village community* (London, 1890), pp. 14–15.

56 Sir Henry Maine, *Ancient law* (London, 1883), pp. 23–4.

57 For an excellent discussion of Maine in relation to other nineteenth-century evolutionary theorists, see J. W. Burrows, *Evolution and society* (Cambridge, 1966), chapter 4.

58 P. Stein, *Legal evolution: the story of an idea* (Cambridge, 1980), pp. 106–7.

59 Maine, *Ancient law*, p. 260.

60 *Ibid.*, pp. 266–7; and for a useful discussion, see P. Gatrell, 'Studies of medieval English society in a Russian context', *Past and Present*, 96 (1982), 28.

61 F. Pollock and F. W. Maitland, *History of English law*, 2nd edn, 2 vols (Cambridge, 1968), pp. 240–2.

62 An argument given further support in B. Philpotts, *Kindred and clan* (Cambridge, 1913); L. Lancaster, 'Kinship in Anglo-Saxon society', *British Journal of Sociology*, 9 (1958), 234–48 and 359–77; H. H. Meinhard, 'The patrilineal principle in early Teutonic kinship' in J. H. M. Beattie and R. G. Leinhardt (eds), *Studies in social anthropology* (Oxford, 1975), pp. 1–29; H. R. Loyn,

'Kinship in Anglo-Saxon England', *Anglo-Saxon England*, 3 (1974), 197-209. For further comments, see R. M. Smith, 'Kin and neighbours in a thirteenth century Suffolk community', *Journal of Family History*, 4 (1979), pp. 253-4.

63 F. W. Maitland, *Domesday Book and beyond* (London, 1965), pp. 404-5.

64 *Ibid.*, pp. 406-15.

65 Dewey, 'Images of the village community', p. 293.

66 For a useful discussion of the writings of late nineteenth-century British idealists such as F. H. Bradley, B. Bosanquet and D. G. Ritchie, and of their criticisms of methodological individualism, see S. Collini, 'Sociology and idealism in Britain 1880-1920', *Archives européennes de sociologie*, 19 (1978), 3-50. Sidgwick's dislike of attempts to write a science of society in Comte's *Politique positive* and Spencer's *The principle of sociology*, is obvious. These efforts for him remained unproven and overblown until they could offer 'something better than a mixture of vague and variously applied physiological analogies, imperfectly verified historical generalisations, and an unwarranted political prediction' (H. Sidgwick, *Miscellaneous essays and addresses* (London, 1904), p. 198). For some pertinent remarks on Maitland's views of a sociology founded on discussions of society in the terms of the physical and natural sciences, see Collini, 'Sociology and idealism', p. 33.

67 Dewey, 'Images of the village community', p. 295.

68 Translated and supplemented by C. P. Loomis, *Community and association* (London, 1955).

69 Although references to Le Play are limited to only three pages of his book, *English villagers of the thirteenth century* (Cambridge, Mass., 1941), pp. 113, 119 and 215, they are highly significant. For instance, when writing of the stem-family organization which he believed to characterize 'champion England', he states: 'This traditional family organization had great virtues . . . every child knew what he had to expect and knew that if he were once given the means of making his living he was secure in holding them. Some certainty and security for the future are necessary to men if they are to be useful members of society' (pp. 214-15).

70 A useful but slightly overdrawn consideration of Le Play's idea is to be found in P. Laslett and R. Wall (eds), *Household and family in past times* (Cambridge, 1972), pp. 16-21. For a more detailed and in general more favourable assessment of Le Play's work see 'Introduction' in R. Wall (ed.), *Family forms in historic Europe* (Cambridge, 1983), pp. 18-28.

71 Homans, *English villages*, pp. 413-14.

72 *Ibid.*, chapter 7; *idem*, 'Terroirs ordonnés et champs orientés: une hypothèse sur le village anglais', *Annales d'histoire économique et sociale*, 8 (1936), 438-48.

73 The principal publications with which we associate this school are J. A. Raftis, *Tenure and mobility: studies in the social history of the medieval village* (Toronto, 1964); *idem*, 'Social structures of five East Midland villages', *Economic History Review*, 18 (1965), 84-99; *idem*, 'The concentration of responsibility in five villages', *Mediaeval Studies*, 28 (1966), 92-118; *idem*, 'Changes in an English village after the Black Death', *Mediaeval Studies*, 29 (1967), 158-77; *idem*, *Warboys: two hundred years in the life of an English mediaeval village* (Toronto, 1974); *idem*, *A small town in late mediaeval England: Godmanchester 1278-1400*

(Toronto, 1982); A. Dewindt, 'Peasant power structures in fourteenth century King's Ripton', *Mediaeval Studies*, 38 (1976), 244–67; E. B. Dewindt, *Land and people in Holywell-cum-Needingworth: structures of tenure and patterns of social organization in an East Midlands village 1252–1457* (Toronto, 1972); E. Britton, *The community of the vill: a study in the history of the family and village life in fourteenth-century England* (Toronto, 1977).

74 Dewindt, *Land and people*, pp. 262–3, 220.

75 For some valuable comments on problems involved in the categorization of individuals and the assumptions underpinning their attempts at 'nominative linkage', see K. Wrightson, 'Medieval villagers in perspective', *Peasant Studies*, 7 (1978), 203–18.

76 For the most hostile of such criticism, see Z. Razi, 'The Toronto School's reconstruction of medieval peasant society: a critical view', *Past and Present*, 85 (1979), 141–57.

77 Views forcefully put in 'Mediaeval peasants: any lessons?', *Journal of Peasant Studies*, 1 (1974), 208, and in *The English peasantry in the later Middle Ages* (Oxford, 1975), p. 12.

78 R. H. Hilton, *A medieval society: the West Midlands at the end of the thirteenth century* (London, 1966), p. 166.

79 'It cannot be too strongly emphasized that at all periods during the middle ages the bulk of the agricultural land was contained within peasant holdings and that these holdings were managed as family concerns' (in his 'Reasons for inequality among medieval peasants', *Journal of Peasant Studies*, 5 (1978), 274).

80 *Ibid.*, p. 278.

81 See his 'Some social and economic evidence in late medieval tax returns' in S. Herbst (ed.), *Spoleczenstwo, gospordarke, Kultura: studia ofiawane M. Malowistowi w czterdzcestolencia pracy nankowej* (Warsaw, 1974), pp. 112–13; *The English peasantry in the later Middle Ages*, p. 28.

82 Hilton, *A medieval society*, pp. 151–2.

83 *Ibid.*, p. 153.

84 *Ibid.*, p. 152 – a view found too in H. Cam, 'The community of the vill', *Lawfinders and lawmakers* (London, 1962), p. 73; and in E. Miller and M. J. Hatcher, *Medieval England: rural society and economic change 1086–1348* (London, 1978), pp. 100–2.

85 '... most of the thirteenth century court rolls give the impression (exaggerated no doubt by the nature of the record) that village life was a continuous series of guerilla actions by the tenants . . .' (*A medieval society*, p. 154). For an account of the kinds of incidents he has in mind, see R. H. Hilton, 'Peasant movements in England before 1381' in E. M. Carus-Wilson (ed.), *Essays in economic history*, *Vol. 2* (London, 1962), pp. 73–90.

86 Hilton, *A medieval society*, p. 151.

87 'A crisis of feudalism', *Past and Present*, 80 (1978), 9.

88 *Ibid.*, p. 17.

89 Dewindt in *Land and people*, pp. 263–75, and Raftis in 'Change in an English village', pp. 159–65, argue for a decline in community spirit after 1350. Hilton would see the period between 1381 and the last half of the fifteenth century as 'intermediate' – a period in which 'the "historic process of dissolution"

[quoting K. Marx, *Pre-capitalist economic formations*, ed. E. Hobsbawm (London, 1964), p. 104] of medieval society had begun with the dissolution of the ties of serfdom but separation of peasants from their land, whether by processes of social differentiation or by force, had not yet happened'; *The English peasantry in the later Middle Ages*, p. 19. For an attempt to give a firm basis to Hilton's arguments and to disprove ideas of an earlier loss of community spirit, see Z. Razi, 'Family, land and the village community in later medieval England', *Past and Present*, 93 (1981), 3–34.

90 A. Macfarlane, *The origins of English individualism: the family, property and social translation* (Oxford, 1978). His view that 'England seems to have been peculiar in that, from at least the fourteenth century, it was inhabited by individuals with highly stressed legal, economic, political and religious rights and duties' has been employed in the analysis of matters to do with the history of the family in England; see his review essay in *History and Theory*, 18 (1979), 103–26; fertility patterns, see 'Modes of reproduction' in G. Hawthorn, *Population and development* (London, 1978), pp. 106–20; the 'law-abiding' nature of English society, see *The Justice and the Mare's Ale* (Oxford, 1980).

91 Macfarlane, *The origins of English individualism*, pp. 170, 206.

92 M. Goldie, 'Old Whiggery, new bottle: Macfarlane's English individualism', *Cambridge Review*, Feb. 1980, p. 111.

93 *Ibid.*

94 See the sources, constituting a *sine qua non* for the early modern village study, described in K. Wrightson ,'Villagers, villages and village studies', *Historical Journal*, 18 (1975), 632–9.

95 For some important issues raised by 'single-source' studies of medieval village communities, see L. R. Poos, 'Peasant "biographies" from medieval England' in N. Bulst and J.-P. Genet (eds), *Medieval prosopography: Proceedings of the Bielefeld Conference, December 1980* (forthcoming).

96 Wrightson, *English society*, p. 226.

97 J. H. Baker, 'Criminal courts and procedures at common law 1500–1800' in J. S. Cockburn (ed.), *Crime in England 1550–1800* (London, 1977), p. 16.

98 Wrightson, 'Two concepts of order', p. 31.

99 Baker, 'Criminal courts and procedures', p. 18.

100 Wrightson, 'Two concepts of order', pp. 34–40.

101 See the comments of J. Sharpe, 'The history of crime in late mediaeval and early modern England', *Social History*, 7 (1982), p. 189.

102 M. Ingram, 'Communities and courts: law and disorder in early seventeenth century Wiltshire', in J. S. Cockburn (ed.), *Crime in England*, pp. 120–3.

103 *Ibid.*, pp. 132–3.

104 A. Harding, *The law courts of mediaeval England* (London, 1973), p. 92.

105 V. H. Galbraith, *Domesday Book: its place in administrative history* (Oxford, 1974), p. 27. See also the essay of J. Campbell, 'Observations on English government from the tenth to the twelfth century', *Transactions of the Royal Historical Society*, 25 (1975), 39–54, in which the Carolingian origins of England's precocity are discussed.

106 An argument developed in Loyn, 'Kinship in Anglo-Saxon England', pp. 199, 203, 204 and 207–9. For a rather different view giving greater emphasis to the

transmission of property within the kin-group and suggesting sharp differences between Anglo-Saxon and Anglo-Norman ways, see J. C. Holt, 'Feudal society and the family in early mediaeval England, I: The revolution of 1066', *Transactions of the Royal Historical Society*, 32 (1982), 193–212.

107 See C. A. Ralegh-Radford, 'The later pre-Conquest boroughs and their defences', *Mediaeval Archaeology*, 14 (1970), 83–103.

108 R. H. M. Dolley and D. M. Metcalf, 'The reform of the English coinage under Edgar', in R. H. M. Dolley (ed.), *Anglo-Saxon coins* (London, 1961), pp. 136–68; C. S. S. Loyn, 'Variations in currency in late Anglo-Saxon England' in R. A. Carson (ed.), *Mints, dies and currency: essays in memory of Albert Baldwin* (London, 1971), pp. 102–20.

109 P. Chaplais, 'The Anglo-Saxon Chancery: from the diploma to the writ', *Journal of the Society of Archivists*, 3 (1966), 160–76.

110 F. H. Harmer (ed.), *Anglo-Saxon writs* (Manchester, 1952), pp. 160, 183–4.

111 H. R. Loyn, 'The hundred in England in the tenth and early eleventh centuries' in H. Hearder and H. R. Loyn (eds), *British government and administration: studies presented to S. B. Chrimes* (Cardiff, 1974), pp. 1–14.

112 D. Whitelock, *English historical documents c. 500–1042* (London, 1955), p. 39.

113 *Ibid.*

114 The system has been neatly described in W. A. Morris, *The frankpledge system*, Harvard Historical Studies, 14 (Cambridge, Mass., 1910), p. 2 as 'compulsory collective bail, fixed for individuals, not after their arrest for a crime, but as a safeguard in anticipation of it'.

115 Galbraith, *Domesday Book*, p. 28.

116 *Ibid.*, pp. 30–41.

117 S. Harvey, 'Domesday Book and its predecessors', *English Historical Review*, 86 (1971), 753–73.

118 Galbraith, *Domesday Book*, pp. 29–30; Harding, *Law courts of mediaeval England*, p. 29; D. M. Stenton, *English justice before the Norman Conquest and the Great Charter* (London, 1965), chapter 1.

119 One can only regret the unfortunate demise of Rutland, especially given Dr Phythian-Adams' recent impressive argument that it represented a very ancient territorial division indeed and not an anomaly as some had previously argued. See C. Phythian-Adams, 'Rutland reconsidered' in A. Dormer (ed.), *Mercian studies* (Leicester, 1977), pp. 63–84.

120 What follows constitutes nothing more than a brief synopsis drawing out certain basic principles of the so-called 'reforms'. For a succinct account, see Harding, *The law courts of mediaeval England*, pp. 32–63. A valuable discussion from a Belgian student of the development of the common law, with much useful comparative material, thereby providing a basis for situating happenings in England within a wider European context is provided by R. C. Van Caenegem, *The birth of the English common law* (Cambridge, 1973). No serious student can, however, avoid F. Pollock and F. W. Maitland, *The history of English law before the time of Edward I*, 2 vols, 2nd edn (Cambridge, 1968) and S. F. C. Milsom's rethinking of that work in *The legal framework of English feudalism* (Cambridge, 1976).

121 M. T. Clanchy, *England and its rulers* (Glasgow, 1983), p. 150.

122 For the full text, see D. Douglas and G. W. Greenaway (eds), *English historical documents*, vol. 2 (London, 1953), pp. 411–13. For more details see N. Hurnard, 'The jury of presentment and the assize of Clarendon', *English Historical Review*, 56 (1941), 374–410; J. C. Holt, 'The assizes of Henry II: the texts' in D. A. Bullough and R. L. Storey (eds), *The study of mediaeval records: essays in honour of Kathleen Major* (Oxford, 1971), pp. 85–106.

123 See the discussion in R. V. Turner, 'The origins of the mediaeval English jury: Frankish, English or Scandinavian', *Journal of British Studies*, 7 (1968), 1–10, which should be supplemented by Van Caenegem, *The birth of the English common law*, pp. 79–81.

124 J. P. Dawson, *A history of lay judges* (Cambridge, Mass., 1960).

125 Clanchy, *England and its rulers*, pp. 149 and 146.

126 E. Le Roy Ladurie, *Montaillou: village occitan de 1294 à 1324* (Paris, 1975), trans. as *Montaillou: Cathars and Catholics in a French village 1294–1324* (Harmondsworth, 1980).

127 B. Lenman and G. Parker, 'The State, the community and the criminal law in early modern Europe' in V. A. C. Gatrell, B. Lenman and G. Parker (eds), *Crime and the law*, pp. 31–2.

128 Dawson, *A history of lay judges*, p. 137.

129 R. H. Hilton, *The decline of serfdom in medieval England*, 2nd edn (London, 1983), p. 18.

130 *Ibid.*, pp. 18–19.

131 An argument more fully developed in 'Freedom and villeinage in England', *Past and Present*, 31 (1965), 184–5, where he considers the sharp 'removal of the *villani* from the ranks of those with free status' as a means by which rising costs in a period of intense fiscal pressure and inflation were 'passed on to the basic producer'.

132 P. R. Hyams, *King, lords and peasants in medieval England: the common law of villeinage in the twelfth and thirteenth centuries* (Oxford, 1980), pp. 255–65.

133 I am using here the concept of surplus associated with Pearson in 'The economy has no surplus: a critique of a theory of development' in K. Polanyi, C. M. Arensberg and H. W. Pearson (eds), *Trade and market in early empires* (New York, 1957), p. 339. Of course, Marxists would always stress the material limits to socially defined surpluses. See B. Ollman, *Alienation: Marx's conception of man in a capitalist society* (Cambridge, 1971), pp. 12–42.

134 E. King, *England, 1175–1425* (London, 1979), p. 50; J. Hatcher, 'English serfdom and villeinage: towards a reassessment', *Past and Present*, 90 (1981), pp. 6–7, both studies building on foundations laid by E. A. Kosminsky, *Studies in the agrarian history of England in the thirteenth century*, ed. R. H. Hilton and trans. R. Kisch (Oxford, 1956).

135 Hilton, 'Freedom and villeinage', pp. 13–17; but see the comments of Hyams, *King, lords and peasants*, pp. 242–3, and Hatcher, 'English serfdom and villeinage', pp. 34–6.

136 Discussed in the introduction to P. D. A. Harvey (ed.), *Manorial records of Cuxham, Oxfordshire circa 1200–1359*, Historical Manuscripts Commission No. 23, Joint Publication (London, 1976). For examples see M. Chibnall (ed.),

Charters and custumals of the Abbey of Holy Trinity Caen, Records of Social and Economic History, New Series, V (Oxford, 1982).

137 Hyams, *King, lords and peasants*, p. 257; see also on this point Hatcher, 'English serfdom and villeinage', p. 23; Homans, *English villagers of the thirteenth century*, pp. 270–2.

138 F. W. Maitland (ed.), *Select pleas in manorial and other seigneurial courts*, Selden Society Publications, 11 (1888), p. xxxvi.

139 On this, see J. S. Beckerman, 'Customary law in manorial courts in the thirteenth and fourteenth centuries', unpublished Ph.D. thesis, University of London, 1972, pp. 47–58.

140 I have considered these developments in greater detail in 'Some thoughts on "hereditary" and "proprietary" rights in land under customary law in thirteenth and fourteenth century England', *Law and History Review*, 1 (1983), 95–128. I intend to consider developments in court procedures and their relationships to practices in other courts in an edition of select pleas from thirteenth- and fourteenth-century manorial courts to be published by the Selden Society.

141 For the characteristics of the 'jury-serving' element among populations of customary tenants, see E. Britton, *Community of the vill*, pp. 94–102; E. Searle, *Lordship and community: Battle Abbey and its banlieu, 1066–1538* (Toronto, 1974), p. 432; Smith, 'Some thoughts on "hereditary" and "proprietary" rights'. For further discussion of the same element's land-marketing activities in the late thirteenth and early fourteenth centuries, see R. M. Smith, 'Some issues concerning families and their properties in rural England, 1200–1800' in R. M. Smith (ed.), *Land, kinship and life-cycle* (London, forthcoming). For certain economic advantages accruing to customary tenants in conditions of inflationary land values see Hatcher, 'English serfdom and villeinage', pp. 14–21.

142 Beckerman, 'Customary law in manorial courts', p. 99. But see a reluctance to accept this point in Z. Razi, 'Family, land and the village community', pp. 12–14.

143 B. Hanawalt, 'Community conflict and social control: crime and justice in the Ramsay Abbey villages', *Mediaeval Studies*, 39 (1977), 402–33.

144 For further discussion, see B. Hanawalt, *Crime and conflict in English communities 1300–1348* (Cambridge, Mass., and London, 1979), pp. 168–83.

145 Hanawalt, 'Community conflict and social control', pp. 407–9, 419–21.

146 Britton, *The community of the vill*, pp. 115–23.

147 Hanawalt, 'Economic influences on the pattern of crime in England, 1300–1348', *The American Journal of Legal History*, 81 (1974), 281–97; *idem, Crime in East Anglia in the fourteenth century: Norfolk gaol delivery rolls, 1307–1316*, Norfolk Record Society, vol. 44 (1976), pp. 13–17. She appears, however, not to have considered in detail the difficulties of applying modern definitions of 'crime' to evidence from the past, although she notes certain indications of variability in the social definition of crime when referring to persons excused of burglary because the 'theft' was committed when they were suffering *fame et inopia*; see *Crime and conflict*, p. 253. See, nonetheless, Sharpe's criticisms in 'The history of crime in late mediaeval and early modern England', pp. 189–90.

148 B. H. Putnam, *The enforcement of the Statute of Labourers during the first decade after the Black Death* (New York, 1908), pp. 24–5.

149 For discussions of the office of township or petty constable in the later four-teenth century, see H. M. Cam, 'Shire officials: coroners, constables and bailiffs' in J. P. Willard, W. A. Morris and W. H. Dunham (eds), *The English government at work, 1327–1336*, vol. 3 (Cambridge, Mass., 1950), pp. 169–71; D. A. Crowley, 'Frankpledge and leet jurisdiction in later-mediaeval Essex', unpublished Ph.D. thesis, University of Sheffield, 1971, pp. 209–42. For a useful discussion of the changing practices of the constable in relation to the court leet and to the State from the fourteenth to the seventeenth century, see J. Kent, 'The English village constable, 1580–1642: the nature and dilemmas of the office', *Journal of British Studies*, 19 (1980), 26–49, although this under-states the conflict of interest in the fourteenth-century constable's position both as officer of the local community and as representative of central government.

150 L. R. Poos, 'The social context of Statute of Labourers enforcement', *Law and History Review*, 1 (1983), pp. 27–52.

151 Razi, 'Family, land and the village community', p. 15.

152 See Z. Razi, 'The struggle between the Abbots of Halesowen and their tenants in the thirteenth and fourteenth centuries' in T. H. Aston, P. R. Coss, C. Dyer and J. Thirsk (eds), *Social relations and ideas: essays in honour of R. H. Hilton* (Cambridge, 1983), pp. 151–68. In only one area does Razi utilize evidence originating in extra-manorial agencies, and this concerns a dispute between the tenants of Halesowen and the abbot that dragged on in the King's Court for almost fifty years, reaching the status of a local *cause célèbre*, the character of which was in part determined by the fact that the manor had been until the early decades of the thirteenth century in royal hands.

153 W. O. Ault, *Private jurisdiction in England* (New Haven, Conn., 1923), pp. 260–6; M. J. O. Kennedy, 'Resourceful villeins: the Cellarer family of Wawne, in Holderness', *The Yorkshire Archaeological Journal*, 48 (1976), 107–17.

154 See R. C. Palmer, *The county courts of mediaeval England* (Princeton, N.J., 1982), pp. 263–307; M. K. McIntosh, 'The privileged villeins of the English ancient demesne', *Viator*, 7 (1976), especially pp. 320–6.

155 See R. B. Dobson, *The Peasants' Revolt of 1381*, 2nd edn (London, 1983), pp. xxxvi–xxxvii.

156 Sharpe, 'The history of crime in late mediaeval and early modern England', pp. 202–3.

157 For Wrightson appears ready to discard the idea of a major break in the social structure as reflected in family forms and demographic–economic relationships, but interprets the early seventeenth century as novel in the way in which cultural differentiation was introduced by religious and educational changes. He notes that 'the effects of these processes could only have happened because their reception was channelled and shaped by pre-existing and persisting characteristics of village society' ('Medieval villagers in perspective', p. 216). Might not we add the possibility of pre-existing and persisting characteristics of village community–State relations as helping to create a certain inevitability in the pattern of shifting allegiances at the local level in the seventeenth century?

158 Harding, *Law courts of mediaeval England*, p. 116.

159 C. Holmes, 'The county community in Stuart historiography', *Journal of British Studies*, 19 (1980), 72.
160 J. R. Maddicott, 'The county community and the making of public opinion in fourteenth century England', *Transactions of the Royal Historical Society*, 27 (1977), 32ff. For further arguments along these same lines, see R. Virgoe, 'Crown, magnates and local government in fifteenth century East Anglia' in J. R. L. Highfield and R. Jeffs (eds), *The Crown and local government in England and France in the fifteenth century* (Gloucester, 1981), p. 59; M. J. Bennett, *Community, class and careerism: Cheshire and Lancashire society in the age of Sir Gawain and the Green Knight* (Cambridge, 1983), chapters 2, 3 and 10.
161 This paper has concentrated on collectivist institutions in the administrative and legal system, but a fuller account would need to include, for instance, the parish, its rituals, ceremonies and processions and those institutions – part religious, part secular – of fraternities and gilds all generating contexts within which individuals functioned in groups. John Bossy has provided some suggestive preliminary remarks highly relevant to such a task in 'Blood and baptism: kinship, community and Christianity in Western Europe from the fourteenth to the seventeenth centuries', in D. Baker (ed.), *Sanctity and secularity: the Church and the world* (Oxford, 1973), pp. 129–43, although in the last analysis his argument is flawed by its tendency to treat north-western and south European societies as indistinguishable in their use of fictive-kin groups as units producing a sense of community. It is, however, a valuable antidote to the ideas of those historians of Puritanism who see that belief system as essentially hostile to a medieval community *esprit de corps*.
162 See a devastating critique of a persistent failure of historians of welfare to keep such a dialectic in mind in D. Thomson, 'Historians and the Welfare State' (forthcoming).
163 For some provisional efforts, see R. M. Smith, 'Fertility, economy, and household formation in England over three centuries', *Population and Development Review*, 7 (1981), 615–19, where there is discussion of the differing demographic behaviour associated with, on the one hand, societies in which institutions work to spread the effects of personal actions by individuals over politically constituted 'communities' and, on the other, those in which kinship, or patron–clientage provides the mediating influence and the linkages between an individual and the wider society.

Notes to Chapter 6

1 This discussion is intended to be both wide-ranging and exploratory, rather than definitive and substantive. Our discussion assumes on the part of its readers a general acquaintance with the literature on the methodology of historical geography. For these two reasons, it has no bibliographical references.

Index